Richard ...nn is an a... .vinn... ... ...,
and author of four best-selling books. His twice-weekly columns in
the *Daily Mail* and the *Sun* earned him a place in the inaugural
Newspaper Hall of Fame as one of the most influential journalists
of the past 40 years.

He has been Fleet Street's Columnist of the Year and was named
Irritant of the Year by the BBC's What The Papers Say awards for
his unrivalled ability to get up the noses of the Establishment. His
extensive radio and television work has brought him both a Sony
award and a Silver Rose of Montreux. He has written for London's
Evening Standard and *Punch* and is still a contributor to the *Spectator*.

Littlejohn's satirical novel *To Hell In A Handcart* was the fastest-
selling fiction paperback on its release in 2001. His highly acclaimed
non-fiction book *You Couldn't Make It Up* skewered John Major's
Conservative government – much the same as the No. 1 bestselling
Littlejohn's Britain did for the Blair years.

Praise for Littlejohn's *House of Fun*

'If you prize free expression, this book is essential reading. I was
unable to find fault with a single sentiment.'

Roger Lewis, *Daily Telegraph*

'Fizzing with outrage, brilliantly scathing, laugh-out-loud hilarious.'
Daily Mail

Also available by Richard Littlejohn

Fiction
To Hell in a Handcart

Non-fiction
You Couldn't Make It Up
Littlejohn's Britain

Littlejohn's
House of Fun

The Coalition Edition

arrow books

Published by Arrow Books in 2010

2 4 6 8 10 9 7 5 3 1

First published in Great Britain in 2010 by Hutchinson
Arrow Books
Random House, 20 Vauxhall Bridge Road,
London SW1V 2SA

www.rbooks.co.uk

Addresses for companies within The Random House Group Limited can be found at:
www.randomhouse.co.uk/offices.htm

The Random House Group Limited Reg. No. 954009

A CIP catalogue record for this book
is available from the British Library

ISBN 9780099547563

The Random House Group Limited supports The Forest Stewardship
Council (FSC), the leading international forest certification organisation.
All our titles that are printed on Greenpeace approved FSC certified paper carry the FSC logo.
Our paper procurement policy can be found at www.rbooks.co.uk/environment

Mixed Sources
Product group from well-managed
forests and other controlled sources
www.fsc.org Cert no. TT-COC-2139
© 1996 Forest Stewardship Council

FSC

Typeset by Palimpsest Book Production Limited,
Falkirk, Stirlingshire

Printed and bound in Great Britain by
CPI Bookmarque, Croydon CR0 4TD

For Mum, Viv and Joyce

Acknowledgements

Heartfelt thanks to Paul Sidey and Wendy Littlejohn for their help, support and patience in the editing and compilation of this book. Thanks, also, to Deke Arlon, Jill Arlon, Terry Connolly, and to all those who have had a hand in the column over the years, including Paul Dacre, Leaf Kalfayan, Alastair Sinclair, Martin Clarke, Jim Gillespie, Tobyn Andreae, Andrew Yates and Chris Stevens. I should also like to thank Claire Cohen and Suzi Walker at the *Daily Mail* and Tess Callaway and Sinead Martin at Random House.

This book would not have been possible without the institutionalised idiocy of official Britain, the pig-headed politicians, jobsworths, Plods and assorted Guardianistas.

I am grateful, especially, to all the readers of the *Daily Mail* and the *Sun*, who have kept the column filled with their contributions to You Couldn't Make It Up, Nice Work, Mind How You Go, Elf'n'Safety and, most recently, Proof of Identity. This one's for you.

Welcome to the House of Fun.

Contents

Introduction

When I sat down to write this book in the summer of 2009, the Conservatives were twenty points ahead in the opinion polls. Labour seemed to be heading for meltdown, despite Gordon Brown's reckless masterplan to creat a vast client state, paid for with an ocean of toxic debt, which would keep his party in power in perpetuity.

Another couple of years and he may even have succeeded. Who can ever tell for certain how things might have turned out?

In the end, his tax-and-spending spree ran out of road, but not without a final, dramatic twist, spread over a long weekend in May 2010.

David Cameron eventually became Prime Minister after cobbling together a deal with the Lib Dems to form the first coalition government since the Second World War.

Littlejohn's House of Fun was orginally intended to close the coffin on Labour's shambolic and damaging thirteen years in power.

This edition contains extra chapters about Brown's final, doomed attempt to cling to power and the dawn of our novel LibCon hybrid government, which is already shaping up nicely to give me plenty of material for another book.

Richard Littlejohn, July 2010.

Overture and Beginners

A few days after Labour's landslide victory in the 1997 general election, two junior members of the new government marched into the piazza at Covent Garden. Civil servants then set up a sink in the square behind the Royal Opera House, complete with soap, water and paper towels.

Tessa Jowell and Jeff Rooker, ministers for public health and food safety respectively, rolled up their sleeves and began washing their hands. To the uninitiated they looked like the street performers who gather in Covent Garden daily to entertain the tourists. Alongside the mime artistes and fire-eaters, they could have been mistaken for a couple of alternative comedians indulging in a little open-air theatre, perhaps to advertise a forthcoming show in one of the many clubs which had sprung up all over London's West End.

Only the presence of film crews suggested there might be something more to it. Soon they were surrounded by camera-clicking Japanese, backpacking Germans and roly-poly, leisure-suited Americans.

'Hey look, Hank, honey, didn't that guy used to be in *Monty Python*? You know, don't mention the war. This is a late parrot. You must know who I mean. Perhaps you're right. He was taller, come to think of it. But I'm sure the woman was in *Benny Hill*.'

Tess and Jeff, though, were deadly serious. They were there to demonstrate the approved method for washing your hands. Their mission, they announced, was to improve standards of personal hygiene.

Thirteen years on, after tens of thousands of NHS patients have died from an epidemic of superbugs such as MRSA, caused primarily by a failure to ensure basic hygiene standards in hospitals, this fatuous stunt looks like a sick joke.

Back then, it was a statement of intent, a clear indication of what was to come. This was the first public cameo of Labour's bully state, which was to infantilise and criminalise us all. No area of our lives, however personal or trivial, was to be off-limits or free from hectoring interference.

Here's what I wrote at the time:

> If they get away with this, pretty soon they'll be issuing guidelines on how often to cut your toenails and change your socks.
>
> Teams of social workers will be empowered to break into homes and confiscate any children who have been allowed to go to bed without cleaning their teeth or have eaten too many chips for supper. For their own safety, you understand.
>
> Scratching your head in a hamburger bar will become a criminal offence, punishable by a fine of £50,000 and up to seven years in prison. We will be prevented by law from preparing any food unless togged out from head to toe in surgeon's uniform, complete with face mask and rubber cap.
>
> Knives and forks must be sterilised and thrown away after each meal. There will be twenty-four-hour surveillance, via closed circuit television links connected to Food Safety Headquarters by the internet.
>
> You'll be sitting down one night watching Coronation Street when a message will flash up on your screen: STOP PICKING YOUR NOSE. YES, WE MEAN YOU. And all this, the government will insist, is for our own good.

As I hope this book will illustrate, all that has come to pass and more. On the day of the 1997 election, I warned in my column in the *Daily Mail*:

> Tony Blair might not frighten you, but if you vote Labour today you will be putting into office a bunch of people with a gut hatred of individual freedom. They want us all to be clients of the state. Around their Islington dinner tables they pour scorn on suburban, family values.
>
> Under Blair, the Labour Party has changed. But these have been changes wrought not of conviction, but of cynical expedience. How do I know this? It's because I've spent my life around the Labour

movement. I have plenty of friends in the Labour Party and they still believe in the same things they believed in two decades ago.

*

I knew what I was talking about. In fact, back in the early 1980s I could have become a Labour MP. During my time as an industrial correspondent on the *Birmingham Evening Mail* and London's *Evening Standard*, I became close to the late Terry Duffy, who was leader of Britain's second biggest union, the 1.5 million-strong AUEW.

I'd known Terry since I started in Brum in 1977 and used to drink with him in a working man's club in Wolverhampton. He was an old-fashioned, right-wing Labour patriot. The support of the *Evening Mail* helped him win first a seat on the union's national executive and, eventually, replace left-wing Hughie Scanlon as the engineers' president.

After he got the top job, he asked me if I'd ever considered a career in politics. To be honest, I hadn't. Then he said if I fancied becoming a Labour MP he'd use his clout to secure me a safe seat.

This was the time when Militant was infiltrating the party and the AUEW was in the vanguard of the fight to stop Labour falling into the hands of quasi-communists.

I'd been instrumental in turning over some of the left-wing plotters. Terry thought I was a perfect candidate to take the fight to the left in the party itself. My politics, such as they were in those days, were on the right of the Labour movement.

In the end, I decided to stick with the day job, where I reckoned I could cause more mischief. Which was the right decision. My job is to sit at the back and throw bottles.

But if I'd taken Terry up on his offer, I'd have entered Parliament in 1983, part of the same intake as Tony Blair and Gordon Brown.

I wonder how that would have worked out.

The Ministry of Silly Stunts

It wasn't all bad news, though. After a few months of New Labour, I began to suspect that someone in government actually liked me. Somewhere in the bowels of Whitehall there had to be a secret department, a Fifth Column, whose sole purpose in life was to keep me in gainful employment.

Perhaps they were trying to discredit me by coming up with outrageous schemes which even I couldn't possibly make up.

They must turn up for work of a Monday morning, pour themselves a large cappuccino, rub their hands together and think:

'Right, then, what are we going to give Littlejohn to write about this week?'

'I know,' says a bright spark at the back, 'why don't we put out a press release saying that the Royal Navy is planning to incorporate the yashmak into the uniform in an attempt to attract Muslim women recruits?'

'He won't fall for that.'

'Of course he will. He'll be desperate for anything to write about.'

'He won't have to fall for it,' says a spotty youth with his head in a copy of the Daily Mail.

'Why not?'

'Well, it's true, innit?'

'What's true.'

'That business about yashmaks.'

'Eh?'

'The navy has beaten us to it.'

'What are you talking about?'

'It's right here on page 31.'

'What is?'

'Listen to this: "Shipshape in a veil. The veil need not be a barrier to life at sea for Muslim women. A major drive has been launched to attract them to join the Royal Navy by altering the Wrens' uniform code to incorporate cultural differences. Muslim women will be told that ways of incorporating the veil, or yashmak, into the uniform are being explored, and they would be permitted to take their swimming test without men being present."'

'Leave off. You're having us on.'

'I'm not. See for yourself. Commander Keith Manchanda, the Royal Navy's ethnic minorities liaison officer, said he hoped the first Asian women recruits would be piped aboard in September.'

'That'll go down like a fatted calf in Luton. They're already threatening to firebomb the local Mecca bingo hall unless it changes its name. Imagine how the mad mullahs are going to react when they find out their women are going to be sharing hammocks with a bunch of sex-mad sailors. Portsmouth will be razed to the ground. Didn't anyone at the MoD check with us first?'

'Not that I'm aware. Mind you, they didn't consult us before they started putting recruiting adverts in Gay Times, either. We were saving that one up for the silly season.'

'Is there any evidence that Muslim women want to join the navy?'

'None whatsoever. Quite the contrary, to be honest.'

'So what's all this about, then?'

'Search me. I suppose it gives that Commander Keith Manchanda geezer something to do.'

'Daft schemes like this are supposed to be down to us. That's what we're here for.'

'Makes you wonder, though, doesn't it? Tell you what I think, they're trying to make us redundant, that's what.'

'How do you arrive at that conclusion?'

'Ask yourself when was the last time we managed to invent anything original.'

'Counselling for gay and lesbian alcoholics.'

'Great idea, but if you remember we discovered Lambeth Council was already doing it.'

'Blind police drivers.'

'Wandsworth.'

'Masturbation lessons for the mentally handicapped.'

'We were too late again.'

'At this rate we're going to be out of a job, unless we can come up with something fast.'

'I've got it – let's ban beef on the bone.'

'Where the hell have you been the past few weeks?'

'On sick leave. My post-traumatic stress counsellor took me windsurfing in Barbados.'

'So you haven't heard?'

'Heard what?'

'They've beaten us to it.'

'To what?'

'Beef on the bone. Two years inside if you're caught selling it.'

'You are bloody kidding.'

'Nope.'

'Well that's that then. We might as well all start looking for a new job. Where did I put that yashmak?'

'He's right, you know.'

'Who is?'

'Littlejohn. You couldn't make it up.'

Gorn to the Corgis

As Tony Blair's premiership came to an end, the Queen was reported to have told friends that she was 'exasperated and frustrated' at the results of his ten years in power. She believes he meddled unnecessarily with Britain's heritage and his policies have been especially damaging to the countryside, as this exclusive fly-on-the-wall recording reveals.

*

Pour me a large Glennhoddle, Philip, I've just had Blair in for his weekly audience. I don't know why I still bother. He might be going but he's taking longer to leave the stage than it took Uncle Edward to abdicate.

They seem to have decided that Scotch accountant chappie is getting the job. You know, the one with the bad haircut and no fingernails. Brown, that's him, like Victoria's gillie.

Anyway, I thought I was supposed to be the one who invites them to form a government. No one has bothered consulting me, even though I've had more Prime Ministers than Blair has had free holidays.

I sometimes wonder what's the point of having a constitutional monarchy. If all they want is someone to do a bit of waving, they might just as well get in that Mirren woman.

Yes, Philip, I know you've always fancied her, ever since *The Long Good Friday*. If you ask me she's a bit of a hussy, getting her kit orf at the drop of a hat.

One wouldn't have been surprised to see her starkers in *The Queen*, given half the chance. And you can wipe that smirk off your face or it's the spare room again tonight.

Common as muck, she is. Gawd knows why one agreed to make her a Dame. Another 'eye-catching' gimmick from Number 10, from what I remember.

Blair seemed such a nice chap at first. Right school, proper manners, but a bit over familiar for my liking.

'Call me Tony,' he said at our first meeting. No thank you very much, Prime Minister. Next thing he'd be calling me Liz and you know how much I hate that.

It's one thing you calling me 'Brenda' but quite another having a complete stranger taking all kinds of liberties.

He even had the cheek to alter the day of our meetings from Tuesday to Wednesday, which is the day I used to like to go shopping at Fortnum's.

I don't think he ever quite got the hang of the Prime Minister/Head of State relationship. Most of the time he acted as if he was the President and I was some kind of skivvy.

Just look at his behaviour when That Woman died. 'She was the People's Princess'. Purleese. Pass the sick bag. Putting it around that he saved the monarchy single-handed, for heaven's sake.

Whatever happened to dignity? That's what I want to know. Blair acted as if the whole country was one of those ghastly daytime television shows that Margaret used to watch in bed.

And how about the time he tried to upstage me at Mummy's funeral? The damned cheek of the man. I should have had Black Rod take him to the dungeons.

I blame that dreadful Campbell man. It says in the paper that he's getting a million for his diaries. I'm surprised he can write his own name.

One of these days I'm going to publish my diaries. That'd shake them all up. How much do you think they'd be worth?

What a tale I could tell. Remember when we invited the Blairs to Balmoral and that awful wife of his refused to curtsey and then stayed up all night singing Beatles' songs round the piano, with Campbell playing the bloody bagpipes. I didn't get a wink of sleep. Then she had the nerve to yawn during the Highland Games the next day.

I don't know who she thinks she is. Just because her dad used to be in *Till Death Us Do Part*. Personally, I couldn't stand the Scouse git, but I know Alf Garnett was a bit of a hero of yours, Philip.

Then there was that 'do' at the Dome, a complete waste of money, as I told Blair at the time. Forcing one to travel on the Underground with that creepy chap whose grandad used to run the LCC and his Brazilian boyfriend. I've never been so humiliated in my life, especially when the

Wicked Witch tried to link arms during 'Auld Lang Syne'. I wanted the ground to open up and swallow me.

Ten years I've had to put up with this. And for what? Nothing works any more. I was stuck in a jam on the M25 for three hours last week.

World-class transport system, he promised, and then put that jumped-up ship's steward in charge. Young Soames had his measure from the start. 'Gin and tonic, please, Giovanni.' One of Bunter's better lines.

I told Blair devolution would end in tears, but did he listen? Of course not; he just blundered in like he always does. Now the whole kingdom is falling to pieces.

Same with the House of Lords. What a complete cock-up. It's supposed to be down to me who gets a peerage. Then I discover Blair's been knocking out seats to the highest bidder. I wouldn't mind, but he didn't even offer me a cut. He's lucky he hasn't had his collar felt. From what I hear, he's not out of the woods yet. He could still end up at the Bailey. That would be a fine legacy, wouldn't it, tee hee.

Education, education, education? That's a laugh. Same with the NHS. Is it any wonder one goes private?

Not that Blair cares, I'm sure. Spends half his time in America, sucking up to that moron Bush. And that's another thing. I'm supposed to be head of the armed forces, but did he ask me before invading Iraq? I could have warned him it would all go pear-shaped, not that he'd have taken any notice.

Frankly, the whole country has gone to the corgis under Blair.

Do you know we had a health and safety inspector round at the Palace telling us to put up 'No Smoking' signs everywhere. I told him to sling his hook.

Why do they want to ban everything? It was bad enough when they voted to outlaw hunting, not that it's made a scrap of difference. I'm exasperated and frustrated, Philip: all this change for change's sake.

Heaven knows I've had to put up with some horrors in my fifty-five years – Harold Wilson and his smelly pipe, that Thatcher woman and her handbag and that grey little man who used to eat his peas off his knife. But at least he knew his place.

For the past ten years, Blair has acted as if he's the bloody Queen, not me. Do you know, he hasn't even had the good grace to invite one to his leaving do.

To be honest, I'm not sure this game's worth the candle any more, not with that Brown taking over. He probably won't even bother turning up for our weekly audience. Maybe I should abdicate, too.

Top up my glass, Philip, there's a dear, and turn on the racing. One's got a horse running in the 3.30 at Haydock.

It's called A Straight Kinda Guy.

Gordon is a Moron

It is never difficult to distinguish between a Scotsman with a grievance and a ray of sunshine – P. G. Wodehouse

Way back at the start of Labour's term in 1997, I wrote that Gordon Brown was destined to be New Labour's Jim Callaghan, a man who became Prime Minister too late, without facing the electorate, and went on to lead his party to crushing defeat. When he finally battered his way into Number 10 his accession was greeted in most quarters like a cross between the second coming of John F. Kennedy and the release of Nelson Mandela. Not by me. I've never done honeymoon periods.

Switching from Blair to Brown was like dumping the wife you hate and then shacking up with her uglier, fatter, even more miserable older sister. At the time I felt as if I was dancing in the dark, as Gordon basked in the glow of post-coital adulation. Here's a taste of what I wrote the week he took over, under the headline: 'Admit It, Gordon, You're Not Up To The Job':

When it comes to being Prime Minister, Gordon just doesn't cut the Colman's. This isn't a 'new' government – it's a collection of has-beens, placemen and people who weren't good enough to be in the last Cabinet.

You'd be hard-pushed to find such a weird array of incompetents, dullards and social inadequates this side of the flight deck of the *Starship Enterprise*. The Miliband brothers even look like Vulcans.

Hilariously, we're asked to believe that Gordon has assembled a government of 'all the talents'. If this is as good as it gets, God help us.

Praise has been heaped on the Home Secretary Jacqui Smith, largely because she seems to have avoided making a complete fool of herself. Most constructive comment has centred on whether she was showing too much cleavage at the dispatch box.

Do you imagine that Osama bin Laden is sitting in his bunker quaking in his flip-flops?

'We'd better surrender, guys, they've just called in that bird who used to be a schoolteacher in Redditch.'

This is a Cabinet of Gordon's Gofers. There's not a man nor woman sitting round that table who would dare to stand up to him.

When the going gets tough, Gordon gets going – in the opposite direction. Now he's Prime Minister, there's nowhere to run. But it won't stop him trying to hide.

The novelty will wear off soon enough. He's running scared. He looks uncomfortable and has the air of a man about to get his collar felt.

It was much easier being the boy sitting at the back of the class, cheating at maths and making himself scarce when his classmates were caught smoking behind the bike sheds.

Gordon knows in his heart that he hasn't got a mandate from the British people. I suspect, too, that now he's finally achieved his ambition of becoming Prime Minister, he's acutely aware that he isn't really up to the job.

If ever there was a classic case of 'be careful what you wish for', this is it. You can smell his fear.

There was a clamour for an early general election to crush the Conservatives once and for all. My hunch all along was that Gordon's innate cowardice would prevail, and I said so. I was virtually alone in insisting that he wouldn't go to the people. When he decided against an election, I had a field day.

You can perform cosmetic dentistry on a leopard, you can put him in a turquoise tie and comb his hair, but you can't get rid of the spots. To paraphrase Robert Browning's aptly titled 'The Lost Leader': never glad confident Gordon again!

The carefully constructed artifice of trust and competence has been blown apart. All the King's Horses and all the King's Men won't put Grumpty Dumpty together again.

Gordon enjoyed an extraordinary and completely unwarranted tide of goodwill, which he has now flushed away.

It's easy to pose as resolute in the face of terrorism when the bombs don't actually go off. Cancelling a casino which hasn't been built isn't exactly a high-risk strategy.

Making a statement on foot and mouth twenty minutes after a sheep sneezes in Lanarkshire doesn't turn you into Winston Churchill.

Come a real crisis, he's the Invisible Man.

The election decision was not about what was good for Britain, it was about what was good for Gordon.

His ridiculous posturing as the father of a grateful nation is shot to pieces. The indecision and naked spivvery have exposed Brown as just another grubby politician on the make. It's going to be a long walk home.

This was his Black Wednesday moment. His graduation gown lies in rags at his feet. He won't get up from this. People aren't as stupid as Gordon thinks.

One thing he has achieved – which many thought nigh on impossible – is to have reinvigorated and reunited the Conservative Party.

Unless I am sorely mistaken, the Tories won't lose that discipline and momentum any time soon. They're now on course to win the next election, whenever it is held.

One of the reasons Tony Blair hung around as long as he did was because he knows Gordon is a loser. Not up to the job. Now the country knows it, too.

I never bought into the prudent son-of-the-manse routine. Gordon has all the sincerity of a bent American televangelist, praising the Lord while simultaneously stealing the congregation's hard-earned cash and chasing every passing cheerleader.

He is a toxic confection of narcissism, naked ambition, spite, bullying, bombast and bubbling resentment, with a self-pitying temper and a yellow streak the width of the Firth of Forth.

His overblown sense of entitlement is only matched by his ludicrously inflated opinion of his own abilities. He has never been able to disguise his pathological contempt for those he considers to be his intellectual inferiors – which pretty much covers the whole of mankind.

He is genetically incapable of accepting any responsibility for his own mistakes and seeks to crush dissent with a ruthlessness which would give a Mafia don pause for thought. Tony Soprano's shrink, Dr Malfi, would have her hands full with Gordon.

For the past thirteen years, New Labour, with Gordon Brown at its dark heart, has misled, bullied, cheated and infantilised the British public.

Brown has bankrupted the country, smashed our once gold-standard private pensions system, sold out our sovereignty to Europe and destroyed the special relationship with the USA over the release of the Lockerbie bomber for the sake of a squalid, sectarian squabble with the Scottish Nationalists.

We have a ruinous welfare culture which rewards the feckless and a taxation system which punishes enterprise and the traditional family.

Economically, he peddled us a prospectus as false as anything which ever came out of the offices of Bernie Madoff. Gordon Brown has succeeded in beggaring the country for generations to come.

Brown's Britain is a failed state, led by an unelected Scottish sociopath and a gruesome gang of crooks, liars, political pygmies and smear-merchants.

Bring me sunshine.

So Who's this Norman Brown Guy?

Brown was the first European leader granted an audience with President Barack Obama. With the excitement mounting, I tuned in to *Eyewitness News*, Palm Beach, for a special preview of this historic meeting.

*

Good morning, America, how are you? This is your favourite son, Chad Hanging, back with another three hours of news you can use. Our top story this hour is the arrival of the President of Englandland in our nation's capital. Joining me now live from London is our special correspondent, Brit Limey.

Good morning, Chad. I'm standing outside Buckingham Palace, the world-famous home of soccer star David Buckingham and his wife, Queen Victoria.

Great to see, you, Brit. Correct me if I'm wrong, but I thought President Tony Blair had already met with President Obama at the National Prayer Breakfast a coupla weeks back.

That's affirmative, Chad. But President Blair isn't President of Englandland any more.

He's not? Then what was he doing in Washington?

Beats me, Chad. Perhaps it was something to do with his new role bringing peace to the Mid East.

How's that going?

Pretty good, Chad, if you don't count the war between Hamas and Israel, Hezbollah firing rockets at civilians and the crazies in Iran going nuclear.

So who's the new guy?

He's called President Norman Brown.

And is he a Conservative, like President Blair?

No, Chad. He's Labour. President Blair wasn't a Conservative, either. He only pretended to be.

So how did Brown get the job?

He just kept shouting at President Blair until he stood down.

But he won an election, right?

No, Chad, there wasn't an election. He did think about calling one, but decided against it because he was frightened he might lose.

How can you change Presidents without having an election? I mean, it's not like President Blair was assassinated.

That's just the way it works in Englandland. The leader of the party with the most seats in the House of Lords gets to be President.

So Norman Brown was elected leader of the Labour Party?

Negative, again, Chad. He did raise money and have a leadership campaign, but no one stood against him.

What, nobody? No primaries, no general election, nothing?

Affirmative, Chad.

Let me get this straight. His party hasn't elected him, the country hasn't elected him, yet he still gets to be President.

Norman Brown doesn't really like anyone being given the chance to vote on anything.

Someone must have voted for him, some time.

Oh, yes. He was elected to the House of Lords by his constituents in Scotlandland.

He's Scoddish, then?

That's a big Ten-Four, Chad.

So is he President of Scotlandland, too?

No, that's a guy called Alan Salmon.

Hang on, if Brown's from Scotlandland, how can he be President of Englandland?

That's just the way it goes in this crazy country, Chad. Brown can make laws for Englandland, but not for his own people in Scotlandland. Not that it matters much because Brown has signed away most of Englandland's law-making powers to unelected European bureaucrats in Brussels, Belgiumland.

That would be like stripping Congress of the power to make laws in America and handing it over to Mexico.

I guess so.

How in the Hell did the people of Englandland vote for that?

They didn't. Brown wouldn't let them, even though it was a solemn promise in his party's manifesto the last time people were allowed to vote.

Couldn't the Supreme Court have stopped him?

Not really. The Supreme Court of Englandland is now in Strasbourg, where the geese come from.

Isn't there any opposition?

There's a guy called Boris.

Sounds Russian.

I wouldn't be surprised, Chad. There are millions of Eastern Europeans living here now, mainly in Peterburl. Englandland has seen mass immigration over the past ten years, but no one voted for that, either.

What in the name of Ulysses S. Grant is going on over there, Brit? We're talking about the country which gave us Magna Carta, saw off the Armada, stood alone against Hitler and invented parliamentary democracy. It sounds more like a Commie dictatorship.

Feels like it some days, too, Chad. There certainly seem to be more armed policemen around these days, and there are surveillance cameras everywhere.

So why is Norman Brown in Washington today?

He's come to tell President Obama to join his crusade to save the world. He thinks he's Superman and has all the answers to the economic crisis.

Englandland has to be doing real good if this guy thinks he can fix the credit crunch.

Not so, Chad. The IMF says Englandland is worst placed of all developed economies to cope. The currency has collapsed, unemployment is headed towards three million and the country is saddled with £2 trillion of debt, which it will take generations to pay off.

So who's responsible for that?

Norman Brown.

Brown's the guy who got Englandland into this mess in the first place?

Affirmative, Chad. When he was Treasury Secretary he encouraged the banks to go on a reckless lending spree which has bankrupted the country, he let public spending rip right out of control, and destroyed

Englandland's private pension system, which was once the envy of the world.

Does he admit he screwed up?

Far from it, Chad. He blames America.

He does what?

Blames America, Chad, for selling sub-prime mortgages, which were then bought by banks in Englandland and turned out not to be worth the paper they were printed on.

No one forced these banks to buy them.

No one stopped them, either, Chad. Ten years ago, Englandland tore up the rules designed to stop banks getting into trouble.

Who was the genius behind that cockamayme scheme?

Norman Brown.

So let me get this straight. This Norman Brown guy wrecks Englandland then flies to Washington to tell us that he's saved the world. And he blames America for his own incompetence?

America and a guy called Sir Fred Goodwin.

Who's he?

Ran the Royal Bank of Scotlandland into the ground.

And they made him a 'sir'? Whose idea was that?

Norman Brown. Now he wants Goodwin to lose his pension.

Can he do that?

No, but seeing as Brown's stolen everyone else's pension in Englandland, it won't stop him trying.

So what's happening in Washington today?

There's a formal meeting at the White House, followed by lunch.

Better tell President Obama to count the spoons.

Much Culling in the Marsh

New Labour was an urban movement, with a thinly disguised hatred of all things rural. From the bungled ban on hunting to the ludicrous overreaction to the foot and mouth crisis, the government has demonstrated time and again that it has no understanding of, and even less sympathy for, the plight of the countryside.

They probably saw the the foot and mouth outbreak as an opportunity, not a crisis, which would enable them to bring forward long-anticipated plans to convert the nation to a wholly vegetarian diet, thus saving the NHS millions in cancer, heart disease, diabetes and obesity treatments.

Furthermore, by slaughtering all cattle, pigs and sheep, we will eliminate up to 50 per cent of flatulent gas emissions, reduce our carbon footprint significantly and enable Britain to meet her commitments under the Kyoto Protocol on climate change.

However, sensitive to accusations that their policies show a callous disregard for the countryside, the Cabinet has decided that despite the most recent foot and mouth opportunity, traditional agricultural shows should go ahead as normal.

Civil servants set about drawing up a set of guidelines to help organisers adapt to the new livestock-free environment. Those who comply are eligible for grants from the Diversity Fund.

*

We now take you over to the Mummerset County Showground, at Much Culling in the Marsh, for the grand opening of the new-look, New Labour Agricultural Fayre.

Due to flooding, the replacement bus service has itself been replaced by a flotilla of dinghies, which will ferry visitors to the event from the roof of the former railway station.

We regret that following the closure of the Much Culling sub-post office and tea room, advance tickets are only available via iPhone.

Those who intend to arrive by Land Rover will be subject to a £25-a-day 'green' tax, payable to Mr Livingstone, chair of the parish council. This charge will also apply to all contestants in the tractor pull.

The government hopes to encourage farmers to abandon their gas-guzzling machines and use horse-drawn ploughs and other alternatives. For instance, it takes only three hundred Albanian labourers to do the job of one combine harvester.

On arrival, after being sprayed with disinfectant and wading through a sheep dip, visitors will be offered a traditional Full English breakfast of muesli and soya milk. Fair Trade coffee will be supplied by Mrs Starbuck, of the WI.

Don't miss the differently-abled tug-of-peace contest on the playing field behind the Much Culling central mosque.

Highlight of the morning will be a daredevil display of wheel-clamping by the intrepid members of the Mummerset Safety Camera Partnership Formation Towing-Away Team.

Following an intervention by the Much Binding Health and Safety Executive, the morris dancing has been cancelled. This is being replaced by a demonstration of basket-weaving and cottaging, brought to you by the Mummerset Gay, Lesbian, Bisexual and Transgendered Switchboard.

Bargain hunters may also be interested in the savings to be made on a wide selection of second-hand luggage, on sale in the British Airways tent.

This afternoon, in the main arena, the sheepdog trials will make way for a heart-stopping exhibition of drive-by shooting, courtesy of the Mummerset Massive.

Once again this year, the show intends to reflect the rich tapestry of the English countryside. We are proud to bring you Polish country dancing and Chinese cockle-picking.

In place of the ploughing contest, members of the Mummerset travelling community will be giving a demonstration of the ancient art of Tarmacking.

No ox roast this year, due to the ongoing foot and mouth opportunity, but hash cakes and nut cutlets will be available from the soft drugs stand.

Take your seats early for a thrilling re-enactment of the annual pitched battle between the Much Culling Hunt and the Mummerset Saboteurs.

We are grateful to Mr Brown, the town clerk, for donating a genuine Camp David leather bomber jacket as a tombola prize.

The Much Culling Boy Scouts will be hosting a vegan buffet and entertaining the crowd with a selection of songs from The Gang Show 2007, including the ever-popular 'We're Riding Along In A Toyota Prius'.

Finally, in a spectacular climax, two doctors from Mummerset Cottage Hospital will drive a 4x4 into the organic beer tent and blow themselves up.

Visitors are reminded that the showground is a no-smoking facility. They should also sort their rubbish into several different categories and use the bonsai bins provided. Failure to do so will result in a fine of not less than £1,000 and having to give a DNA sample.

We thank you for your attendance but regret this will be the last Much Culling Agricultural Fayre, as the Mummerset County Showground has been sold to developers for starter homes and a new secure unit for failed asylum seekers.

Don't forget to dip your feet on the way out.

Rebranding St George

Over the past decade, they've tried rebranding everything from the Spastics' Society to the Marriage Guidance Council and the Hunchback of Notre Dame for fear of giving offence.

The government even bunged the Protestant Orange Order in Northern Ireland £100,000 to give the annual marching season a touchy-feely makeover.

Some bright spark thought it would be more 'inclusive' if the traditional celebration of King Billy's victory over the Catholics at the Battle of the Boyne were to be relaunched as 'Orangefest' – a sort of Unionist Blue Nose Day, complete with a bouncy Hillsborough Castle.

That way, Republicans might feel less inclined to throw petrol bombs at it.

Nothing is safe from the revisionists. So I suppose it wasn't going to be long before they got round to England's patron saint. Sure enough, just in time for St George's Day 2007, there were calls to give him a political version of the Trinny and Susannah treatment.

The proposal was outlined in a new report from an ecclesiastical think-tank, entitled: *When The Saints Go Marching Out: Redefining St George for a new era.*

Simon Barrow, one of its authors, declared: 'It is time that St George was reclaimed from the dragon, from past associations with racism and the far right, and from images of arrogant flag-waving.'

Writing in the *Church of England Newspaper*, he said St George's Day should become a 'day of dissent' – celebrating 'the pro-democracy Putney Debates, the equality-seeking Levellers, the anti-slavery abolitionists, the women's suffrage movement, conscientious objectors and peacemakers, anti-racism campaigners, human rights activists and those struggling against debt and poverty'.

He seems to have missed out the Tolpuddle Martyrs, the Bryant & May match girls, the Birmingham Six, the Dave Clark Five, the Guildford Four, the Fun Boy Three, the Forest Gate Two and Winston Silcott, but never mind.

It's the thought that counts.

This is St George, patron saint of the Guardianistas.

Funny how they never want to rebrand St Paddy's Day, to make it more acceptable to Glasgow Rangers supporters; or the Notting Hill Carnival, to make it less Caribbean.

Forgive me, that was 'unhelpful'.

So what would a modern tick-all-the-boxes St George look like? The report said he should be recast as a champion of the oppressed and disadvantaged.

He'd probably be some kind of asylum seeker – sorry, 'undocumented' immigrant.

The red cross would have to go, for a start. Far too, well, English. And with its association with the Crusades, incredibly offensive to Muslims.

Maybe it could be replaced by an EU flag; or a CND badge; a set of Make Poverty History wrist bands; or a Greenpeace logo.

Instead of a helmet and visor, he'd be wearing one of those modish Afghan peasant hats, so popular with the lentil-munching classes in Islington.

Rather than a broadsword, George could carry a NOT IN MY NAME placard, or – even better – a WE ARE ALL HEZBOLLAH NOW banner, sponsored by the *Independent*.

Perhaps an intifada headscarf and a fake suicide belt. They seem to be all the rage these days. A pair of Call Me Dave recycled sneakers, specially designed to minimise his carbon footprint, would be *de rigueur*.

Oh, and don't forget the iPod.

There'd be no fire-breathing dragon, either, not in a smoke-free environment. No dragon of any description, for that matter.

Dragons are probably on the endangered species list, anyway. George would be a paid-up member of the Dragon Liberation Front, roaming the land freeing dragons from animal testing laboratories, pausing only to sell the *Big Issue* on his way to kicking in the front window of McDonald's as part of an anti-globalisation protest.

Instead of slaying dragons, he'd smash up Range Rovers and other assorted 4x4s to demonstrate his deep concern for the planet.

His trusty steed would be replaced by an eco-friendly mountain bike.

George and his same-sex civil partner would adopt a child from Malawi over the internet and live happily ever after in a solar-powered squat in Stoke Newington with a B&Q windmill on the roof.

What the hell, why not get rid of George altogether and replace him with a differently-abled, mixed-race, wimmin's rites co-ordinator called Georgina?

That should satify even the most pernickety revisionist.

Cry 'God Help Harry, England and St George'.

That Bugger Swift

When I started out in journalism on a local paper in 1971, the leader of the local council was an engine driver called Charlie Swift, who ran the city in his spare time.

Meetings were always held in the evenings and he'd frequently hitch a ride to the Town Hall with me in the office van, in exchange for a scoop for next week's paper. He was his own press officer.

Charlie's surgery was the front room of his terraced house in the ward he represented. He didn't receive a penny from the ratepayers in either salary or expenses. Neither did any of his fellow councillors, who all had real-world jobs and gave their time voluntarily.

Everyone knew Charlie – and he wasn't universally popular. Round town he was known as That Bugger Swift.

But the streets were clean, the parks immaculate, the corporation buses ran on time, the roads were in good repair, the schools had a pretty decent record, the car parks were free and the dustbins were emptied twice a week.

That was about all anyone wanted from their local authority.

The Town Hall was an impressive edifice, slap bang in the city centre, a symbol of solidity, stability and civic pride. I can still remember the name of the town clerk, which was proudly enscribed on the side of all municipal vehicles.

As it happens, I'm writing about Peterborough, where I cut my journalistic teeth. But it could be any town or city in Britain in the early seventies.

Within a few years, the system of local government which had served us so well was swept away in a frenzy of Heathite corporatism and 'modernisation'.

Traditional borough boundaries were erased and historic local authorities were merged into gigantic supercouncils. A new era of 'professionalism' was ushered in.

The old breed of town clerk with a sense of duty was replaced by a managerial class of chief executives out of the *Guardian* jobs pages, who pretended they were employed to run major commercial organisations – and expected to be paid accordingly.

Councillors began to receive 'out-of-pocket' expenses and allowances, paving the way for full-time council leaders earning £60,000 a year.

Imposing Victorian Town Halls found themselves redundant, as shiny new – uniformly ugly – civic centres sprang up everywhere and councils embarked on a recruitment and spending spree which would do justice to a sailor on shore leave.

Out went frugal 'ways and means' departments, devoted to keeping costs down. In came corporate finance divisions, money no object.

The parks committee became the 'leisure and amenities' directorate. Bandstands, swings and roundabouts were neglected, while hideous new 'leisure centres' were built at vast expense.

And so we arrived where we find ourselves today – with grandiose council 'cabinets', vast PR departments, local authorities with foreign policies and anti-nuclear zones, 'diversity' directorates and 'carbon footprint' committees.

The sanitation department morphed into 'Environmental Health'. These days they'd rather employ inspectors to rifle through your bin for the 'wrong kind' of rubbish than dustmen to take it away.

Staff are hired on the basis of sexuality, disability or ethnicity, not their ability to do the job. If they must have a quota of lesbians, give them all a broom and send them out to sweep the streets once in a while.

Councils are run for the benefit of those who work there, not for the people who pay for them. Is it any wonder council tax has doubled under Labour?

Where once the council chamber contained butchers, bakers and builders, we now have a generation of full-time councillors who have never held down a proper job in their lives.

Planning decisions are taken not by someone who lives round

the corner – and is therefore accountable to his neighbours – but miles away by faceless bureaucrats and rubber-stamp political lobby fodder, acting on a central government directive.

So remote have local authorities become from the paying public, in both political and geographical terms, that few think it even worth bothering voting in local elections any more, because they don't believe it will make the slightest difference.

Turnout has dropped so low that there's talk of bribing people to vote by giving them free doughnuts and lottery tickets.

Is this really what women chained themselves to the railings and dived under racehorses for?

In an outrageous scam, New Labour even proposed jacking up Town Hall allowances and salaries still further and giving councillors a £10,000 'parachute payment' when they're kicked out of office.

The ludicrous Hazel Blears, then Local Government Secretary, even suggested councillors should get ratepayer-funded pensions.

Meanwhile the 'services' we pay for are appalling. Town Halls employ legions of jobsworths to find out what we want to do and then stop us.

Over the years, I've made a good living pillorying and poking fun at this never-ending carnival of politically motivated profligacy. My columns and TV shows have featured regular Nice Work If You Can Get It sections, diligently spotlighting the ingenious and often hilarious jobs invented by councils and quangos to expand their empires and devour our taxes.

But with the country deep in the financial mire, it ceased to be a joke. Unemployment is at a fourteen-year high and is predicted to hit three million before there is any prospect of an economic recovery.

Those kind of numbers haven't been seen for a quarter of a century, when as a young industrial correspondent I would shuffle along to the Department of Employment once a month dutifully to record the latest jobless total.

Back then, the jobs being lost came overwhelmingly from inefficient, loss-making state-owned steel mills, car factories and coal mines, after Mrs Thatcher decided the government had no business running businesses.

Today, the inevitable attrition is decimating the productive, wealth-creating sectors of the economy. Skilled craftsmen, chartered accountants, chemists, bank staff, estate agents and investment analysts have all made the long trek to the job centre.

But there's one lucky group of people who have no such worries about losing their livelihood, their pension or the roof over their head.

Britain's five-a-day co-ordinators, diversity managers, equality officers, elf'n'safety enforcers and carbon-footprint campaigners can all sleep easily in their beds.

While private companies are either contracting or going to the wall, the public sector continues to party like it's 1999. There's been no shake-out in the Town Halls, no Christmas parties cancelled in quangoland.

Far from it. While the productive sector of the economy was disappearing down the plughole, taking with it millions of jobs, the public sector carried on hiring merrily as if the near-collapse of the global banking system never happened.

With the private sector shedding jobs at the rate of a thousand a day, the *Guardian* carried more than thirty pages of adverts for assorted project managers, facilitators, co-ordinators, support workers and general factotums, as it has done every week for at least the past two decades.

So when the government announced plans to encourage people to abandon their cars and walk to work, I predicted that it would spawn a whole new job creation scheme.

Needless to say, within weeks the *Guardian* was running adverts for 'community walking co-ordinators'.

But it didn't stop there. At a time of mounting unemployment in the private sector, it was revealed that Town Halls have spent more than £3 million over the past year on so-called 'lifestyle' advisers.

These newly invented non-jobs include a £41,000-a-year 'promoting healthy weight' adviser in Lewisham and a £19,000-a-year 'temporary mass participation' worker in Bromsgrove.

Mid-Suffolk has recruited a development officer to teach juggling to youngsters, to 'improve hand-eye co-ordination'. Fife has a cheerleader and a 'teen funk' instructor.

Dozens of councils have hired staff to guide crocodiles of children and parents to school. They called them 'walking buses'.

In Oldham, the council is laying on dance lessons, anticipating the fatuous appointment of Arlene Phillips as Gordon Brown's 'dance tsar'.

All this is as insulting as it is superfluous. But a Local Government Association spokesman said: 'Councils will make no apology for actively working to give people better health.'

Where did councils get the idea that 'actively working to give people better health' is any of their damn business, especially when they can't do the jobs they are paid for, such as keeping the streets clean and emptying the dustbins?

Perhaps, while they're at it, they will apologise for closing swimming pools; banning ball games in the street; for neglecting parks and playgrounds, turning them into no-go areas; and for selling off school playing fields to property developers.

It was reported over the weekend that graduates of Labour's pretend universities are more successful at finding work when they leave than those who have attended traditional universities.

What it didn't say was what kind of gainful employment they've found. Now we know. The government has simply invented work for them.

Most of them haven't got proper jobs at all. They're 'lifestyle' advisers and 'walking co-ordinators'.

This non-stop recruitment drive at our expense has gone through a number of different phases. There was the great AIDS scare, when no self-respecting council could bear to be without an army of HIV prevention workers. At one stage, I worked out that there were more people in Britain earning a good living from AIDS than were actually dying from it.

That was followed by the crazy multiculturalism obsession, which could be satisfied only by hiring thousands of equality and diversity commissars.

Today's driving force is the great global warming scam, entailing the recruitment of legions of eco-warriors and enviro-crime fighters, on salaries commensurate with their self-righteousness.

In between, we've had such lunacy as real nappy co-ordinators, tasked with encouraging women to use washable nappies instead of disposable – until someone worked out that all the detergent being used to wash dirty nappies was actually doing more harm to the environment than throwing them away.

We've had everything from condom commandos to advisers hired to address the very special needs of gay alcoholics.

For instance, on the day Virgin Media and Glaxo announced 2,200 redundancies, Barnet Council, in north London, was desperately seeking a Head of Internal Audit and Ethical Governance, on £80,000 a year, plus the usual perks. How on earth have they managed without one all these years?

This is just one example of utterly unnecessary spending on jobs which didn't exist until now and serve no real purpose.

None of these new public servants is providing anything most people would remotely consider to be a public service. Local government is increasingly a conspiracy against the paying public, extracting ever more taxes in exchange for an ever-worsening level of provision.

They're more interested in dreaming up exciting new rules, fines and punishments and finding elaborate excuses for not doing what we pay them for.

Take Guildford Council, in Surrey, threatening to close down burger vans which don't offer 'healthy options'. What gives them the right to do that? It's none of their damn business what people eat.

Time was that I used to have fun with some of the more insane jobs advertised in the *Guardian* – lesbian self-defence instructors, transgender policy co-ordinators, nuclear-free zone inspectors. These days I tend towards rage when the *Guardian* drops on the doormat, its news pages bringing more gloom about job losses in the private sector on page one, while the recruitment section promises a paradise of gold-plated, recession-proof public sector employment opportunities.

Now more than ever, with the economy going to hell in a hand-cart, we simply can't afford this circus of taxpayer-funded excess, if we ever could.

This is what Gordon Brown really means when he boasts about 'prudence' and 'investment'. It's his reckless spending, putting 800,000 more people on the public payroll, which has left Britain the worst equipped of all industrialised countries to deal with the downturn.

We are now two nations: those who have to make a living in the real world and the army of subsidised public 'servants' guaranteed their jobs and index-linked pensions regardless of cost.

While millions of us in the competitive sector of the economy stare down the barrel of redundancy, the feather-bedded inhabitants of Brown's bloated client state are insulated from the realities of his economic mismanagement. They won't be joining the three million unemployed any time soon.

The Conservatives should promise an end to this racket. If elected, Call Me Dave should say that councillors will no longer receive anything, other than coffee and biscuits and a bus pass for attending meetings.

He should then set about dismantling our grotesque super-councils and replace them with slimmed-down operations based on the old borough boundaries, so that those charged with providing services actually live among those paying for them. If they're local, they're accountable.

Here's a real opportunity for Cameron. But I wouldn't hold your breath. Tory-run councils are just as bad.

It's a crying shame the Town Halls aren't still run part-time by engine drivers, not by self-regarding, pious Guardianistas.

Where's That Bugger Swift when you need him?

To Hell in a Dustcart

From the Littlejohn column, November 29, 2002, following another of Gordon Brown's sneaky pre-Budget statements. While it was hailed, as usual, as a work of genius, there was a nasty surprise lurking within the small print. Here's what I wrote:

Tucked away in Gordon Brown's pre-Budget statement is a proposal for an exciting new tax on rubbish.

Householders will be fined if they don't sort their waste into separate bags for recycling. And new charges will be levied according to the weight of each bin bag.

This could be as high as £1 a sack. Just think, only twenty billion bags to go and Gordon's filled in his black hole. The men in sandals insist that recycling is the only way to save the planet. They may have a point. I've got nothing against recycling. I'm one of their best customers at our local bottle bank.

But this is about money, not the environment. Gordon's big problem is that he wants to meddle in every single aspect of our lives. If it moves, or even if it doesn't, he'll tax it. Has he given a moment's thought to how this scheme would work in practice?

It's not as if the average Town Hall refuse department is a model of efficiency. They can't even keep the streets clean. In my neck of the woods the recycling containers in the local car park are hardly ever emptied and people just dump their bottles and papers by the side of them, creating an ugly eyesore. Gives the rats somewhere to sleep, though.

How are the dustmen supposed to know whether each bag contains what it's supposed to without ripping them open and rifling through the contents? Perhaps we are to be issued with transparent bin bags to make the job easier.

And what if we just deny it's our rubbish? Will they trawl

through each bag looking for a discarded envelope or some other evidence of who dumped it? In most streets they won't be able to tell who chucked out what once the foxes have been at it.

Then there's the question of weighing it. How are we supposed to know how much each bag weighs?

Are there going to be scales on the back of every dustcart? And are we expected to take their word for it? Or will we all have to fork out for our own individual set of rubbish scales?

Will the binmen be on some sort of incentive scheme, like traffic wardens? Since most of them have now been privatised will they be set targets for overweight bags or stray plastic bottles in sacks of cardboard?

What's to stop them slipping a rogue fizzy drinks can into a sack full of rotting fruit and veg? That'll be a quid, missus.

Who is going to adjudicate? Stand by for thousands of adverts in the *Guardian* for rubbish inspectors – or rather Environmental Protection Enforcement Co-ordinators – on twenty-five grand a year and a Mondeo.

How long before some old lady is sent to prison for refusing to pay a fine for forgetting to separate a yogurt pot from her Fruit'n' Fibre cartons or putting out a bag weighing a couple of ounces over the limit?

Think I'm joking? These are the same people prosecuting greengrocers for flogging apples in weights and measures their customers understand.

Then there are the practical considerations. In many areas the dustman already comes round about as often as Father Christmas. Imagine how much longer it's all going to take if they have to sift through and weigh every single bag.

My guess is that this will have the exact opposite effect to that which it is claimed to be intended.

When the government slapped a tax on old cars taken to scrapyards, the numbers dropped. End result – abandoned old cars at the side of every road. Once this tax kicks in some people will simply chuck their rubbish in hedges, a bit like they do now.

And no one has yet pointed out that we already pay through the nose in council tax to get our rubbish collected. This is just another way of making us pay twice.

We are all going to hell in a dustcart.

Bring Out Your Dead

When I was a boy we lived in a bungalow in Essex, on a neat suburban street leading down to the railway station. Every week the dustmen would empty our two metal bins: one for household waste, the other for the ashes from our Creda boiler.

They'd walk round the back of the house, hoist the bins on to their shoulders and, having emptied them on to their cart, would bring them back to where they belonged, behind the coal bunker.

Another man went in their wake with a broom, sweeping up anything that had fallen out and scooping it up on a giant shovel. I can still see them now in my mind's eye, wearing donkey jackets with heavy-duty leather patches across their shoulders.

Strong men, doing men's work. The kind of English yeomen you'd always want alongside you in a fight. When it came to doling out Christmas boxes, the dustmen were first in line for a mince pie and a half-crown.

They were admired, stock characters in popular culture. So how on earth did we get from there to a situation where, in Britain in 2008, there were a record 228 assaults on dustmen?

Both physical and verbal attacks were up by a fifth over the year, as a consequence of this government's decision to put refuse collection in the front line of the punishment culture.

In Hertfordshire, an angry resident attacked a dustcart with a broom – reminiscent, as I wrote at the time, of Basil Fawlty's manic thrashing of a dead Austin 1100.

In Southampton, armed police were called out after a green-grocer held a dustman hostage at gunpoint.

In Coventry, a schoolteacher who made a mild complaint about her dustmen was to be barricaded in her home by fifteen wheelie bins dragged from all over the neighbourhood and strategically positioned across her driveway.

The lunacy of the recycling rules and the Stalinist zeal with which they are enforced has the capacity to unleash the inner Basil Fawlty in us all.

*

Elf'n'safety was the excuse given for not emptying a wheelie bin that turned out to contain a corpse. It had been lying undisturbed for three weeks.

Neighbours reported that refuse crews working for Elmbridge Council would turn up at the house in Cobham, Surrey, every Friday, shake the bin and then decide it was too heavy to pull the few feet to their cart.

It was halfway up the drive and council rules state that it must be placed on the pavement on the day of collection, otherwise the rubbish won't be collected.

Only when the bin was knocked over, probably by scavenging urban foxes, was the body of the thirty-year-old woman revealed after a passer-by saw a foot sticking out of the lid and phoned the police.

Goodness knows how long her corpse would have remained there if it hadn't toppled over.

A post mortem showed she had suffered a serious head injury and police launched a manhunt for the suspected murderer, who was believed to have legged it to Malta.

If the dustmen had been doing their job properly, he wouldn't have had three weeks to make good his escape.

You can only begin to imagine the bovine stupidity which contributed to the delay in finding the body.

Didn't it occur to the dustmen to have a look inside the bin to find out what was weighing it down?

Given that they inspected the bin three times, you'd have thought they might have noticed something was amiss. A corpse does tend to get a bit ripe after a few days, particularly if not wrapped securely in a regulation black plastic bin liner.

'Oi, Sid, have a butcher's at this. Looks like a dead body.'

'Why are you telling me? I'm a dustman, not a bloomin' undertaker.'

'But we can't just leave it here.'

'Why not? If they wanted it lugging away, they should have put it by the kerb. It's halfway up the drive.'

'It don't half pen and ink.'

'That's a good enough reason for leaving it be. You dunno where it's been.'

'Come on, Sid, give us a hand.'

'What, with my back? I'm not lifting that. Elf'n'safety, innit?'

But it's unfair to lay all the blame on the dustmen.

They were only obeying orders.

Perhaps Elmbridge Council has a policy of only collecting corpses on alternate Tuesdays. A dead body probably counts as the 'wrong' kind of rubbish.

I'm surprised the murderer wasn't also fined for putting it out in the wrong container on the wrong day.

*

Incidentally, the last time I drove past my old bungalow, all the pretty, well-tended front gardens in the street were disfigured by ugly wheelie bins.

A friend who still lives there says the local refuse and recycling regime would test the patience of a saint.

He regularly has to walk to the station through piles of rubbish on pavements strewn with everything from pizza crusts to sanitary towels torn from plastic sacks overnight by predatory suburban foxes.

I wonder what the dustmen of my childhood would have made of it all.

'My Old Man's A Dustman'

Not a lot of people know this, but I was Britain's first 'green' journalist. I've been recycling all my old columns for years. So I couldn't help wondering what Lonnie Donegan would have made of our modern refuse collection regime, had he been writing his classic hit 'My Old Man's A Dustman' today. A one, a two, a one, two, three, four . . .

Now here's a little story
I can't believe it's true
About how local councils
Won't do what they're paid to do.
Our bins are overflowing
And though they stink and leak
They'll only come and empty 'em
Every other week.

Oh, my old man's a dustman
He wears a dustman's hat
With 'Environmental Protection Team'
Written on the back.
He used to drive a dustcart
And always came on time
Now he searches dustbins
For signs of eco-crime.

Some folks they recycle
And some of them forget
So if they use the wrong bin
He leaves it on the step.

One old boy got sloppy
And didn't close his lid
So my old man went round there
And fined him fifty quid.

Oh, my old man's a dustman
The planet he must save
He wears recycled trainers
Just like Call Me Dave.

I say, I say, I say
(Yeah)
I found a bug in my dustbin
(Did you kill it?)
No, it was an electronic bug.

Now one old girl in Rochdale
Had trouble with her feet
So she couldn't push her dustbin
Right into the street.
My old man got his tape measure out
And checked it on his list
Said: 'That's not out for collection
So it's staying where it is.'

Though my old man's a dustman
He's getting rather grand
Thinks he's an eco-warrior
Under General Miliband.

I say, I say, I say
(What?)
I found a rat in my dustbin
(You sure it's not an inspector from the council?)
That's what I said: I found a rat in my dustbin.

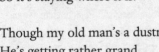

One day while in a hurry
He missed a lady's bin
He'd only gone a few yards
When she chased after him.
She said: 'It's full of chicken bones
It isn't going to keep.'
He said: 'I'm only doing bottles today,
See you Tuesday week.'

Oh, my old man's a dustman
He wears a Greenpeace pin
He's fighting global warming
But he won't empty your bin.

A buxom housewife on his round asked:
'Why won't you take my sacks?'
My old man said: 'Don't blame me, love
Blame Gordon's landfill tax.'
They make us sort our rubbish
It's gone beyond a joke
Then they send it off to China
Where it all goes up in smoke.

I say, I say, I say
(Yes?)
I've just found a gas bill in my compost box
(Then put your trousers on, chummy,
You're bleedin' nicked.)

One day I said to my old man
'Dad, don't you find it strange?
That they'd endanger public health
In the name of climate change?'
He said: 'Now you look here, my son,
They couldn't give a toss.
It's nowt to do with climate change,
It's showing you who's boss.'

Oh, my old man was a dustman
He wore a dustman's hat
Now he's an Alternate Week Co-ordinator
And he lives in a penthouse flat.
So if your bin is full to the brim
And you just can't stand the smell
Don't bother ringing my old man
'Cos you can go to hell.

A Convenient Lie

The justification for the great recycling terror is the belief that the earth is being destroyed by man-made climate change. If the floods don't get you, the Saharan temperatures will. So the legions of global warming loonies and polar bear huggers here in Britain should have seized on this report in the *New York Times*:

> Soviet scientists on board an icebreaker drifting just three hundred miles from the North Pole have concluded that the world is getting hotter.
>
> Warm-water fish are appearing in increasing numbers in Arctic seas as temperatures have risen, melting the ice caps.
>
> The Russian explorers believe that very soon ships will be able to sail right across the Pole.

Unfortunately for the 'man-made climate change' headbangers, the report actually appeared on 12 December 1938. It was republished on a website run by a former TV meteorologist, who treats the whole 'climate change' racket with a healthy dose of sea salt.

The Soviet scientists also concluded that the warmer weather was almost certainly down to the rays of the sun. And they added that it would be rash to prophesy the duration of these higher temperatures, since the Ice Age was followed immediately by a period of much hotter summers than they were experiencing in the thirties – the warmest decade of the twentieth century, as it turned out.

A few short years later, by 1947, the ice caps were restored to their former glory and Britain experienced one of the harshest winters on record, lasting well into March.

Even as the warmists were drawing up new laws, fines and taxes to stop the earth going into meltdown, we were going through another cold spell.

November 2008 was the coldest for three decades. We even had snow in October, on the very day the House of Commons was debating its ludicrous, self-important 'climate change' bill.

That was the same month China's official news agency reported that Tibet had suffered its 'worst snowfall ever'.

Across the world, temperatures plummeted, just as they have been falling for ten years. There was snow in the Las Vegas desert in October and much of North America was hit by an ice storm.

Since then the evidence against the warmists has been coming thick and fast. As thick as the ice in Canada, where during the winter of 2008–9 it covered two million square kilometres more than it did the past three winters and is between 10 and 20 millimetres thicker than last year

According to NASA scientists in Maryland, the polar ice caps, far from shrinking, are actually increasing in size.

In the Alps, where one mild winter sparked a wave of hysteria about 'global warming', they had their best snowfall for twenty years and the skiing season kicked off two weeks early.

None of this has in any way deterred the 'global warming' fascists. They simply dismissed this glaring, incontrovertible evidence as a 'blip' and continue to insist the world is burning up.

Around the same time, 31,000 scientists had signed an online petition challenging the conventional wisdom that man-made CO_2 emissions were causing 'global warming'.

Dr Arthur Robinson, of the University of Oregon, announced this to a packed press conference in Washington. He said he was aware that critics would claim this list was phoney, but said signatories had been carefully vetted and at least nine thousand had PhDs.

This went largely unreported on either side of the Atlantic. Any dissent from the great global warming scam, however valid, is dismissed as heresy.

In the words of Rod Stewart's 'Mandolin Wind':

> The coldest winter in almost fourteen years,
> Could never, never change your mind.

Never mind fourteen years, we're talking about the coldest winter in thirty years.

And still they wouldn't admit to even a smidgeon of doubt. In an increasingly secular Britain, 'climate change' is the new religion.

As the wise old G. K. Chesterton observed: when people stop believing in God, they don't believe in nothing – they believe in anything.

*

Inevitably, more than five thousand new jobs – and counting – have been created by local authorities to cash in on the 'global warming' hysteria. Town Halls across Britain are estimated to have spent more than £100 million recruiting an army of green warriors.

Take the the People's Republic of Islington, where the council kicked things off by advertising for a 'Carbon Reduction Adviser' on thirty grand a year.

The advert read: 'Islington Council is leading the way in tackling climate change . . .'

You could have fooled me. Islington may be leading the way in deliberately creating traffic congestion, vindictive parking enforcement and turning almost every road in the borough into a crazy golf course.

It could mount a convincing case for leading the way in stabbing, street crime, litter, graffiti and child molestation in council care homes.

But saving the planet? No one would ever confuse the Holloway Road with the Brazilian rainforest, even without the CCTV cameras every five yards.

Where Islington has always led the way is in hiring graduates of pretend 'universities' for lucrative non-jobs at the taxpayer's expense. But it doesn't have the field to itself.

In Tower Hamlets, the poorest borough in London and arguably the most deprived in Britain, fifty-eight employees have job titles which contain the words 'climate change' or 'global warming'. Nevertheless, Tower Hamlets still has the worst recycling record in the country.

Last time I looked, Nottingham had twenty-two staff dedicated to dealing with 'issues around global warming'. The city also boasts seventy 'green champions'. We're not talking Robin Hood and his Merry Men here.

Salford decided to hire a Principal Planning Officer (Climate Change) on £32,487 a year. Just in case you wondered why this grandiose new position is being created, the advert explained: 'The climate in Salford is changing . . .'

Oh, yeah? The last time I was up there, most of Britain was basking in a spring heatwave and I was wearing an open-necked shirt and lightweight suit. By the time I got to Salford, it was freezing and I had to resort to my heavy overcoat. There was a howling wind and rain was forecast.

So no climate change there, then.

Thirty grand seems to be about the going rate for an eco-warrior. Bedford Borough Council advertised for a climate change officer dedicated to cutting greenhouse gases. The post pays £33,328 a year and all the usual perks, including – wait for it – an 'essential car user allowance'.

You couldn't make it up.

Hull now has thirty full-time staff beavering away on 'environmental issues'. It's just a pity they weren't beavering away building dams, instead of dreaming up exciting new punishments for enviro-criminals.

When floods swept through the city a couple of summers ago, the council was woefully unprepared. Residents washed out of house and home were left to fend for themselves.

*

In fact, during the widespread flooding which hit many parts of Britain in the summer of 2008, all these climate champions proved to be utterly, hopelessly, bloody useless.

When the heavens opened, it was the same old story, just as it is when it snows in the winter. No evacuation plans, no flood defences, simply the usual headless-chicken incompetence. Anything above light drizzle has our so-called 'emergency' response teams frozen in the headlights.

While we're worrying ourselves sick about 'global warming', we still haven't got a clue what to do about the weather.

*

Oh, and after I described global warming as a new religion, the Archbishop of Canterbury threw his mitre into the ring.

To be honest, Dr Rowan Williams has always looked more like a Druid than a clergyman.

So it was no surprise when he signed up to the whole 'climate change' swindle, warning that not even God can save us from the effects of global warming.

He doesn't seem to have noticed that the world has managed to look after itself for the past few million years through plague, pestilence and Ice Age.

Meanwhile, if further confirmation were needed, an Oxford environmentalist was given permission to claim that he was unfairly sacked because of his views on climate change.

Tim Nicholson was made redundant from his job as head of sustainability at a local firm. He refuses to take flights because of the harm he alleges planes do to the planet.

A tribunal ruled that he could make a claim for religious discrimination under the Employment Equality (Religion and Belief) Regulations 2003.

*

Most of this madness is predicated upon Al Gore's alarmist enviro-movie, *An Inconvenient Truth*.

But no less an authority that the founder of the Weather Channel in the US says Al Gore should be sued for fraud. John Coleman maintains that's the only way all the evidence about 'climate change' can be properly challenged. He insists the great global warming scare is a huge scam, and says he has scientific proof to back him up.

Coleman doesn't deny that weather cycles change, and he admits that carbon emissions are higher than they were, say, three hundred years ago. But he says carbon in the atmosphere amounts to only 38 particles in 100,000. Far from 'global warming', the earth is actually in a cooling-down phase.

It's fair to assume he has some idea of what he's talking about, since – unlike most of the hysterical doom-mongers – he's been a meteorologist all his life.

Sometimes you do need a weatherman to know which way the wind blows.

An Inconvenient Truth has been tested in court in Britain and a judge ruled that it is both biased and contains proven inaccuracies. But, disgracefully, he wouldn't issue an order preventing it being shown in British schools by propagandists hell-bent on brainwashing our children.

Friends of the Earth actually admit there are nine factual errors in the movie, but say that doesn't matter – lies are allowed in pursuit of their quasi-religious crusade. Maybe they should change their name to Enemies of the Truth.

*

Incidentally, back in 1938 they weren't quite so sentimental about polar bears as we are today.

The *New York Times* reported that whenever the Soviet expedition came across a polar bear they shot it for food.

> Several bears had been encountered and they provided
> fresh meat for the party.

Given that we are told 'global warming' presents such an ominous threat to agriculture, and the exhaust gases of cattle contribute greatly to the non-existent hole in the ozone layer, maybe we should start farming polar bears.

The Slop-Bucket Kid

A few years ago I was introduced to the then environment secretary David Miliband at a reception. He pumped my hand and invited me to visit his office for a drink.

Why would I want to do that?

Miliband explained that he would appreciate the opportunity to convince me I had got it all wrong over AWCs.

I had no idea what he was talking about. Wasn't an AWC some kind of early warning missile defence shield? And, if so, what had it got to do with the Department of the Environment?

I was well wide of the mark. In Labour's La-La Land, AWC stands for Alternate Weekly Collections. The penny dropped.

'Oh, I get it. You mean not emptying the dustbins.'

Far from it, said Miliband. We are emptying the dustbins, just once a fortnight instead of once a week. If only I could spare him half an hour of my time, he could convince me that this was a brilliant, efficient way of saving the planet.

As he droned on, promising that he could support his case with hard evidence, I lost the will to live. This boy's a fool, as Eric Morecambe used to say.

Once his feet were under the table at Environment, this hated initiative became Miliband's flagship programme. Indeed, it is just about the only significant contribution of his brief ministerial career.

At one stage, so taken was he with his own genius, that he even suggested we all buy a slop bucket for our leftovers. My reaction was:

It's just what we've always wanted – a bucket of leftover food slurping around under the sink for a fortnight, just waiting to be sent for something called 'anaerobic digestion'.

Yum, yum. Slop buckets sound like something straight out of a Hogarth painting. Why not go the whole hog and abolish flush toilets, too?

Let's all keep potties under our beds and empty them once every couple of weeks. The contents could also go for 'anaerobic digestion' to be turned into 'bio-gas' or spread on the rose bed.

Having introduced this ludicrous policy, he simply walked away from the carnage into the Foreign Office, leaving the rest of us – literally – to sweep up behind him.

Yet, incredibly, as Brown wobbled, this other-worldy wonker was being touted for the highest office in the land. I've never understood why the Westminster Village Idiots take politicians at their own estimation – which is probably why I ended up as a song and dance man instead of a revered political commentator.

Frankly, I can think of no politician of Miliband's generation less suited to becoming Prime Minister – unless you count his kid brother Ed, New Labour's Private Pike.

Miliband Major is living proof that anyone who wants the job so desperately should be immediately disqualified from getting it. Just look at the train wreck which is Gordon Brown.

The Boy David was raised in a north London socialist hothouse, crammed with 'intellectuals' – which helps explain everything. You have to be really clever to invent something so stupid as scrapping weekly refuse collections. These people deal in theory, not reality.

His glittering career has taken him from studying politics at university, through working as a policy researcher to running the policy unit at 10 Downing Street, before being parachuted into a safe seat in one of Labour's rotten boroughs in Geordieland. He's never had a proper job in his life.

Yet all this 'policy' experience didn't prevent him coming up with one of the most unpopular, unworkable policies ever introduced by any government.

That's because he only ever meets people like himself – insular, self-regarding obsessives who live and breathe politics and have little or no interaction with the people they purport to represent. It's life, Jim, but not as we know it.

Perhaps he is worried that if he does venture out of the bubble, someone might actually recognise him and tip a slop bucket over his head.

Let me assure him, here in the real world no one, but no one, is saying: What we want is David Miliband. Most people have no idea who he is, otherwise they would pelt him with rotten food from their overflowing dustbins every time he dared show his face in public.

*

When Miliband started introducing slop buckets, I can remember asking at the time: why stop there? Why not force every home to keep a pot-bellied pig in the kitchen. Pigs will eat anything and thus, if all our household waste was fed to them, we could abolish refuse collections altogether and the polar bears would live happily ever after.

It was supposed to be a joke. But now it seems a pig in your back garden is the new suburban, must-have accessory, as people seek alternative ways of disposing of their rotting household waste.

The only drawback is that elf'n'safety won't let you feed it on kitchen scraps, which rather defeats the object. Still, plenty of people are apparently prepared to raise domestic pigs for the table in these economically straitened times.

Has anyone thought this through? What about swine flu? And how long before someone decides that keeping pigs might offend Muslim neighbours?

*

Despite the ever-present possibility of being assaulted by an angry householder, Havant Borough Council received 238 applications for a single £14,000-a-year job as a dustman. How many of those came from the 238 Labour MPs certain to lose their seats at the next election? It's the only other career most of them are qualified for. Since David Miliband is such an enthusiast for recycling and will be out of a job after the next election, I wondered if he had applied. Imagine the interview.

Tell me, Mr Miliband, why do you want to become a dustman?

Because I have a keen interest in climate change and I see the envi-

ronmental protection operative as a key front-line player in the fight against global warming.

We're in the front line, all right – against angry householders, thanks to you lot.

What do you mean?

Ever since you sent out that edict on alternate weekly collections when you was Environment Secretary, we've become the most hated men in Britain.

But don't people understand that we must reduce our carbon foot-print?

Frankly, Mr Miliband, most people don't give a stuff. They just want their bins emptied.

They get them emptied, every other week.

You try cramming two weeks' rubbish into one wheelie bin. You've even cut the size of those in half. No wonder they're overflowing. You should see the state of the pavements.

People must learn to recycle more. It's for the good of the planet.

That's all very well, but what the hell are people supposed to do with their food waste when we only come round once a fortnight?

I've already suggested that everyone should have a kitchen caddy under their sink, for their food scraps.

You mean a slop bucket.

Well, I wouldn't exactly put it like that.

I bloody would. We tried that and abandoned it after a week. Housewives were tipping them over the lads' heads. We almost had a strike on our hands.

People are just going to have to learn to adapt if we're to save the polar bears.

Folk do their best, but now you've started fining them for putting the odd envelope in the bottle bank by mistake, they don't even bother recycling. They just dump everything at the side of the road and leave us to pick the bones out of it. You wouldn't believe what we have to deal with – hypodermic needles, half-eaten tubs of Pot Noodles, it's disgusting. I'll tell you, when we come across a pile of dirty disposable nappies, it's like a breath of fresh air.

That's why we've given you extra powers, surveillance, microchips in the bins.

This is the refuse collection service, young man, not MI5. You've been watching too much Spooks. You've turned decent, law-abiding taxpayers into criminals.

But under the terms of the Kyoto Protocol . . .

Don't Kyoto me. Some of us have to live in the real world. This used to be a simple, straightforward, steady line of work. People put their rubbish out once a week, we collected it. Job done and a nice Christmas box every year from a grateful public.

But we have to move on. This is the twenty-first century. The earth is in mortal danger.

I don't know about that, but my lads is in mortal danger, what with the rats and foxes and her at Number 48 on the warpath. I'm losing men who have worked here for nigh on twenty years. Why do you think we're having to advertise?

Can we talk about my job application?

If you must, but get a move on. I've got another 237 people out there in the waiting room.

How much does it pay?

Basic £14,000.

That's a month, is it?

Month? That's £14,000 a year.

Oh, I see. What are the hours?

Six in the morning to three-thirty in the afternoon, half an hour for lunch.

Every day?

Every day. Used to be plenty of overtime, too, but that went up the spout when you halved the number of collections.

What about holidays?

Four weeks a year, plus bank holidays and seventeen guaranteed sickies, no questions asked.

It's not exactly what I'm used to.

How's that?

At Westminster, we get three months off in the summer and never work Fridays.

Nice work if you can get it.

But there's allowances, obviously.

You get two sets of overalls and a new pair of boots every year.

And that's it?

Yep.

No £150 a day just for turning up?

Sorry.

No second-home expenses?

Nope.

No money for patio heaters, flat-screen televisions, kitchen sinks, bath plugs, porno films?

No. But Dirty Barry back at the depot does a nice line in mucky DVDs, if you're into that kind of thing.

Subsidised first-class travel?

You can get dropped off home, provided the cart is going past your door on the way back from the tip. But you'll have to get someone else to sign you out.

Oh, well. Beggars can't be choosers. I'll take it, until something better turns up. At least it means I won't have to pay 50p in the pound income tax.

I'm sorry, Mr Miliband, but I'm afraid you've had a wasted journey.

Why's that?

I've just had this circular from Harriet Harman saying I've got to give the job to a woman. On your way out, would you send in Jacqui Smith?

Bring on the Red-bearded Dwarves

Beachcomber was the *nom de plume* of the brilliant satirist J. B. Morton, who wrote the surreal By The Way column in the old broadsheet *Daily Express* for more than half a century until 1975. He would have had a field day under New Labour.

Morton ridiculed petty bureaucracy and the idiocies of the law. He inspired a whole generation of comedians, from Peter Cook and the Monty Python team to Spike Milligan, who brought Beachcomber to television.

His subversive inventions included the 'horrible welfare worker' Mrs Wretch, the disastrous civil servant Charlie Suet and the Ministry of Bubbleblowing. He also created the humourless, interfering oaf Prodnose.

Perhaps his most famous character was Mr Justice Cocklecarrot, a well-meaning but useless judge, whose lot in life was to listen to a series of farcical cases brought before the courts by vexatious litigants – including the ubiquitous Red-bearded Dwarves, who gloried in names such as Scorpion de Rooftrouser and Churm Rincewind.

Most of it is as relevant today as it was when Beachcomber first wrote it. Which of us hasn't encountered Mrs Wretch, Charlie Suet and Prodnose? They are our constant companions.

These days Baroness Wretch would be sitting in the House of Lords and Sir Charles Suet would be head of the diversity directorate at the European Bubbleblowing Commission.

Prodnose seems to be running everything else, up to and including elf'n'safety. Maybe that should be dwarf'n'safety.

The Case of the Discarded Apple Core, which was sent for trial at Crown Court, would have been tailor-made for Mr Justice Cocklecarrot.

It stars a young lady called Kate Badger, who even sounds like a

Beachcomber character. She works in promotions, which would have amused Morton.

Miss Badger was accused of tossing an apple core out of the window of her parked car on to the pavement in Wolverhampton town centre.

Her VW Golf was photographed and she was traced with the use of number plate recognition software and issued with a £60 fixed penalty fine, which she is refusing to pay because she says she was in a shop – namely River Island, m'lud; I believe it is a clothing emporium – at the precise time the alleged offence was committed.

Miss Badger maintained the apple core must have been discarded by a friend, but she can't remember who she was with on the day in question, even though she can remember being in River Island. It may have been someone who has subsequently moved away from the Wolverhampton area.

The case ran for eleven months and consumed thousands of pounds in legal fees. Instead of telling everyone to grow up, go home and stop wasting the court's time and taxpayers' money, magistrates agreed to send the matter to Mr Justice Cocklecarrot.

If convicted, Miss Badger faced a maximum penalty of £20,000 and six months in prison.

Twenty grand and six months in the slammer does seem a bit harsh for littering. But Miss Badger wasn't charged with littering.

In an indictment which could have come straight from the wildest Beachcomber flight of fancy, she was accused of 'knowingly causing the deposit of controlled waste, namely an apple core, on land which did not have a waste management licence' and of 'failing to provide information' as to who did throw said apple core, contrary to Section 33 of the Environmental Protection Act 1990.

Charlie Suet would have been proud of them. Just as well William Tell didn't live in Wolverhampton:

My lord, the defendant is charged with child endangerment and possession of a deadly weapon, namely one crossbow. He is also in breach of several provisions of the Health and Safety Regulations.

Furthermore he knowingly caused the deposit of controlled waste, namely an apple, on land which did not have a waste management licence, contrary to Section 33 of the Environmental Protection Act.

We ask for him to be remanded in custody pending a full trial. His son is the subject of a protection order and is currently in the care of Ms Wretch, of the social services directorate.

Bring on the Red-bearded Dwarves.

Ye Olde Globalle Warminge

from Ye Guardian, of 1663

As Mr Samuel Pepys records in his Diary today: 'There was last night the greatest tide that ever was remembered in England to have been in this river, all Whitehall having been drowned.'

Now that the waters of the Thames are lapping at the very doors of ye Palace of Westminster, will the King awake to ye very real threat globalle warminge poses to his realm?

For centuries expertes have been warning of climate change. As long ago as 1236, there was a great deluge which caused the halls of Westminster to flood. Many soothsayers predict that unless drastic provisions are enacted within two hundred years, the Thames will cease to freeze over in winter, bringing to an end to the annual frost fayres.

This journal, in particulair through the musings of Mistress Toynbee and Master Monbiot, has attempted to alert Parliament of the necessity to confront the man-made catastrophe soon to engulf this sceptred isle.

While we make no secret of our preference for Puritan rule over the monarchy, we did harbour hope that the accession of Charles, King of Scots, to the throne of England would usher in a new age of enlightenment, modernisation and diversity.

Yet our best wishes remain unfulfilled as his Royal Highness lives up to his reputation as Ye Merrie Monarch and leads a life of hedonism while ye crisis worsens.

Today, ye Guardian calls on Charles II to recall parliament urgently to sanction a confection of emergency measures designed specifically to eradicate globalle warminge.

Firstly, there must be an immediate prohibition on the smoking of tobacco products in public places; namely ale houses, theatres and bear-baiting pits. Master Monbiot calculates that the effluent from this filthy habit is causing a hole the size of Wessex in ye ozone layer.

Furthermore, ye new-fangled 'patyoe heaters' being erected in coachyards and beer gardenes for the comfort of imbibers in inclement weather must be discouraged through the imposition of a special tariff; the proceeds of which should be expended on the recruitment of a dedicated army of globalle warminge co-ordinatores under the direction of a Carbonfinder General, to be appointed by ye King and given powers to hang, draw and quarter all Enemyes of Ye Earthe.

Ye ecologistes are concerned about the emissions of harmful gases from livestock being kept in the environs of the Citye. Domestic cattle, pigges and sheepes, are giving off enough poisons to destroy ye rainforest of Epping, which has already been ravished by rapacious developers of property in ye Manor of Chigwelle.

Ministers must therefore order the populace to switch to a diet consisting exclusively of vegetables and grains; providing not just a reduction in greenhouse gasses but also a virtuous enhancement of well-beinge.

The burning of fossile fuelles for heating and cooking is a major cause of concern. Introducing a compulsory vegan diet should eliminate the need for much cooking.

Instead of putting another log on the fire, citizens should be urged to wear an extra tunic. We must follow the example of our Celtic neighbours and extract more of our energye from renewable sources, such as peat.

Transporte continues to leave a scar upon ye environmente. The highways and byways are littered with the exhaust droppings of horses and donkeys, giving rise to noxious fumes which ascend up unto the Heavens and further erode the layer of ozone.

We call upon the Keeper of the Exchequer to levy an immedi-ate 'green' tax on biofuels such as hay, which are contributing to the problem.

In addition, the populace must be discouraged from travelling in any horse-drawn vehicle, particularly in the Citye. We propose that a 'congestion charge' zone be established between Ye Olde Balls Ponde Road in the north; Lambeth Walke in the south; Nottinge Hill in the west, and Wappinge in the east. All vehicles entering the Citye will be subject to a daily fee of admission , thus encouraging more journeyes by foot and lower emissions.

Much more must be done to recycle domestic waste. Currently, housewyves are disposing of rotten food by feedyng it to their livestock. Once the livestock is removed by law, other arrangements must be made.

Ye Corporation of Ye Citye of London should supply wheelye bins to each household, together with strict instructions on the sorting of waste into categories such as parchment and bottels, which will be collected once every two years.

Any citizen repeatedly depositing materiels in the wrong receptacle; ie: tipping the contents of a chamber pot into a bottel banke; will be hanged.

Lastly, returning to the present floods, work must begin at once on the construction of Ye Thames Barriere, at Greenwich, first proposed over 150 years ago by Mayor Whittington, but cruelly postponed indefinitely because of ye olde Torye spending cuts.

We ignore at our peril the eerily accurate prediction of one of the first ecologistes, St Swithin. He wrote, perceptively that on:

> St Swithin's Day, if it does rain,
> Full forty days, it will remain.

We must act now. If we don't, the consequences could be dire and in less than five hundred years the whole of Englande could be under water.

Nice Walk If You Can Get It

At the height of the climate change hysteria, the government announced plans to offer free travel advice to encourage us to walk, cycle or take the bus in an effort to cut down on 'greenhouse emissions'.

At a cost of 'only' £10 million, 92,000 people were to be counselled on how to reduce their car use by 'up to' 14 per cent. I rode shotgun on one pilot scheme.

Good morning, madam. I'm from the council. I've come to advise you on your personal travel plans. May I suggest leaving your gas-guzzling Suzuki jeep at home and taking the bus on the school run instead.

What's that you say? You've got three children under fifteen and they all go to different schools?

No problem, we're here to help.

Have you considered one of those bicycles that the Goodies used to ride on television?

You can get three up and Halford's will sell you a trailer to go on the back, made out of recycled toenails from Afghanistan, which comes with the Greenpeace seal of approval. Yours for only £999.99 plus VAT.

Don't worry if you can't ride a bike: we can offer full training, in twenty-three different languages, including scribble.

In certain circumstances we are able to provide a grant to encourage you to shift from carbon-hungry modes of transport to a more ecologically friendly lifestyle.

You don't happen to be an asylum seeker, do you? Pity.

Member of an ethnic minority?

Sorry, madam, white English doesn't count, I'm afraid, ha, ha, not many of us left, if you know what I mean, but don't quote me, more than my job's worth.

No room on the form for it, anyway.

You're not a lesbian, are you? No, please don't be offended, not that there's any reason why you should be offended, nothing wrong with it in this day and age, I might even give it a go myself if I was a woman.

I should have realised, you having three kids and all that, but these days you never know what with UVF or whatever they call it.

Anyway, best not to go there, you can't be sure who's listening.

Apparently they've got these satellites what can see from outer space whether you've got a gazebo? No, that's not the word, you know, conservative thingy on the back of your house, so you have to pay more council tax and this bloke at the Town Hall said they can hear every word you say, even through the loft insulation they insist on now.

All I'm saying, like, is that if you was a sexually diverse person then we could get you 50 per cent off the price of your next tandem.

Same goes for the pikeys, sorry, members of the travelling community, as we have to call them now.

You're not one of them, are you?

Course not, otherwise you'd have a Toyota Land Cruiser, running on red diesel, not a Suzuki hairdresser's job, plus a horse and cart, which also qualifies under the ozone-reduction scheme.

Transgendered? Me, neither. Not a clue.

There's a box for it, though.

Sorry, this isn't getting us anywhere, well not you anyway, nor your kids to school.

I suggest you take the number 69 from the bottom of Nelson Mandela Way, that's about twenty minutes' walk from here with a fair wind. It goes straight past the nursery, you can drop off your youngest.

That runs every two hours on the quarter hour, unless there's a strike, which there usually is, though not as often as on the Tube.

Then take the W9 Shoppa Hoppa, don't mind standing, do you? 'Cos they've taken out all the seats to get more people in and meet the department's targets on optimum occupancy in line with the European standard agreed at Limoges last Tuesday and to help them get wheelchairs on, not that you ever get anyone in a wheelchair on a bus, they all get minicabs paid for by the council.

Change at the Steve Biko Shopping Precinct on to the number 27, which will get to the front gate of your daughter's school by about lunchtime, it's cottage pie Tuesdays, or vegetarian alternative, which I wouldn't advise frankly, tastes like carpet underlay, my Kylie says.

Then your eldest can catch the bendy bus to the Desmond Tutu Comprehensive and should be there in time for the going-home bell. How much is all this going to cost, I can hear you saying.

Well, a single journey is £4, unless you buy one of them London Transport Lobster Cards, if you don't mind handing over your e-mail address, your blood group and your mother's maiden name. Why they want to know all that for a bus pass is beyond me.

But the good news is that your eldest won't have to pay anything because no one does on those bendy buses, ever since they did away with conductors, though I'd get him a stab vest just in case, to be on the safe side.

Take no notice of the scraping sound, that'll be a pedestrian being dragged along underneath, or else a cyclist, bloody nuisance if you ask me, with any luck it will be Boris Wossname or that Call Me Dave bloke with the windmill.

Now, I know what you're going to say: how are you supposed to do your grocery shopping, since all the local shops have been turned into Carphone Warehouses or Starbucks, or places what only sell fireworks, and the nearest Tesco is five miles away, off the ring road at the back of the Keir Hardie Industrial Estate?

You could always walk.

That would be a great way of offsetting your carbon footprint and getting fit, not that I'm implying, madam, and think of how much you'd be saving in petrol.

Just think of all the polar bears what's being saved from dying of ozones, though.

How did I get into this line of work?

Since you ask, I used to be a black-cab driver until Red Ken ripped up the Knowledge and started fast-tracking immigrants into the trade and flooding the streets with bloody rickshaws.

Soho looks like downtown Kowloon these days, there's no money in it, not even to the airport, that's always assuming you can get a fare back to Ilford.

And then there's the bus lanes and the bloody traffic lights which only change on to green for about five seconds.

The congestion charge was supposed to help but from where I'm sitting it's only made things ten times worse and now he wants to charge twenty-five quid a day for SUVs, which is another reason, madam, for leaving the Suzuki at home.

So I sees this 'green personal transport co-ordinator' being advertised in the *Walthamstow Guardian* and I think with my thirty years of experience I'll give it a go.

Be a fool not to, actually, at forty grand a year, plus index-linked pension and London weighting, it's more than I used to clear at the cab game and the hours are better, no more late nights or drunks throwing up all over the upholstery.

I had that Al Gore in the back of my cab once . . .

Two Jags Rides Again

Two Jags got a comprehensive coating in *Littlejohn's Britain* and I assumed – or, rather, hoped – that we'd seen the last of him when he stood down as Deputy Prime Minister.

But in the summer of 2009 this preposterous figure was reincarnated as something called the Council of Europe's 'rapporteur' on climate change.

That's a new one on me. Wasn't the dwarf in *Time Bandits* called Rapporteur?

I've no idea what a rapporteur does, but I would imagine it involves a lot of first-class air travel, five-star hotels and lobster suppers. There's probably a bird thrown in, too. Somewhere along the line.

In his new capacity, Two Jags flew to China to deliver a lecture on global warming. That's right: he jetted halfway round the world and back to talk about the need to cut carbon emissions.

Don't these people have any idea how ridiculous they are?

What astonishes me is that anyone, especially in my trade, takes him seriously. Two Jags is a circus act. Come to think of it, the dwarf in *Time Bandits* had considerably more gravitas than Prescott.

Yet in some quarters he's still treated as a proper person. The *Independent* carried an interview with him in which he announced that Europe's target of cutting emissions by 80 per cent was nowhere near tough enough. The paper even ran an editorial praising Prescott's authenticity.

The only thing authentic about this old fraud is his ocean-going, ozone-puncturing hypocrisy and self-importance.

I didn't christen him Two Jags without reason. This was the man who insisted on having not one, but two, 'gas-guzzling' limousines.

He had his wife chauffeured 200 yards along the seafront at the Labour conference so that her hairdo wouldn't get windswept.

Pauline's creosote-thick hairspray has probably done more damage to the atmosphere than a fleet of SUVs.

Two Jags took a helicopter back to central London from the rugby league final at Wembley and commandeered an RAF flight to turn on the Blackpool Illuminations.

After giving a speech on the importance of public transport to the railwaymen's union in Scarborough, he made an ostentatious display of boarding a train home. He then got off at the next station, where his driver was waiting with the Jag to convey him back to London in air-conditioned, eight-cylinder, fifteen-miles-to-the-gallon luxury.

Once he returned from China, he embarked on a tour of Britain, lecturing schoolchildren about global warming. He didn't travel by bike.

When he was 'in charge' of the environment, he was so concerned about the delicate eco balance that he ordered tens of thousands of houses to be built on flood plains.

Yet now we are asked to believe that he is a born-again Al Gore. According to the *Indy*, he is the brilliant global player who brokered the Kyoto deal in 1997 and was 'returning to a major role in climate change politics'.

All you need to know about the Kyoto 'deal' is that the rest of the world ignored it, while here in Britain it has been used as a catch-all excuse for everything from the extortionate tax on petrol to fining people £500 for putting out their dustbin on the wrong day.

In one sense, I suppose you could argue that Kyoto was a success, since the world has actually been getting colder over the past decade, despite China opening a new coal-fired power station every five minutes.

Britain's ridiculous obsession with 'man-made global warming' has prevented our building a new generation of power stations. As a result, we are facing the looming prospect of rolling power cuts in the not too distant future.

But you won't find a forest of windmills in the back garden of Two Jags' turreted mansion.

Just as Al Gore consumes enough electricity to power a small town and flies by private jet to deliver his lavishly rewarded pieties on polar bears, so Two Jags, too, thinks that cutting your carbon footprint is for the little people.

In the same week as Two Jags' adventures in China, the *Guardian* carried a spread about everyday people who were doing their bit for the planet. They boasted about how they were going to eat more root vegetables, wear thicker undies and travel by train more often. But even though I think they're all barking mad, at least they are prepared to make some kind of self-sacrifice in pursuit of their quasi-religious crusade.

Two Jags was conspicuous by his absence. While those poor, deluded saps are turning down the thermostat, shivering in their thermals and eating their own toenail clippings, you won't catch him chowing down on turnips or taking a slow boat to China.

Our esteemed 'rapporteur' will relax at the front of the plane, or in the rear seat of his limo, tucking into the finest food flown in from around the world. And to hell with the ice caps.

He will continue to leave a trail of yeti-sized carbon footprints as he tours the globe lecturing the rest of us on how we're all responsible for razing the rainforests.

In the great debate about non-existent global warming, this freeloading, flatulent, frequent-flying fool is about as relevant as the polar bear on Fox's Glacier Mints.

The Prescott Diaries

Two Jags has always insisted he had been unfairly maligned, especially by me, and sat down to compose his own version of events to put the record straight. I was lucky enough to receive an early draft of his diaries. They begin on 2 May 1997.

VICTORY AT LAST. The days of Tory toffs with their snouts in the trough, their mistresses, their chauffeur-driven cars and big houses in the country is over. It's our turn now. I am appointed Deputy Prime Minister and given the keys to Chorleywood. Tony tells me I can have a brand new Vauxhall Omega, too, but I put me foot down and says that I want another Jag. If it were good enough for Michael Hazeldene, it's good enough for me.

FIRST DAY AT my new ministry, the Department of Transport, Environment and the Regions. Staff all cheer and clap me when I arrive. One cheeky little piece gives me a kiss on the cheek. Stacey, I think she said her name were. I shall have to keep an eye on her. You know how some women find powerful men irresistible.

TO SCARBOROUGH, to address the annual conference of the railway workers' union. Owing to engineering work at Peterborough, the result of eighteen years of Tory neglect, I take the Jag. Well, you don't think I'm going on a coach, do you? Not a man in my position. Loud applause as I promise to build a world-class transport network and announce cancellation of Tory plans for widening of North Circular.

IF WE ARE to save the environment we have to get people out of their cars, I tell Stacey as I dictate a letter to her in the back of the Jag. It's Tracey, Mr Deputy Prime Minister, sir, she tells me. Not so formal, pet, I says, you can call me DPM, giving her a reassuring pat on her knee. These modern girls have to know we're not like them stuck-up, randy Tories, always tekkin' advantage of their secretaries. New Labour, New Man, that's me.

WHAT AN HONOUR. I've been asked to present the rugby league cup at Wembley. Fancy. Me, a humble working-class lad from Hull in the Royal Box. My chauffeur tells me that there is gridlock on the North Circular, so I take a helicopter back to Chorleywood, where I have to prepare my speech on cutting emissions.

IT'S THAT BLOODY snob Bunter Soames again. Gin and tonic, please, waiter. Just because I used to be a steward on the ferries. Damn good one I was, too. They say I was the inspiration for Kate O'Mara's Triangle. Typical Tories, treat you like skivvies, I says to Tracey as I send her hurrying off to get me a pork pie and a bottle of brown ale from the canteen.

PICK UP SUNDAY papers to read that Robin Cook has dumped his wife and run off with his personal assistant, Glorious Gaynor. At least he's done the decent thing, more than can be said for those sleazy Tories like Cyril Parkinson. Pauline tells me she's had Robin Cook's missus on the phone in floods of tears. I better not catch you carrying on with a woman in the office, Pauline says. Don't worry, luv, you won't catch me.

GET HELD UP on M4 on way to airport to fly to the Earth Summit in India. Almost miss me plane. I've got to do something about all this congestion. Just think of all them indignitaries suffering the indignity of getting stuck on the main road to Heathrow. There's only one thing for it – a priority bus lane. Make a note of that, I says to Tracey, who is accompanying me to India as my personal assistant. Pauline would've come but she don't like the food.

NO SUCH TROUBLE in India. I am whisked to conference centre in an eleven-car motorcade, with a police escort. If this is what a third-world transport system is like, bring it on. Them Indians know how to give proper respect to a world statesman like meself. After my brilliant speech on reducing our carbon footprint, I collect my Global Award for the Betterment of the World Environment from the chairman of the Bhopal Chemical Corporation.

BACK HOME, I have the privilege to have been chosen to turn on this year's Blackpool Illuminations, Bernard Manning being unavailable due to an operation for piles. The train is out of the question, all services having been cancelled on West Coast Main Line due to strike by railway union members in protest at Labour transport policies. M6 is bumper-to-bumper, so I calls up the RAF and commandeers a plane of the Royal Flight. If it's good enough for the bloody Queen, it's good enough for the workers.

TO NUMBER 10, where Tony is getting tantric foot massage from Karen Chaplin. Must get Tracey to give that a whirl while she's down there. He says he's in trouble over taking money from that Formula One chap, Bertie Ecclescake. If only he'd asked me first, I'd have steered him well clear of accepting gifts from billionaires. Best thing to do is bluff it out, tell 'em he's a straight kinda guy, not like them Tory crooks with their hands always out to big business in return for peerages, knighthoods and special favours.

RELAXING WITH TRACEY over a plate of oysters and a glass of champagne at Chorleywood, telephone rings to tell me that Peter Mendelsohn has been forced to resign from the Cabinet over a dodgy mortgage to buy a house in Nottingham Hill. Never liked him, or his Brazilian boyfriend. What does he need a fancy big house for, anyway?

MILLENNIUM EVE and we're all off to Greenwich for a party at the Dome. Pauline's not happy because Tony won't let us take the Jag, says we've all got to go on the Tube to set an example to the ordinary people. Pauline complains her hair gets blown all over the place and it's not as if she's got a personal hairdresser like Cherry. Had to admire the way Tony's missus barged aside the Queen during 'Old Lang Syne', though. Mind you, I can't see this place ever making any money, not unless they turn it into a casino or summat.

ON THE ELECTION trail, some punter lobs an egg at me and I give him a slap. What's the big deal? Shows I'm a man of the people, not stuck-up like these oyster-scoffing, champagne swilling Tory public school snobs. You can't imagine John Major giving anyone a slap, unless it was that Edwina woman what wrote a book saying they'd been having an affair for years. There you go again, told yer, them Tories can't keep it in their trousers for five minutes.

MY OLD MATE Joe Ashton, MP for Bassetlaw, is caught getting a personal massage in a Siamese sauna in Northampton. I don't know what got into him, paying for sex like some sleazebag Conservative. Why pay for it when you can get it for nowt?

MANDY PETERSEON is forced to resign again, this time for helping some super-rich Indian businessmen obtain passports. How many more times have I got to say it? Labour politicians have no business accepting owt from billionaires. Still, it means he's got to get out of Hillsborough Castle. I wonder if Tony will let me have it as a weekend home, sort of companion piece to Chorleywood. I can't take Pauline to the flat in Admiralty House, not with Tracey being there all the time, and the union's kicked me out of the place in Clapham.

TONY ASKS ME to give up the Transport brief and concentrate on saving the planet. He says I'll be remembered for doing to the railways more than anyone since Dr Beecham. First job is to tackle the flood plains in the south-east of England. I know, I'll build hundreds of thousands of houses on them, that should stop 'em flooding.

AT CLIMATE CHANGE Summit in Rio, I meet George W. Bush for the first time. I dunno what Tony sees in him, but after Seven-11 I suppose we've got to stand by America, even if they probably asked for it by refusing to sign Kyoto Protocol on global warming. For a US President, he's pretty thick, can't even speak the Queen's English properlably. Bush has always struck me as a bit of a cowboy. You can just see him riding round a dude ranch in Colorado, wearing a big Stetson and hand-tooled boots.

CLARE SHORT RESIGNS on principle. That's something you won't ever get me doing. Pauline calls on the mobile and wants to know who was that woman she's just seen me on telly with at Iraq War Memorial Service? Oh, nobody, I says. And why didn't I take her along, she being my lady wife? Sorry, pet, I explain, I thought you was booked in for a perm at Maison Giovanni in Hull that afternoon.

ADMIRALTY HOUSE. Tracey brings me the newspapers, along with my regular chipolata sandwich. Bit of bacon might be nice every now and again, I says. No, DPM, she comes back, chipolatas will always remind me of you. On the front of one of the scummy tabloids it says David Blunkett has been caught having it off with a woman what's only publisher of that Tory rag the Speculator. You can't trust these stuck-up Tory birds to keep their mouths shut, eh Tracey? I wonder how much she got for her story, she says.

HAVE YOU SEEN papers? Pauline screamed down phone. You and that trollop all over front pages, you fat bastard. I can't believe Tracey has spilled the beef. Still, I thought it were a good picture of me. Call chauffeur to start the Jag for mercy dash to Hull, East Coast Main Line buggered again and it being too difficult for RAF to land helicopter in St James's Park, owing to mass demonstration by transport unions over station closures. I managed to calm her down, bit of fun, nothing in it, you know. It must have worked, because before I left to come back to London, she cooked us me tea. More chipolatas. But then she slipped and accidentally dumped it in me lap, along with a scalding mug of coffee.

SORRY, JOHN, says Tony, but I'm going to have to wind up your department. Can I keep Chorleywood? I asks. All right, he says, but no more hanky-panky. Take up sport, divert your surplus energies that way. I know, I thought, there's a cricket pitch at Chorleywood, I'll see if the Special Branch lads fancy a game. When I got the cricket set out there was only one stump and some funny shaped bats, like hammers. And wooden balls, too. Still, it passed a quiet afternoon.

CALL YOURSELF A Deputy Prime Minister, I can't turn my back for five minutes, says Tony, after picture of me playing cricket turns up in *Mail on Sunday*, bloody Tory rag. This is your last chance, John, I want you to fly to Colorado and meet a man who wants to buy the Dome off us. No, you can't take Tracey. And this time, I'm warning you, try to stay out of trouble . . .

*

I'm glad I got my version out early. In the event, the official Two Jags Diaries were priceless. My friend Hunter Davies, his ghost writer, did a magnificent job of capturing the authentic voice of Prescott.

The best stuff was in the detail. No one cared about Two Jags boasting how he brokered the peace between Blair and Brown. But his account of getting drunk at an awards lunch with journalist Petronella Wyatt is priceless, this line in particular: 'I was seated next to this young woman from the *Spectator* – Petrofino, Peregrino, something like that.'

Well, you know what them stuck-up Tory birds from the *Speculator* is like!

Revenge of Safety Elves

Hundreds of people from Kendal, in the Lake District, turned out for a Freddie Mercury tribute concert at a local leisure centre. As the band reached its finale, the singer urged everyone to get up and dance.

This was a jig too far for the venue's manager, who switched on the main lights and pulled the plug on the sound system, mid-song.

Dancing is apparently in breach of elf'n'safety regulations. A spokesman for the local council said: 'We hope this did not take away the enjoyment of the event.'

And another one bites the dust. This was just one example of the elf'n'safety tyranny which has grown up under Labour and from which no aspect of human activity, however harmless, however innocent, is immune.

In Afghanistan, the Taliban banned dancing because it was anti-Islamic. In Britain, the elf'n'safety nazis are banning dancing everywhere because it's dangerous.

Blackpool Council ordered that the dance floors at sixteen community centres used by pensioners should be carpeted over in case they slip and hurt themselves during weekly ballroom dancing sessions.

Peter Jefferson, chief executive of Blackpool Coastal Housing, which manages the centres, said: 'We needed new flooring to fall in line with the Disability Discrimination Act. Carpet is the best option. I know it is not ideal for dancing, but it is perfect for karate.'

So it's too dangerous for a little light foxtrot, but OK for martial arts?

Apparently not according to several readers who wrote to me after I reported this story, saying that it's positively dangerous to practise karate on carpet, with a high risk of twisted ankles, torn ligaments and burns.

Anyway, I know eighty is supposed to be the new thirty, but how many OAPs do you know who want to go to karate classes?

It didn't stop there, either. At one of the community centres, enterprising OAPs hired a temporary dance floor, which they laid over the carpet on top of the original dance floor.

Nice to see someone dancing rings round elf'n'safety for once. But there's no end to this kind of lunacy.

Even the chief executive of the Royal Society for the Prevention of Accidents said his worthy cause has been hijacked by extremists.

Tom Mullarkey complained that children are being deprived of their childhood because they are prevented from doing anything which carries even a scintilla of risk.

Everything from playing conkers to wearing football boots with studs and swimming with snorkels has been outlawed in the name of keeping our kids safe.

'We do not believe in extremist health and safety ideas which would keep children wrapped in cotton wool,' said Mr Mullarkey.

'Our argument is that a skinned knee or twisted ankle in a challenging and exciting play environment is not just acceptable, it is a positive necessity.'

Let's overlook the tortuous use of language. In the real world, children play in parks. In officialdom, they utilise 'challenging and exciting play environments'.

Though Mullarkey was rather late to the party, his intervention was nonetheless welcome. Not that it will do any good.

We are facing an obesity epidemic, but government at every level conspires against any form of physical activity, especially if it involves children. I thought ministers had repented when it was announced that councils were being encouraged to hire 'street football co-ordinators'. I should have known better.

Turns out the real purpose of these new jobsworths was not to encourage kids to play football, but to ban it.

The Communities Department sent out a fifty-three-page memo ordering local authorities to carry out risk assessments before allowing ball games on municipal property.

The guidance stated: 'If not planned properly, football can be divisive and trigger conflict. Passions can get high and physical contact can easily lead to confrontations.'

That's the whole point of street football. It's to encourage boys to burn off excess energy. And if it descends into a punch-up, so what?

Some of the worst fights I've ever seen have been on Sunday morning football fields. No harm done. I can remember a referee – who sent off three players from the same side within the first ten minutes – having to flee for his life from supporters on motorbikes. This is all part of the meddlesome Guardianista plot to eliminate all risk and spontaneity from every aspect of our lives.

It was bad enough when professional football introduced the superfluous fourth official. By the time Labour has finished, there'll be so many risk assessors, elf'n'safety advisers, diversity monitors and anti-social behaviour counsellors on the touchline, there won't be room on the pitch for anyone else.

How long before they legislate on the use of jumpers for goal-posts?

You won't be able to use jumpers from budget retailers because they're made by slave labour in the Third World. Next, they'll be insisting that teams have to reflect the gender, ethnic origin and sexuality of the surrounding area. And no one will be allowed to win, because it could traumatise the losers.

After I wrote about schools banning sack races and three-legged races on elf'n'safety grounds, I added: 'I'm tempted to speculate that it'll be egg-and-spoon races next, except these things have a horrible habit of coming true. No, not elf'n'safety. Salmonella.'

Cue a barrage of letters from readers all over Britain informing me that their local schools have already beaten me to it.

Teacher Annie Hayward said real eggs have been replaced with rubber eggs because of – you guessed – salmonella scares. Maureen Emerson went to her grandson's sports day to discover him taking part in a jelly-and-spoon race. John Reeve reported that his four-year-old son's nursery school is now holding a potato-and-spoon race.

And from South Ayrshire, Mags told me she recently took part in an updated version which involved balancing a big rubber ball on the end of the spoon. They said some children were allergic to eggs. But this was the mothers' race.

When it comes to elf'n'safety, even I can't make it up. Then again, I don't have to.

*

In Fleetwood, Lancashire, the council has banned hopscotch. Cleaners were sent in to scrub away a chalk grid on the pavement.

Ruth Hunter, who describes herself as a 'Streetscene Manager', said: 'The hopscotch grid took up the width of a narrow strip of pavement very close to shops and there was an important safety issue with children playing on the grid, particularly for people walking on the pavement, who would have to step into the very busy road to avoid them.'

*

Nowhere is sacred. The elf'n'safety nazis have already invaded places of worship, making bell-ringers wear safety helmets and ear-muffs.

Maurice James, from Cardiff, attended a wedding in a lovely little fourteenth-century church in a tiny village in the back of beyond.

Before the ceremony began, the vicar said he was obliged to tell the congregation that in the event of an emergency there were two ways of escape, through the vestry and through the main door.

Also, he added, like some ecclesiastical trolley dolly, mind the step. How long before vicars conducting funeral services have to advise the departed to make sure they take all their belongings with them?

*

St Peter's Church, Derby, had to remove hassocks on the orders of elf'n'safety.

They said the church would be held responsible if anyone tripped over a hassock or fell off one and hurt themselves. Have you ever heard of anyone falling off a hassock? Are A&E departments the length and breadth of Britain teeming with people suffering prayer-related injuries?

It won't be long before they're insisting that all members of the congregation have to wear skateboard-style knee pads before taking communion.

*

And St Patrick's Catholic Church, Wellington, in Shropshire, was threatened with closure after being presented with a safety report which claimed that after a hundred years, a build-up of incense smoke may have caused the air in the church to become toxic and possibly carcinogenic.

Ye gods.

*

A crematorium in Nottinghamshire was told it must remove all its memorial benches because they are three inches too low. Kevin Browne, the crematorium manager, said: 'An inspector went around with a tape measure, measuring everything for compliance with the Disability Discrimination Act 2005.

'Apparently, it means that the buttocks of infirm people are below the point at which they can easily return to a standing position.'

So they all had be replaced, at a cost of £200,000. And every other memorial bench in every other crematorium and cemetery in Britain will now have to be checked. The bill could run into millions.

Jayne Allen paid £400 for a bench bearing a plaque in memory of her late husband. The first she became aware of any problem was when a letter arrived telling her that the bench was being returned to her.

'It was all very undignified and quite insulting. It shows little respect for the dead,' she said. Not that elf'n'safety gives a toss about respecting the dead, or the bereaved. These are the same maniacs who authorised the wholesale bulldozing of headstones for fear that they might topple over and hurt someone.

Who decides what is, or what isn't, an optimum height for a park bench? People come in all shapes and sizes. One man's 'too low' is another's 'too high'.

What kind of job is it crawling around a cemetery measuring benches and then ordering them to be removed? One which pays thirty grand plus and a motor, and an index-linked pension for life. And to justify their existence they keep having to invent ever more absurd and expensive rules.

The cost of home repairs is soaring because elf'n'safety is forcing contractors to hire scaffolding instead of using ladders for even the most minor job.

Guidelines state: 'When working from a ladder, three points of contact should be maintained.

'That means both feet and one hand in contact with the ladder or stepladder. Do not work off the top three rungs – they provide a handhold.'

These imbeciles has obviously never been anywhere near a building site. If both feet and one hand have to be in contact with the ladder, how the hell can anyone even hammer a nail into a wall?

The same rules apply to window cleaners, who are now reduced to cleaning upstairs panes with hosepipes.

I can only think of one good reason for erecting a scaffold. And that's to string up whoever comes up with these absurd laws.

In Cheshire, for instance, elf'n'safety banned knitting needles at a hospital in Cheshire, just in case someone pokes their eye out. Which, of course, they never have.

Director of nursing Bernie Salisbury said: 'We believe this sensible and proactive measure will avoid preventable accidents.'

I wonder where she stands on superbugs, which kill thousands of hospital patients every year – not so much 'preventable accidents' as criminally negligent homicide.

In the middle of an alleged swine flu epidemic, the government sent out thirty million leaflets urging us to wash our hands. Across the country, hospitals have installed alcohol-based, anti-bacterial handwash dispensers to stop the spread of diseases and superbugs.

But after a risk assessment, St Margaret's Hospital in Epping removed the dispensers over fears that alcoholics might rip them off the wall, drink the contents and poison themselves.

Talk about foaming at the mouth.

*

One of my favourite elf'n'safety stories was the attempt by an amateur dramatic company in Brierley Hill, West Midlands, to stage a performance of *Jack and the Beanstalk*.

They were told that despite the beanstalk being 30 foot tall, Jack would be allowed to ascend just 4 foot of it – and only then with a harness and hard hat.

Ridiculous, I thought to myself. How many people have ever hurt themselves in *Jack and the Beanstalk*?

Out of curiosity, I Googled 'Beanstalk'. The first thing that popped up was a report that Wee Jimmy Krankie had been rushed to the Glasgow Royal Infirmary after falling 20 feet from a beanstalk during a matinee at the Pavilion Theatre.

Oh, no he wasn't! Oh, yes he was!

*

Elf'n'safety turned out in force at the 2009 London Marathon. Inevitable, I suppose, given that the streets of London are an obstacle course at the best of times.

As the competitors negotiated roads littered with traffic-calming measures, officials could be seen standing at the side of the course with signs reading 'Beware, Hump' and an arrow pointing downwards.

I'm astonished that the Marathon has survived the march of the safety nazis for this long, given the potential for exhaustion, dehydration, sprained ankles and getting run over by a lunatic in a giant chicken costume.

Now that the government has given the go-ahead for 20mph limits in all residential areas, don't be surprised if next year's Marathon doesn't feature speed traps and random breath tests round every corner.

*

You can't even go out for a quiet meal these days. I heard from one reader in Portsmouth who was refused an after-dinner flaming sambuca, because the local council had warned the restaurant that flaming sambucas constitute a fire risk under safety guidelines.

My local Indian, Tandoori Nights, received a visit from elf'n'safety which threatened prosecution unless the chef stopped topping his signature dish with gold leaf.

And across the country doggy bags have been banned, along with feeding kitchen scraps to pigs. After a column on waste, I wrote: 'One man's waste is another man's pig swill'.

Not any more.

I heard from Peter Luther, who had a thriving business in Dorset, collecting scraps from schools and hospitals and boiling it before selling it on for animal feed.

He was the fifth generation of his family in the swill business. That all ended after the foot and mouth panic.

Now it all has to go for landfill, just to be on the safe side. Apparently, it's also illegal for supermarkets to give food past its sell-by date to farms and zoos.

*

On the advice of insurers and the elf'n'safety nazis, South Hams Council, in Devon installed a warning notice on the beach at Castle Cove, which reads: 'Beware of Incoming Tide'.

Some seaside councils have already scrapped donkey rides on the grounds of animal cruelty and Punch and Judy because it glorifies domestic violence.

How long before they get round to banning paddling and sunbathing, backed by fines of £5,000? Building sandcastles will soon require hard hats and hi-vis jackets, scaffolding and a visit from the building inspectors.

But 'Beware of Incoming Tide'? In Devon, King Canute wouldn't be a local legend, he'd be a court case.

*

The ultimate absurdity came when MI6 fell to elf'n'safety. The Secret Intelligence Service advertised for an occupational health adviser, immediately christened Dr No, No, No.

The £40,000-a-year job encompasses everything from foreign travel briefings to 'health surveillance' and alcohol abuse.

Bond's budgie-smuggler swimming trunks, as worn by Daniel Craig, will have to go – replaced by a wet suit and lifejacket.

You can just imagine 007's next visit to Q's laboratory to collect his specially adapted Toyota Pious.

He won't be allowed to carry a gun, or to go undercover without a hard hat and high-vis jacket.

Gyrocopters, mini-submarines, moon buggies and exploding alarm clocks are out of the question.

Far too dangerous. Laser pens can only be used with a full welding mask and gauntlets.

Bond's licence to kill will be revoked under the yuman rites act. There'll be no unprotected sex with exotic beauties.

No smoking, obviously. And no martinis, either, shaken or stirred. Remember, 007, you only live once.

Teddy Bears' Picnic

If you go down to the woods today, forget about disguise. You'd better wear a hard hat and a hi-vis jacket. Dingly Dell has finally fallen to the elf 'n' safety nazis.

For twelve years, retired builder Mike Kamp had been collecting firewood from the forest near his home at Betws-y-coed, North Wales.

It's a right enshrined in Magna Carta of 1215, the template for democracies around the world. Free men down the centuries have been granted the liberty to gather dead wood from common land to fuel their stoves, repair their homes and make charcoal.

That was before the Forestry Commission came along and started demanding that anyone wanting to collect wood would need a licence to forage.

Subsequently it imposed an outright ban, stating: 'This is an area where we are subject to increasing constraints in terms of health and safety. We have a duty of care to people in our wood.'

Note the use of the possessive 'our' wood. It isn't their wood. It's common land and it belongs to everyone.

As Mr Kamp said: 'They are claiming there are health and safety issues. But people have walked through the woods collecting firewood for hundreds of years without too many safety problems.'

Precisely. I doubt there is one recorded incident of a firewood-related fatality in North Wales.

This, as usual, is about bureaucrats justifying their own sad existence and protecting their backs in the event of someone turning their ankle in a rabbit hole, ringing Blame Direct, and suing for com-pen-say-shun.

We take you over now to a briefing at the multi-million pound headquarters of the government's Firewood Prevention, Elf 'n' Safety and Child Protection Joint Task Force.

'Listen up, team. We've had a tip-off that a number of teddy bears are going down to the woods today and we want to maintain the element of surprise. So you'd better go in disguise.'

'Why's that, guv?'

'For every bear that ever there was will gather there for certain because today's the day the teddy bears have their picnic.

'Every teddy bear who's been good is sure of a treat today. There's lots of marvellous things to eat and wonderful games to play.

'But they don't have a catering licence or a safety certificate. If anything goes wrong we could have carnage on our hands. Food poisoning, sprained ankles, it doesn't bear thinking about, if you'll pardon the pun.'

'Oh, very good, sir.'

'I want the tactical support unit beneath the trees where nobody sees them. They'll hide and seek as long as they please, 'cause that's the way the teddy bears have their picnic.

'And I don't want any heroics, either. If you go down to the woods today, you better not go alone. It's lovely down in the woods today, but safer to stay at home.'

'What do you want us to do, guv?'

'Watch them, catch them unawares. See them gaily gad about, they love to play and shout, they never have any care.

'At six o'clock their mummies and daddies will take them home to bed, because they're tired little teddy bears. That's when we move in.'

'Why wait until six o'clock, guv?'

'We suspect a major paedophile ring is operating in the area. After all, we've only got their word for it that they are mummies and daddies. Remember little Maddie?

'I want names and addresses and don't forget to read them their rights. I'm not having any of them getting off on a technicality.

'Social services are providing armed back-up, the helicopter is on standby and I'm bringing in the firewood squad. We believe that some of the contraband wood is being used to make offensive weapons – i.e. witches' brooms.

'So let's do it to them, before they do it to themselves. And, hey, hey, hey. Let's be careful out there.'

The Trumpet Taliban

Some years ago, after trapeze artists on a tour of Britain with the Moscow State Circus were ordered to wear crash helmets by the elf'n'safety nazis at Haringey Council, I remember speculating upon what other indignities would soon be imposed upon performers in the Big Top.

I imagined them being forced to lay the tightrope on the ground, so that no one would ever fall off.

Jugglers would have to wear hard hats and lion-taming wouldn't be able to survive the animal rights zealots. I also wondered where elf'n'safety stood on the hazard presented by flying custard pies. As usual, this was only half in jest.

A few months later, seventy clowns held a mass meeting at Zippo's Circus in Blackheath, south London, over fears that they could be sued if they continued throwing custard pies and buckets of water at the audience.

Which only served to prove, yet again, that you couldn't make it up.

After that, it all went quiet on the circus front. For a while.

Zippo's Circus was back in the news in 2008 after falling foul of both the animal rights brigade and Birmingham City Council.

In Yorkshire, something calling itself the Sheffield Animal Friends tried to get the circus shut down on the grounds of cruelty to 'exotic' animals.

For the record, Zippo's has four horses, three ponies, a dozen budgies and a Jack Russell. It doesn't get more exotic than that. Anyway, Zippo's has been held up as a model of animal welfare.

And did anyone bother asking the budgies if they were being exploited? I'd have thought it was more fun being in a circus than cooped up in a cage all day.

When the circus set up in Birmingham, half an hour before the show was to start, plans for the grand finale had to be revised after an intervention by a council official.

This is how the show panned out. Three clowns – Nicol, Michael and Pappa – normally introduce themselves with a trumpet blast.

In the build-up to the climax, Nicol sounds three notes on a tuba, which then explodes and lands, horn down, on one of the other clowns' heads, while Nicol simultaneously blows a puff of smoke out of his backside.

So far, so harmless.

But the council official ruled that if Zippo's insisted on including trumpets and the exploding tuba, then the show could not go on.

Use of musical instruments meant it would be classified as a 'live musical performance' and would therefore be in breach of licensing regulations. Going ahead without a licence would mean the circus facing a fine of £1,000.

Reluctantly, Martin Burton – who doubles as Zippo the Clown and proprietor of the circus – dropped the music and the show went on in silence. He was even ordered not to play a soundtrack recording of flamenco music during the act.

'I'm a big fan of silent comedy, but this is ridiculous,' said Martin.

He thought that he'd been given a clean bill of health by the local authority before the circus even came to town.

Some circuses have closed for good, rather than comply with the new licensing rules. But Martin is a believer in negotiation and was determined to keep the show on the road. He'd already had lengthy discussions in advance with Birmingham's elf'n'safety department.

There was a problem over whether skipping on a tightrope was dancing, or walking. Dance is classed as regulated entertainment and must be licensed, but you don't need a licence to walk. Not yet, at least.

In the end, after what we used to call in my day covering the unions, a free and frank exchange of views in a spirit of meaningful negotiation, and taking due cognisance of all the facts – it was agreed that tight-rope skipping does not constitute dancing within the meaning of the Act.

Another potential conflict arose over the resident Jack Russell, name of Clopsky, who leaps in the air and lands on the feet of a German acrobat performing a handstand.

Here, the debate centred not on the cruelty to Clopsky, but on whether the acrobat could be considered to be taking part in professional sport, which would also require a licence, application in triplicate, three months' notice, non-refundable fee payable in advance, etc.

Having seen the rehearsal, the council kindly withdrew its objections, deciding that said acrobat was unlikely to feature in the 2012 Olympics and therefore did not qualify as a professional sportsman.

After that, Zippo thought he'd been given the all-clear. But although he'd squared elf'n'safety, he hadn't reckoned on the last-minute ambush by the Trumpet Taliban – who, needless to say, come under a different department.

Jacqui Kennedy, who described herself as director of regulatory services at Birmingham City Council, defended the decision to halt the music.

'Under the Licensing Act 2003, elements of the programme proposed by Zippo's would fall into the category of regulated entertainment and such events would require either a licence under the Act or a temporary event notice.'

I bet she's a laugh a minute at the Christmas party. If ever a woman needed a custard pie in her face . . .

Our council tax has doubled under Labour to pay for all this madness, most of it dedicated to finding out what people want to do and then inventing ways of stopping them. Despite the economic crisis, there's never any problem finding £50,000 a year to pay a madwoman to adjudicate on whether or not a Jack Russell standing on the feet of an acrobat doing a handstand requires a licence.

Or to threaten to prosecute a circus because a clown playing an exploding tuba is classified as a 'live musical performance' and therefore in breach of subsection II; clause VI; paragraph XVII; pursuant to the Licensing Act of 2003.

I'm only surprised that when he blew smoke out of his backside he didn't trigger a raid by the paramilitary wing of the council's smoking cessation unit.

★

All members of the Wick Royal British Legion Scotland Pipe Band were issued with earplugs to stop them going deaf, after music at a practice session was measured at 122 decibels – 2 decibels louder than a private jet. Whatever happened to Scotland The Brave?

★

The Trumpet Taliban have hit squads everywhere. Fresh from threatening Zippo with prosecution they turned their attention to school music lessons.

Teachers have been told to wear earmuffs or stand behind noise-absorbing screens when supervising pupils playing musical instruments. Schools which fail to comply can be taken to court under noise regulations.

One honk on a cornet is alleged to be enough to cause permanent hearing loss. Standing next to a saxophone is supposed to be as dangerous as a firing a field cannon.

Young children are the biggest menace. In their enthusiasm to learn, they can take out a music teacher's eardrums from fifty paces.

'Sound levels produced by groups of student instrumentalists are likely to be higher than those produced by a professional group of players because of less developed technical abilities and natural exuberance', according to the Health and Safety Executive.

After just nineteen minutes' exposure to a school orchestra, you might as well start learning sign language and lip-reading.

The Trumpet Taliban have been storming classrooms armed with decibel meters and concluded that listening to a quick blast of 'Seventy-Six Trombones' from 4B is more lethal than operating a pneumatic drill or standing next to a jumbo jet while it is taking off.

Which begs the question, if they're right, why isn't Britain swarming with stone-deaf former music teachers? Why aren't our world-famous conductors all wearing hearing aids?

I can understand why having to listen to little Kylie struggling to squeeze a tune out of a recorder might constitute mental torture, but if teachers are forced to wear earmuffs or stand behind baffle boards, how are they supposed to teach when they can't hear what's being played?

And if they do erect screens, they have to take care to ensure that the sound is not reflected back towards the children.

At the time I suggested, laughingly, that they should make the pupils wear earmuffs, too. That way, no one will come home from school with his ears bleeding.

While they're at it, they could insist all music teachers wear hard hats, just in case they get hit on the head with a flying drum-stick.

A stray violin bow could take your eye out, so children learning to play one should all be forced to wear protective glasses. Don't want anyone going blind, as well as deaf, halfway through Vivaldi's *The Four Seasons*.

Yet again, I should have known I was tempting fate.

A professional musician, who had been working in the West End and touring shows for ten years, wrote to tell me of the pre-posterous precautions now being forced on production companies by the Trumpet Taliban.

Producers are so terrified of being sued for hearing loss that musicians are forced to wear strapped-on decibel meters, earplugs and noise reduction headphones.

At his most recent engagement, the drummer was no longer allowed to play a traditional drum kit: he had to play silent elec-tronic drum pads, while the guitar and bass players also had to do without amplifiers.

And, yes, the brass section all had to wear earmuffs. The artificial output is then fed into a sound desk, where it is mixed to 'safe' levels. When he questioned this madness, he was told it was now a criminal offence to play a saxophone without noise-reducing headgear.

Needless to say, it defeats the whole object of playing together as an orchestra, since they can't hear each other.

It doesn't only destroy the morale of the musicians, it cheats the paying public. How long before it will only be legal to perform a piano concerto on one of those silent keyboards which older readers will remember Joseph Cooper playing during the mystery tune round on *Face the Music*?

Better still, why not just ban music altogether? That's what the real Taliban did in Afghanistan.

*

My headline on the column wondering if musicians would soon have to start wearing protective glasses, helmets and gloves to guard against injuries was: 'A Swift Kick in the Orchestras'.

Some readers may have recognised this as old-fashioned Cockney rhyming slang: orchestra stalls . . .

The very next day came news of a condition called 'cello scrotum', which was said to afflict cellists and was caused by the vibration of their instrument against their groin.

Subsequently, it was revealed to be a hoax, invented thirty-four years ago in a spoof medical journal report.

But don't be surprised if the Trumpet Taliban latch on to this fictitious affliction and start demanding that cellists have to perform wearing cricket boxes and skateboarders' knee pads.

*

The Trumpet Taliban also struck at the famous Cove House Inn on Chesil Beach, Dorset, rumoured to be the setting for Ian McEwan's bestselling novel *On Chesil Beach*, which features folk music every Thursday night.

An enforcement officer from Weymouth and Portland Council visited the landlord and told him that whenever live music is played in the pub, all bar staff will have to wear earmuffs to prevent them going deaf.

How they are supposed to hear anyone ordering a drink was not explained.

Two pints of lager and a packet of crisps, PLEASE!

The Condiment Nazis

After the government announced what it described as a 'comprehensive shake-up' of local government priorities, some councils decided to take the guidance literally. Officials in Gateshead began touring chip shops confiscating salt shakers with more than five holes in them.

They spent £2,000 on replacements, which were given away free. Fish and chip shops were issued with five-hole salt shakers instead of the normal seventeen-hole ones in an effort to get people to use less salt on their meals.

According to a spokesman: 'Research carried out by us discovered customers were often receiving huge quantities of salt with their fish and chips – up to half their daily allowance.

'The council was so disturbed it decided to commission a manufacturer to produce a salt shaker with fewer holes, which it distributed free to every fish and chip shop and hot food takeaway in Gateshead. We believe the cost to be a small price to pay for potentially saving lives.'

Officials claimed that cutting the number of holes from the traditional seventeen to just five reduces by up to 60 per cent the amount of salt shaken on to a fish supper.

They carried out fifteen days of research, obtaining samples of fish and chips, measuring salt content and conducting experiments 'to determine how the problem of excessive salt being dispensed could be overcome by design' while still ensuring a 'visibly attractive sprinkle'.

What they hadn't factored in was the ingenuity of chip shop customers, who will sprinkle on however much salt they fancy. Fewer holes simply means they shake for longer.

Chip-shop owners reported punters unscrewing the caps of the shakers to save time, smothering their food with salt. People will always find a way of beating the system. But even that's not the point.

It's none of the council's damn business how much salt people choose to consume. If the taxpayers of Gateshead wish to sit around eating salt by the tubload until their arteries resemble a Siberian mineshaft, that's entirely a matter for them.

Their GP might want a quiet word with them, but it has absolutely nothing to do with the tinpot condiment nazis at the Town Hall. It turns out that this scheme was the brainchild of something called the Local Authorities Co-ordinators of Regulatory Services, which is responsible for ensuring councils follow food hygiene rules.

What's the betting this will spread like wildfire until five-hole salt shakers are compulsory, non-compliance punishable by a £5,000 fine and six months in Strangeways?

A spokesman for this obscure hygiene quango said: 'Heart disease costs taxpayers £7 billion a year, so to say that projects such as this are a waste of money is mind-boggling.'

No, old son, what's 'mind-boggling' is that you think you have any right to dictate to the chip-lovers of Gateshead – or anywhere else for that matter – how much salt they can put on their supper.

This has nothing to do with food hygiene. It's meddling for the sake of it.

Speaking of food hygiene, the Local Government Association unveiled a national poster campaign featuring, among other delightful images, a man sitting in a restaurant with the caption: 'My council makes sure this romantic meal won't give us the trots'.

Very tasteful. The Trots who dreamed that up must be very pleased with themselves. It's part of a campaign to raise awareness of the range of services provided by Town Halls.

Another featured a drunken slapper in fishnet tights, squatting on the pavement, clutching a beer bottle, while projectile vomiting. The caption read: 'My council clears up my mess'.

These posters were hoisted across the country, at a cost of goodness knows how much. Is it any wonder that council tax has doubled under Labour, while what we really think of as 'services' have got worse.

Local authorities seem to have pretty much abandoned most of the tasks they were set up for in the first place, while expanding into areas which should be none of their concern.

This is just another small example of the way in which they are engaged full-time in empire building, finding new ruses by which to interfere in our lives and inventing exciting schemes for monitoring, regulating, taxing, fining, punishing and spying on us.

As for the government's 'shake-up', I doubt their list of priorities matches yours.

In at number two is: reducing teenage pregnancy. What the hell has handing out the morning-after pill got to do with your local council?

Also in the Top 10: cutting the crime rate. Isn't that a job for the Old Bill?

Then there's 'per capita reductions in CO_2' – which translates into cripplingly expensive car parking charges and pay-as-you-throw taxes.

High up in the charts is combating obesity among primary school children – which would be much easier if councils hadn't banned competitive games in schools and sold off thousands of playing fields to supermarkets and spiv property developers.

All you need to know is that it will involve more taxes, more fines, more powers for officials, more bureaucracy, more staff hired out of the *Guardian* and more interference.

Hilariously, a press release trumpeting the new initiative said: 'This means less red tape and more freedom for local authorities to deliver what local people want.'

If I were you, I'd take that with a very large pinch of salt.

*

If the condiment nazis don't get you, the sandwich stasi will. Frank Hughes, who runs a small scaffolding hire company in Liverpool, received a visit from enforcement officers working for a public-private agency set up by the council and was asked to explain in detail how he disposes of his industrial waste.

Frank said he doesn't. He told the official that scaffolding is a relatively simple business which doesn't generate waste.

But you must eat lunch, the inspector retaliated.

I bring sandwiches, Frank told him. And before you ask, I take the wrapping home with me.

In which case, you're breaking the law, the jobsworth informed him. Sandwich wrappings are classified as industrial waste within the meaning of the Act. You need a licence to dispose of them.

And since you don't have one, you are committing a criminal offence. Frank would be hearing from the litigation department in connection with this heinous crime and could expect a minimum fine of £300.

With that, the official ticked all the relevant boxes and took his leave, another job well done. It wouldn't have surprised me if the inspector had produced a roll of *CSI*-style crime scene tape, cordoned off the building, declared the whole business off-limits, called for armed police back-up and ordered Frank to cease trading immediately.

Frank wrote to me in despair. 'I am not making this up.' I didn't think you were for a moment, guv.

The Fridge Fascists

As if we're not already overrun with thousands of five-a-day co-ordinators, nagging us to eat our greens, and legions of recycling enforcers, sifting through our dustbins for evidence of carelessly discarded potato peelings, plans were unveiled for a new standing army of food police, charged with cutting down waste.

Inspectors were to be paid £8.50 a hour, with double time on Saturdays, to visit our homes and offer 'advice' on what we eat and what we throw away.

Soon there will be eight thousand of these food fascists hammering on every one of Britain's twenty-five million front doors and demanding to inspect the contents of our fridges and pedal bins, at a cost of tens of millions of pounds the country simply can't afford.

This crazy scheme has been dreamed up by the same quango which wants to force each and every household to instal a slop bucket under the sink. The justification is to bring about a reduction in the amount of food we waste.

After just one day's training, this new breed of busybody was given the power to turn up on our doorsteps unannounced and demand answers to an intrusive series of questions about our food consumption.

They also hand out guidance on optimum portion sizes and what to do with leftovers, as well as explaining the difference between 'best before', 'use by' and 'sell by' dates.

How stupid do they think we are? We can read. Just a guess, but I would imagine that 'best before' means best eaten before the date specified. Similarly 'use by' is the date said item is likely to go off and start to whiff a bit. If something in a supermarket has passed its 'sell by' date, don't buy it.

This is all part of the infantilisation of Britain, the belief that we are incapable of running our own lives without government guidance, interference and regulation.

A spokesman for the health department said: 'By hitting people at home, rather than in supermarkets, we can get inside their lives. It's only by knocking on doors you can find out what they are having for their tea and offer some healthy suggestions.'

Listen, chum, we don't want you getting inside our lives. If I choose to eat four rashers of bacon and three eggs for breakfast, that's my heart attack. And I can assure you that if any of these inspectors comes knocking on the door of Littlejohn Towers at teatime, he'll be sent away with his head in a slop bucket.

You can bet your life that this scheme won't stop at just offering handy hints on how to make an appetising supper out of last night's leftovers. Soon it will be backed up with fines and punishments. Under this government 'voluntary' schemes have an inevitable habit of becoming compulsory.

How long before the polite knock on the door becomes a battering ram and the leaflet offering 'advice' turns into a warrant?

Think I'm exaggerating? Look at how 'encouragement' to recycle led to a vast enforcement industry, with householders being punished for leaving their dustbin lids ajar – with inspectors climbing over garden walls and using anti-terror laws to spy on those suspected of slipping plastic containers into the box marked 'glass only' or inadvertently dropping a used envelope into their garden waste.

As I keep telling you: once you give anyone in authority any kind of power, they will always, always, always abuse it.

'Open the door, madam. Armed food police. We have a warrant to search your refrigerator. Anything you don't eat may be taken away and used against you in court.'

This is where you end up when a government has no idea what to do about the big issues, so occupies itself meddling in ever more intimate and irrelevant areas of our lives. I believe the expression is 'past its sell by date'.

Brown Windsor Soup

When the Prime Minister starts handing out advice on what to do with your leftover vegetables it's time to start counting the spoons.

But at a saving-the-planet summit in Japan, the Prime Minister declared that we'd all be £8 a week better off if we didn't throw away so much food.

We've had Gordon as the Iron Chancellor, we've had The Man Who Stole Your Old Age. We've had Stalin and Mr Bean. And now we had Gordon as Delia Smith.

Talk about a classic case of activity displacement. Brown didn't have a clue what to do about the big issues, so he took to lecturing us about the food we leave on the side of our plates. The impertinence of his hair-shirt statism has always been breathtaking.

When you think of all the billions of pounds of our money he has wasted over the past eleven years, it takes a special lack of self-awareness to chide us about wasting £8 worth of food a week. Gordon on thrift is like Pete Doherty on sobriety.

I couldn't wait for his next party political broadcast.

Hulloo. I'm talking to you from the kitchen of Number 10 Downing Street, making the right long-term decisions and getting on with the job of turning last night's leftover potato peelings into a delicious supper.

For many years, I have been saving money on the weekly shop by eating my own fingernails, a healthy, sustainable and nutritious alternative to turkey twizzlers and other environmentally unfriendly ready meals packed with salt, which cost the NHS billions of pounds a year.

Housewives are already acquainted with the practice of adding the water used to boil peas and carrots to their gravy.

Based on this sound principle, Sarah and I are now drinking our own bathwater and, in line with the pioneering efforts made by local authorities to meet our commitments to tackle climate change, my government will as a matter of urgency bring forward a bill which will make it a criminal offence to flush your toilet more than once a fortnight.

Alternate weekly flushing will not only help us meet our commitments under the Kyoto Protocol, it will also ease the pressure on Britain's Victorian sewage infrastructure, so woefully neglected by the Conservatives.

It is in the area of discarded foodstuffs that we can bring about most change. Billions of tons of food are wasted every year, irresponsibly consigned to landfill sites, producing greenhouse gases which massacre millions of polar bears.

From next Monday, our teams of inspectors will be sifting through your rubbish bins, not only searching for items which have been wrongly assigned to incorrect recycling receptacles, but also to identify and catalogue any household detritus which has been callously and wilfully consigned to the dump, but which otherwise could have been used in a more prudent and economical fashion.

Our highly motivated co-ordinators will be knocking on doors in an attempt to re-educate domestic stakeholders in the better deployment of previously used comestibles.

All items which have not yet realised their full potential will be returned to the householder, together with detailed instructions on the recommended method of second and third use, for instance, boiling chicken bones to make stock or turning the outer leaves of iceberg lettuces into lampshades.

Initially, compliance will be voluntary, but after a trial period of three months in which the scheme has been rolled out across Britain, anyone failing to obey a legitimate order from a foodstuffs recycling official will be subject to a fine of no less than £5,000 and a period of imprisonment, not exceeding twenty-five years.

Once citizens are well versed in the new system, we will be moving towards a programme encouraging people to eat all surplus packaging and carrier bags, as well as the food contained therein, thus realising the nutritional benefits of previously wasted cardboard and Styrofoam.

This will allow us to abolish rubbish collections altogether, at a stroke repairing the hole in the ozone layer, saving the rainforests and ending our dependence on imported kiwi fruits.

No one will be allowed to buy food unless they have a certificate from a trained recycling professional proving that all their previous groceries have been exhausted within the meaning of the Act.

Later this week, in the House of Commons, I shall be unveiling our plans to reintroduce rationing. Please go to our website for a delicious and simple recipe for Woolton Pie and a hearty yet economical Brown Windsor Soup.

Plodwatch

We didn't need a report from Her Majesty's Inspectorate of Constabulary to tell us that standards of front-line policing are crumbling.

Sir Ronnie Flanagan, Chief Inspector of Police, merely confirmed what I'd been saying for years when he admitted that officers have become so bogged down in form-filling that they 'over-record and under-deliver'.

Time was being spent on paperwork rather than getting out on the street, solving crimes and catching criminals, he concluded. But that's only part of the problem.

I've made a respectable living chronicling the assorted officiousness, incompetence and bovine stupidity which has come to characterise the modern police 'service'.

There's no shortage of material. The difficult bit is deciding what to leave out. Half the stuff which appears in my column comes from serving officers, furious and frustrated at what their noble vocation has become.

On the coppersblog website, policemen and women gather in cyberspace to exchange tales of useless 'management' and hopelessly out-of-touch senior officers, obsessed with meaningless targets, 'diversity' and 'risk assessment'.

The coppersblog was set up by a serving policeman using the pseudonym PC David Copperfield, who blew the whistle on the lunatic bureaucracy and moronic, target-driven culture in a Midlands force – sorry, 'service'. He later unmasked himself as thirty-six-year-old Stuart Davidson, when he resigned from Staffordshire Police and emigrated to Canada.

In a parting shot, he said he was sick of the madness and political interference which infests British constabularies. Here's what he wrote:

Thousands of front-line officers like me have to fight a daily battle just to get out of the office, before we even think of going after criminals. I'm lucky if I spend more than an hour a day on patrol.

My initial training in Britain was as dissatisfying as the selection procedures. We learned very little about crime, all too much about multi-cultural awareness and sensitivity towards bisexuals.

During my course, I spent just half an hour on burglaries, but three whole days on diversity, where we were encouraged to confront our supposed prejudices about Muslims, travellers or transgendered peoples, though, in reality, you would never find a less prejudiced group than my fellow recruits.

None of this highly politicised training prepared us for going out on the streets to take on thugs and thieves.

But, as I grew to learn over the subsequent four years, such tasks were only a small part of policing.

Our main work, it turned out, comprised watching our backs, answering questions from procedure-fixated superiors, and doing the bidding of deskbound bureaucrats. Even the most trivial offences would result in a blizzard of forms and hours behind the desk.

Take one example. Earlier this year, I was called to the house of a woman who claimed her boyfriend had stolen her dog. The supposed crime turned out to be little more than a minor domestic tiff and the dog was soon returned.

I thought that was the end of the matter. But no. A deluge of paperwork followed. I had to fill in forms covering witness statements, domestic incidents, 'no crime reported' and attempted detection.

In all, this nonsense covered twelve pages of written documentation. It was a meaningless pantomime, for we all knew that no action was necessary.

On another occasion, I had to go to an incident where a boy was alleged to have thrown a football at another.

By the time I got to the scene, the supposed victim could barely remember anything about this trivial event but, even so, all the painful, needless bureaucratic steps had to be followed, including a videoed interview.

> An obsession with targets and box-ticking meant we get exactly
> the same points for cautioning a girl for pulling another girl's hair as
> we get for a burglary.

He revealed that in Edmonton, Canada, it takes about sixty minutes to process a criminal and the officers are quickly back on the street. In Edmonton, north London, it takes an average of 606 minutes – that's over ten hours.

Cops like PC Davidson may reveal the ghastly truth. Ronnie Flanagan may highlight the problems in an official report, yet it won't make the slightest bit of difference. The Guardianistas who run the Home Office and the new breed of social workers who masquerade as senior policemen won't allow it to change. This is the police force they want.

Over the past thirteen years the police have gone from being citizens in uniform to the politically correct provisional wing of New Labour, more concerned with social engineering than fighting crime.

And as the *Life on Mars* generation has retired, it seems to have been replaced by a new breed of cocky, scruffy young guns, sometimes scarcely distinguishable from the thugs and morons they're paid to police.

For instance, eighteen Metropolitan Police officers turned up on Facebook boasting about crashes they've had while on duty. Even though the bragging included driving at 75mph in a bus lane, running over a drunk and wrapping a car round a lamp post, none of the officers was sacked – merely reprimanded or given 'words of advice'.

Elsewhere, on YouTube, a PC from Humberside was seen performing wheelies on a pavement while riding a motorbike (confiscated in a criminal inquiry) as his colleagues fell about laughing.

You might argue that all these officers were doing was engaging in the mindless, in-yer-face showing-off which is the hallmark of the cyberspace 'social networking' generation. The difference is that they are put in a position of trust and must be held to a higher standard.

Little wonder, then, that the report from HM's Inspectorate of

Constabulary concluded that the 'traditional ethos of discipline' has been hopelessly eroded.

Thanks to yuman rites legislation, sergeants are terrified of bringing insubordinate Plods under control for fear of being branded 'workplace bullies' and dragged through an industrial tribunal.

That's on top of the minefield of 'racism' and 'sexism' allegations and trebles-all-round damages claims from officers for perceived slights – everything from a Muslim assistant commissioner on £180,000 a year being passed over for further promotion to a soppy WPC throwing a wobbly because she was asked to make a cup of tea for an inspector.

Canteen culture has become com-pen-say-shun culture. The prevailing ethos is more social services than *Sweeney*. While the blame sits squarely with the hopeless, venal Labour government and the left-wing establishment in the Home Office, the responsibility is directly that of the new breed of chief police officers, none more so than former Met commissioner Ian Blair.

He warranted a whole chapter to himself in my last book. Greasing up to Labour and ingratiating himself with the Guardianistas as the self-flagellating face of 'progressive' policing got him the job in the first place.

Not that it did him much good subsequently. He managed to fall out with the Black Police Association and the Met's most senior gay officer, Brian Paddick, who first came to prominence after he popped up on a Wolfie Smith website boasting of his attraction to anarchy. Paddick also survived charges of misconduct, went on to preside over the disastrous policy of turning the streets of a south London into an open-air drugs den and ended up as an assistant commissioner before standing unsuccessfully as the Lib Dem candidate for London Mayor.

Blair also upset Britain's most prominent Muslim cop, who resigned with a fat pay-off. Most of his top brass despaired of him and the other ranks think he betrayed them. They can smell weakness.

Blair is the least copper-like copper I've ever met, managing to make Brian Paddick look like Jack Regan.

Back when I did a bit of broadcasting, I interviewed a few senior cops. Blair's predecessor, Sir John (now Lord) Stevens – aka Captain Beaujolais – and his protégé, the late Mike Todd, from Greater Manchester, both turned up on TV in full, reassuring regalia: gold braid, scrambled egg, all knife-sharp creases and buffed black boots. They looked and sounded every inch what you expect from an old-fashioned policeman.

When it was Blair's turn, he arrived in a grey suit and loafers and spoke in that curious, evasive management jargon, beloved of New Labour. I could have been interviewing Jack Straw or any other brown-nosing junior minister.

Blair did more than anyone to politicise policing. He thought he could run the Met like a branch of Haringey Town Hall. He repaid Labour's patronage by everything from lobbying hard for extended detention without trial to lending Tony Blair a police Range Rover emblazoned with 'Vote Labour' stickers at the 2005 general election.

In Blair's last year, £122 million was spent on paperwork – and another, astonishing, £26 million 'checking paperwork' – and the number of bobbies on the beat actually fell. The amount spent on routine patrols was cut by £20 million.

After being sacked – just as I predicted – by the new Tory Mayor Boris Johnson, Blair left behind an embittered, demoralised, ill-disciplined force and a capital city riddled with boarded-up police stations, gun crime, stabbings and general mayhem, while officers spend most of their time filling in forms, ticking boxes or suing each other.

Blair's days were numbered after the Met was found guilty at the Old Bailey of endangering the public over the shooting of the Brazilian electrician Jean Charles de Menezes, and he suffered a vote of no confidence from the Met Police Federation and the London Assembly and was criticised by an Independent [Labour] Police Complaints Commission report. But he clung on and kept insisting: I will survive.

You know where I'm going with this, don't you?

As always, and with apologies to Gloria Gaynor, it helps if you sing along . . .

At first I was afraid
I'd be crucified
Kept thinking that I would be sacked
When that Brazilian died.
I went missing on the day
I just hid myself away
And I went home
And I unplugged the phone.
I turned my back
I didn't want to know
I just walked away from Scotland Yard
Had nowhere else to go.
I know I've said some stupid things
Like you can leave your doors unlocked
But you don't expect a cock-up
When you're playing out of your socks.

'Go on, now go
Just clear your desk
We've no confidence that you, Sir Ian
Can sort out this bloody mess.'
Weren't they the ones who were always praising me
For all the work I've done
To promote diversity?
Oh no, not I
I won't resign
As long as Red Ken's on my side
I know that I'll be fine.
Because I've done nothing wrong
I've got the file on Cash for Gongs
So I'll survive
I will survive
(hey, hey).

I took all the vile abuse
The press could throw my way
They never were this horrible
To Captain Beaujolais.
They said I was a berk
Who should be doing social work
I used to cry
Over that business with Dizaei.
But now you see
A human being
Though far away from Stockwell Tube
It looks as if I'm fleeing.
I've got my faults, I've made mistakes
I admit that they exist
But contrary to some reports
I'm not permanently pissed.

Go on, then go
And do your worst
But I will never quit the Job
'Cos my career comes first.
Wasn't I the one who put the PC in the Met?
Do you think I'd put my papers in
When I've a bonus to collect?
Oh no, not I
I won't resign
Because of one unfortunate incident
Down on the Northern Line.
Although I am Chief Constable
I am not responsible
I won't resign
I won't resign
(hey, hey).

Mind how you go
And close the door
I'm still in charge, I'm staying put
I'm not saying any more.
Wasn't I the one who taped the Attorney General's calls?
As long as I'm Labour's favourite cop
I've got them by the balls.
And that is why
I will survive
Unlike Jean Charles de Menezes
I know I'll stay alive
Though they've got me by the throat
I still won't get my coat
I won't resign
I won't resign
(hey, hey).

The day this was published in the *Mail* I was told the song was posted on every notice board in every nick in the Met, and Scotland Yard echoed to the sound of giggling cops singing 'I Will Survive' behind closed squad room doors. It's the little things that make my job worthwhile.

They Tasered a Sheep!

If Blair was the poster boy for the political policeman, the other face of Plod belonged to Richard Brunstrom, chief constable of North Wales, whose deranged obsession with persecuting motorists led me to nickname him the Mad Mullah of the Traffic Taliban.

Brunstrom, too, has his own chapter in *Littlejohn's Britain*. One of his last stunts before retiring was hoisting himself up on some scaffolding and breaking into his own headquarters to test security. He turned North Wales Police into one of those weird cults you find in the remoter mountain ranges of North America.

It wasn't just drivers, either.

Brunstrom's men arrested, fingerprinted, photographed and took a DNA swab from a man accused of the heinous crime of canoeing without a permit. Nigel Conway refused on principle to pay the £3 demanded by a rafting company to paddle along an 830-yard stretch of the River Dee in Llangollen. The company leases the bank from a local landowner and believes it is entitled to charge others to use the river.

Mr Conway said: 'I refused to pay because everyone should have the right to access water free of charge.'

The firm reported him to the police and a week later he had his collar felt. He was taken to the station and interviewed for two hours in connection with 'obtaining services dishonestly' under Section 11 of the Fraud Act.

This was despite the fact that there is no specific law relating to access to rivers in England and Wales.

'It was such a joke, even the officers at the station were laughing,' said Mr Conway.

Sorry, but it's not funny. The rafting firm should have been told to take a running jump. At the very best, this was a mere civil dispute.

How dare the police arrest an innocent canoeist and treat him like a criminal? I'm only surprised Mr Conway wasn't breathalysed, too. But Brunstrom was unrepentant.

And although the Mad Mullah has gone, the madness goes on. The North Wales Plod surpassed themselves when called to a sheep blocking the A55 near Bodelwyddan.

There are a number of ways to shift a sheep, which are not known for their propensity to violence.

You could try bribing it with a handful of freshly mown grass. You could kick it up the backside. Or you could lob a lasso round its neck and drag it away.

They Tasered it.

You can just imagine the scene, with the cops crouching behind their patrol cars, *Life on Mars*-style, Tasers at the ready.

'You are surrounded by armed bastards. Surrender now or we'll shoot. I'm warning you, chummy, give yourself up or you're dead meat.'

Baa-aaaarrrgh!!

*

In Norfolk, officers arrested a scarecrow dressed in a police uniform and holding a speed camera made out of plastic bottles. It had been put there to advertise a fête in the village of Brancaster.

Inspector Dave Buckley said the speed gun could confuse drivers. 'We appreciate the spirit of the family-orientated festival but our priority is the safety of motorists.'

Where do they find these people? Maybe there's something in the water in Norfolk.

Over in Norwich, the vintage car used in *Chitty Chitty Bang Bang* was banned from a parade because it hadn't got an MOT certificate.

Meanwhile, it was revealed that the chief constable of Norfolk had received a £70,000 bonus on top of his £125,000 salary.

The chairman of the police authority said the bonus was necessary to attract the right candidate.

'We were looking for someone who could think outside the box.'

*

In Liverpool company director Gary Sanders was stopped by the Mersey Tunnel police for laughing while driving.

Gary wasn't driving dangerously or speeding, but the officer said he was laughing 'excessively' at a joke a friend had told him over a hands-free phone.

Since when has laughing behind the wheel been a criminal offence?

And as if that wasn't ludicrous enough, the officer then questioned him for thirty-five minutes about everything from his ethnic origin to his hair colour – even though Gary suffers from alopecia.

This stroppy, officious, humourless Plod caused Gary to miss an important business meeting and insisted he produce his documents at a police station, despite eventually admitting that no offence had actually been committed.

*

Grampian Police spent £170,000 trying to convict male stripper Stuart Kennedy – aka Sergeant Eros – for impersonating a police officer.

They have arrested him six times since March 2007, and he has appeared in court twenty-two times, without them securing a single conviction.

They even charged him with possessing an offensive weapon. Is that a rubber truncheon in your pocket . . . ?

*

A sniffer dog was stolen from under the noses of its handlers at Lancashire Police headquarters. Actually, the police managed to lose three dogs in 2008, including a cocker spaniel being specially trained by Northumbria Constabulary.

*

In Nottinghamshire, officers set up a shrine outside their headquarters to honour two police dogs which were roasted to death in a sweltering police car during the recent heatwave.

*

And speaking, or, rather, whispering, of dogs . . . at Ashford, in Kent, a former police sergeant with a rare voice disorder sued for compensation after being turned down for a job as a dog handler.

As a result of muscle spasms in her vocal chords, Catherine Gilbert can only whisper, which means she can't shout commands.

She claims she has suffered discrimination and should have been offered counselling.

But why would anyone apply for a job which ordinarily involved shouting if they could only whisper? Her condition also meant she had difficulty communicating with colleagues and using the telephone.

She has our sympathy, but why join the police in the first place?

Maybe Kent Police felt members of the whispering community were under-represented in the force, like transsexuals and people with Tourette's syndrome.

Surely she would have been happier working as a dog whisperer or a court stenographer, which is what she is doing now after resigning from the police to spend more time with her lawyers.

Incredibly, eight days have now been set aside to hear this case. Even if she loses it will cost taxpayers tens of thousands of pounds in court time and legal fees.

She should be charged with wasting police time.

'You have the right to remain silent . . .'

*

No such silence in Northampton, where officers have been equipped with loudhailers and ordered to tour the streets shouting at householders who leave their doors and windows open. It follows a spate of burglaries in Northampton, which police claim 'cost' them three grand a time to investigate. No, it doesn't. That's their job. The one we pay them for.

I've heard of megaphone diplomacy, but megaphone policing is ridiculous.

*

In Preston, PC Tony Cobban refused to sit on a bike and pose for publicity photos – because he hadn't been on a cycling proficiency course. He said: 'I was just being cautious. My concern would be if anything happens to me while on the bike and it hadn't been risk-assessed or insured. In this day and age, you have to cover all the bases.' He received the full support of Lancashire Police.

*

In Devon, police scrambled five patrol cars and a helicopter to apprehend a man suspected of being drunk in charge of a tractor. He was driving erratically at speeds of up to 12mph.

*

In Ayr, Scotland, a man was fined for dropping a £10 note. Arthritis sufferer Stewart Smith had just left a charity shop when he was called back by two policemen, who pointed to the note and a till receipt lying on the pavement.

Stewart thought he'd put the money, part of his change from buying a T-shirt, in his back pocket, but it must have fallen out.

Thanking the officers, he retrieved the note and prepared to go about his lawful business. Not so fast, chummy.

The cops informed Stewart he had committed an offence and gave him a £50 fixed-penalty notice for littering. We're not exactly talking *Taggart* here, are we?

'Hulloo, is that the polis? Come quickly, there's been a murrdah!'

'Nae can do, pal, all our officers are out nicking litter bugs.'

Stewart, a former warehouse worker who has to live on disability payments because of his arthritis, was stunned. A £50 fine is more than half his weekly benefit.

He tried telling them it was an honest mistake. No one in his position can afford to wander the streets throwing £10 notes away. But the police in Ayr operate a zero-tolerance policy when it comes to littering. Stewart has been told that unless he pays up he could face further action.

His solicitor is calling for the fine to be rescinded and an apology issued, describing the incident as 'a scandalous use of police resources'.

Strathclyde Constabulary refused to back down. No doubt the Case of the Felonious Tenner counts as another crime solved, another box ticked.

*

Bournemouth Police banged up a grandmother for the night after she complained about being terrorised by young thugs. Mrs Brenda Robinson, aged sixty-six, was arrested for clipping the ear of a yob who threatened her with a lump of wood and called her an expletive-deleted bitch.

This came just days after an elderly neighbour, Edward Keene, suffered a broken nose and severe bruising after being punched and headbutted by a pair of teenage hooligans.

*

Dyfed Powys Constabulary dispatched an officer at the crack of dawn to interview a local taxpayer who sent a copy of the famous German pastor Martin Niemöller poem about tyranny ('Then they came for the Jews', etc) to councillors.

Sales manager Stan Rogers was read the riot act and told that he could be prosecuted for 'harassment'.

*

In a similar case in July, a seventy-seven-year-old grandmother in Bursledon, Hants, was warned that she would be arrested for inciting religious hatred unless she took down a jokey sign on her gate reading: 'Our dogs are fed on Jehovah's Witnesses'.

*

Both Herefordshire and West Sussex forces used the Public Order Act to attempt to prosecute toy-shop owners for selling golliwogs. Worthing Police said hunting down those trading in 'threatening, insulting and abusive' cuddly toys was a 'priority'.

*

In Birmingham, an Osama bin Laden lookalike who took a job as a recruitment officer sued for religious discrimination because his colleagues teased him that he looked like, er, Osama bin Laden.

*

MI5 and Special Branch were staking out a St Trinian's-style school in the Sussex countryside, suspected of being used to train al-Qaeda bombers. Among those they spotted trooping in and out were uniformed members of the Sussex Constabulary.

For a while they thought their surveillance operation was blown – until they realised the Sussex Plods were being sent there for 'diversity' training.

*

Devon and Cornwall Police pulled out of a televised appeal aimed at catching an Afghan wanted for sexual assault after protests from a race watchdog.

Detectives were livid when the Chief Constable Stephen Otter caved in to pressure from the local racial equality council.

Officers were due to appear on an episode of ITV's *Manhunt* to ask for help in apprehending the prisoner, who absconded from bail after being arrested in connection with the rape of one woman and the sexual assault of three others.

He was believed to be working as an unlicensed taxi driver somewhere in the South of England. So that narrows it down.

Mr Otter, a graduate of the 'diversity' school at the Met, ordered detectives not to take part.

Sonia Francis-Mills, the director of the Devon race council, said: 'I don't think they were happy. I think the police often just want to feel collars.'

Now there's a novelty. She claimed that if this man's description was made public, there could be a 'violent backlash' against other members of ethnic minorities. Why?

We've had Islamic terrorists blowing themselves up in London without a violent backlash against the wider Muslim community. We've had Asian doctors charged with conspiring to set off car bombs in London and Glasgow without any reports of law-abiding Pakistani surgeons being beaten up at random.

This particular Afghani, whose alleged victims were all assaulted after they got into his minicab, had been on the run for months and the TV appeal may have been the police's best hope of catching him.

But his chances of getting away with it just got better, because a spineless chief constable was frightened of upsetting some self-righteous Guardianista.

The Commission for Racial Equality nationally says, sensibly, that it has no problem with police describing a suspect's race and skin colour if it's relevant.

So why didn't Otter just tell Miss Francis-Mills to Foxtrot Oscar? When did she get the veto over policing?

This is a woman who thinks the trouble with the police is that they 'just want to feel collars'.

Call me old fashioned, but isn't that what we pay them for?

*

Apparently not. Cheshire Constabulary actually employs a 'Demand Management Unit Manager' to write to robbery victims telling them why their cases won't be investigated.

*

A number of forces started issuing women police officers with smaller motorbikes and lighter weapons to encourage more female recruits.

Crêche and breastfeeding facilities are also provided in police stations to encourage a more 'family-friendly' atmosphere.

City of London, Gwent and Cleveland Police introduced quiet areas in their stations to allow mothers to express breast milk and installed fridges to store bottles.

At this rate, I joked, they'll be taking their children out on the beat in pushchairs. I should have known better.

Soon afterwards I discovered that Cumbria Constabulary has even commissioned a range of maternity wear for pregnant policewomen.

The outfits are described as 'stylish, practical and comfortable, ideal for mothers-to-be who are fighting crime with the modern police force'.

The new uniform came in response to complaints from expectant mums that they were being forced to wear unflattering XL-sized trousers and blouses.

Call me old-fashioned, but why are pregnant women 'fighting crime' on the streets of Cumbria? I'm all for equal opportunities, but what use is an eight-months-gone WPC when it comes to chasing shoplifters or tackling football hooligans?

And how long before Mothercare starts stocking stab vests?

*

After it was reported that North Wales police dogs were being taught to headbutt suspects rather than bite them, news came that K-9 units were being issued with stab vests.

But it was the dogs getting the body armour, not the handlers.

*

Thames Valley Police demanded to know a vicar's ethnic background before they would send out an officer to investigate a burglary at his church.

If he refused to co-operate, he wouldn't even get a crime number for the insurance.

The police said the questions were part of 'best practice' aimed at determining which types of people are the victims of particular crimes.

It is now a legal requirement to record the ethnicity of victims. Why?

Would it be any more, or less, of a crime if someone who had been burgled was Chinese, Jamaican or a native of Honduras?

In this case, it's fair to assume that the Rev. Simon Lane, vicar of St Andrew's parish church, is unlikely to have been an illegal immigrant from Somalia – although, given the state of the Church of England these days, you never know.

*

Emma Lucas was stricken with guilt after stealing £3,000 from Sainsbury's, in Chestfield, Kent, where she worked.

Twice she tried to give herself up, first at Herne Bay police station, then at Canterbury.

Both times she was told to go away because there was no one available to arrest her, as it was a Bank Holiday. It took her another two days to get her collar felt.

*

In London, officers have been issued with special cards to help them beat the stress of tackling crime.

As part of an initiative called Shrinking Clouds, they will also be shown a DVD on relaxation and be encouraged to eat more fruit and vegetables.

Whenever they feel under pressure, they are instructed to take a deep breath and consult the card. That should come in handy when you find yourself face to face with an armed robber.

I always thought stress management in the Met involved fishing a bottle of Bell's from the bottom drawer in the squad room, followed by a few pints in the Feathers.

*

Then there was the directive to all officers to stop using regional dialects and slang because they can't be understood by colleagues in other parts of the country.

It followed the introduction of a new national radio system which allows officers to communicate across force boundaries for the first time.

So no more: 'Chummy's on the plot, guv', or 'He's bang to rights'.

The police commissioned a linguist who identified fifty ways in which coppers say 'yes' over the airwaves – including 'OK', 'Wilco' and 'Affirmative'. All of these will have to be abandoned for just three terms – 'Received' for 'I have understood'; 'Yes Yes' for 'I agree'; and 'Will do' for 'I shall carry out the task.'

So that's 'Z-Victor One to BD' out of the window. And I still don't know what 'BD' stood for.

Meanwhile, the government is encouraging victims of crime to contact the police by text.

For instance: 'Hlp 5-0 sum1 hs brokN n2 my hous' apparently means 'Help, police, someone has broken into my house'.

If they can't understand regional dialects, how on earth are they going to work that out?

*

If you've ever watched *The Bill*, you'll know that police slang for a road accident involving a police car or officer is POLAC – short for 'police accident'. Not any more, at least in Gloucestershire. When I first heard the reason, I thought it was a wind-up.

But a spokesman for Gloucestershire Constabulary said: 'We are aware the term POLAC, when heard verbally, can be interpreted as a racial slur against people of Polish background.'

*

And here's an outrageous example of how the obsession with diversity can ruin careers. The first person I heard describe a BMW as 'Black Man's Wheels' was a black man. It's an expression which has been in common parlance on the street for donkey's years.

But a senior policeman in Birmingham was reprimanded for using it and had his pay cut as a result.

Superintendent Chris Pretty was demoted one rank to chief inspector. Two officers complained that when he opened a leaving present containing a toy BMW at a party to mark his last day as head of training, he quipped: 'Oh, Black Man's Wheels.'

It was a harmless joke. But instead of telling the complainants to grow up, West Midlands Police took it seriously.

Bini Brown, from the African Caribbean Self Help Organisation in Birmingham, said: 'These particular comments made by a high-ranking police officer merely add fuel to the myth that BMWs are driven only by black criminals.'

No, they don't. It's simply a humorous acknowledgement of the enthusiasm some young black men have for blinged-up Beamers.

Mr Pretty is no racist. He's done much for the region's black community as a former head of the 'black-on-black' crime taskforce and solved several murders.

A police spokesman said: 'He has been dealt with in an appropriate manner.'

Actually, he was dealt with in an absurd, heavy-handed, vindictive, utterly inappropriate manner. No wonder so many dedicated police officers are walking away from the job.

*

Because the police spend so much time sitting around the station filling in forms or staring at CCTV screens, you rarely see a bobby on the beat. That reassuring physical presence has long gone.

So in Grimsby, police stationed a life-sized cardboard cut-out of a community support officer in a branch at Tesco, in the hope that it would deter shoplifters.

Someone nicked it.

Life on Venus

The BBC's time-travel cop show *Life on Mars* was watched by seven million viewers. It was a post-ironic take on *The Sweeney* and featured a modern policeman, DI Sam Tyler, who fell into a coma and woke up in 1973. He was horrified by the crude racism, sexism and casual brutality of seventies' DCI Gene Hunt, of the Manchester CID.

But what if a 1970s copper was transported forward in time? What would he make of New Scotland Yard in the twenty-first century?

*

(Scene One: Hunt wakes with a raging hangover to find himself slumped over a desk. He reaches into his pocket, pulls out a packet of Kensitas and lights up)

Where the hell am I?

Put that out.

What?

This is a designated no-smoking facility.

What are you bloody talking about?

I ask the questions.

Who the hell are you, darling?

Detective Inspector Suzi Obafemwi. And this is my squad room.

YOUR squad room? Stop messing about, petal, and get us a drink, there's a good girl. My gob feels as if a rabid badger has crawled in there and died.

Don't you 'good girl' me, you patronising bastard.

Come on, luv, stop playing games. You're not a bloody DI. For a start, you're a tart. And you're coloured, unless this hangover is playing havoc with my eyesight.

How dare you call me a prostitute, you racist pig?

No offence, flower. When I said 'tart', I didn't mean, er, it's a term of endearment, like.

Not round here it isn't. And I'm not 'coloured', I'm black.

Only trying to be polite, sweetheart. It took me five years to learn to say 'coloured'.

Who are you?

DCI Gene Hunt, from Manchester.

You must be the new guvnor. We've been expecting you.

Sorry, luv, I don't mean to be rude. It's just that where I come from we haven't got any black, female detective inspectors.

What, in Manchester? In 2010?

Two thousand and what?

Ten, SIR.

You make 'sir' sound like a toe-end in the goolies, luv. Who do you think I am?

Our new guvnor.

But I only came down here for a leaving-do at the Feathers. Old Barlow, first-class thief-taker.

Who?

Chief Superintendant Ken Barlow.

Never heard of him.

He's a bloody legend, flower. Cracked the 1971 diamond vaults job.

I wouldn't know. I wasn't born then.

Eh?

This is 2010, remember?

Bloody Nora, I know this weak southern beer doesn't agree with me, but someone must have spiked my drinks.

You certainly stink of booze.

My head's banging like a bloody Lambeg drum in an Orange Lodge parade. Pour us a Scotch, there's a luv.

This is also an alcohol-free working environment. You don't want to let the Commissioner catch you smelling like that.

I thought he liked a drink.

No, that was the last one, Captain Beaujolais.

Captain Birdseye?

No, Beaujolais. He went off to run the Diana inquiry.

Diana Dors? She hangs around with some pretty dodgy characters. That Alan Lake, he's a wrong 'un.

No, Princess Diana.

And I've never heard of HER. If this really is 2010, I must have fallen into a coma.

You were certainly comatose when I found you.

Anyway, seeing as I'm here, we might as well get on with it. What are you working on at the moment?

Cash for ermine.

Someone fencing stolen fur coats?

No, the Prime Minister's been accused of selling seats in the House of Lords in exchange for political donations.

They've always done that, flower. You might as well try to stop dogs licking their wossnames. What else?

There's been a spate of homophobic crime.

Homo-what?

Phobic, sir. A writer went on Radio 4 and said she thought gay marriages were abhorrent.

So what? There's no law against it.

There is, sir. It's a hate crime.

I hate crime, too. Anyway, who ever heard of two poofs getting married?

It's all the rage. Civil partnerships, they call it. And I wouldn't let anyone in this building hear you using language like that.

Like what?

Poofs, sir. Some might find it offensive.

Come off it. There aren't any brown-hatters in Scotland Yard.

Oh, yes there are, sir, at the very highest level. There's even a Gay Police Association.

You'll be telling me next that there's a Black Police Association, as well.

Correct, sir. I'm the vice-chair.

Bloody hell. Anyway, where is everyone – down the pub? I could do with a large one myself.

Out on inquiries, or attending diversity training. At least, those who aren't off sick.

Sick? What, sleeping off a session, you mean?

No, stress, mainly. Half the Met took at least three weeks off sick last year. Cost £36 million.

Jeesus. I've never missed a day in my life. I'd sack the lot of them.

You can't do that; they'd sue for wrongful dismissal on the grounds of racial or sexual discrimination.

You're kidding. What about those who aren't throwing a sickie?

A couple of officers are interviewing a ten-year-old boy who sent an e-mail to another boy, calling him 'gay'.

You're NOT kidding, are you?

No, sir. And Simpkins has been seconded to the golliwog squad.

The WHAT?

It's a special unit set up to prosecute shopkeepers found to be selling racially inflammatory soft toys.

Aren't we nicking any real villains?

DS Harper arrested a man on the Underground for carrying an offensive weapon.

A knife or something?

No, sir, a cricket ball. And we felt the collar of a man reading out the names of war dead next to the Cenotaph.

That's what it's bloody there for.

It's inside the exclusion zone, to prevent terrorism.

Effin' IRA, again.

No, sir, that's over.

Don't tell me – Gerry Adams is the Prime Minister of Northern Ireland.

Of course not, sir. He's deputy to Ian Paisley.

Are you sure you haven't got any Scotch?

'Fraid not. I can offer you a tea.

Milk and three sugars, please, treacle.

No treacle, just camomile and ylang-ylang.

If not the bog-trotters, then who?

Who what, sir?

Terrorism.

Al-Qaeda.

Who's this Al geezer when he's at home?

International Islamic jihadists. They've already let off four suicide bombs on London Transport.

We should shoot them on sight.

We did, sir, only we shot the wrong man. He was a Brazilian.

So what are we doing?

We're gathering all the intelligence we can. Some of the lads are staking out a suspected bomb factory.

Why don't we just surround the place with a couple of hundred armed officers, steam in and take the place apart.

Tried that, too. In Forest Gate. Took it apart brick by brick. One of the suspects took a bullet.

You make that sound like a BAD thing. I'd drive them to the nearest multi-storey car park and dangle them off the side by their ankles until they confessed.

Don't quote me, sir, so would I. But the Commissioner would never allow that. You really are quite a throwback.

That's the nicest thing you've said all day. Come on, Suzi, sod this for a game of soldiers, you can buy me a drink and then we'll go out and see who we can fit up.

You've been watching too much Life on Mars, *sir.*

Life on Mars, petal? This is more like Life on Venus.

Flip Flop

Torbay Police came up with a novel idea to help drunken young women get home safely. They stood outside pubs distributing free flip-flops because they were worried that these sozzled sluts might fall off their high heels and hurt themselves.

Inspector Adrian Leisk said: 'Sometimes people get drunk and you see them carrying footwear, which is inappropriate. The emphasis is on providing replacement footwear for people to go home in, should they find their footwear uncomfortable or soiled.'

Nice. Thank you for sharing that. Surely the police would be better advised to storm the pubs before women can drink themselves senseless — and threaten to strip the licences of the landlords who continue to serve them when they are visibly drunk and incapable.

These flip-flops were paid for out of a £30,000 grant from the Home Office. Imagine how much that would add up to if the idea catches on and every police force in the country decides to start handing out 'safe footwear'.

The government can't afford to buy proper boots for our troops on active service, but has no problem forking out for flip-flops for floozies too boozed-up to walk home in their Matalan peep-toe platforms.

A spokesman for Safer Communities Torbay said they were targeting 'vulnerable people, particularly females, in need of support' as part of their campaign to clean up the streets.

What's wrong with water cannon?

When I first reported this story back at Christmas 2008, I had assumed it was an isolated piece of localised lunacy, confined to the English Riviera. Predictably, I was wrong.

I soon learned from coppers all over Britain that the provision of flip-flops was seen not just as an essential template for modern, progressive policing, but as your starter for ten.

Sussex Police not only followed up enthusiastically on the Torbay initiative, they expanded upon it.

Front-line officers were being sent out on patrol equipped with goody bags to be handed to Christmas revellers at closing time and ordered to distribute them to drunks tipping out of pubs and night clubs. There were black bags for females, red for males. No doubt in Brighton they had a pink version, too.

In addition to flip-flops, the lay-deez' goody bag contained a bottle of water, a lollipop, guidance on 'safe' levels of alcohol consumption and, inevitably, a condom.

The gentlemen's had everything but the flip-flops, plus a leaflet giving instructions, in the unlikely event of successful deployment of condom, on the necessity of obtaining consent from the other party.

Try to imagine the thought process which went into this. The chief constable is wrapping up a 'management' meeting at Sussex Police headquarters.

There's heroin being sold outside schools, a spate of muggings at the Arndale Centre, joy-riding and burned-out cars on the Jasmine Allen Estate, a county-wide epidemic of burglary and vandalism and half a dozen unsolved murders.

The committee has just approved a full-scale anti-terrorist operation into who has been leaking to the *Brighton Argus* confidential details of the council's top-secret plans to cut back household rubbish collections to once a month.

'Any other business?'

'Yes, guv, as part of our drive against anti-social behaviour, community liaison is proposing that we hand out goody bags to drunks.

'This is a Home Office initiative which has been successfully trialled in the Torbay area and is being rolled out across the country. You may have read about it in the Daily Mail.

'Each bag will contain a complimentary pair of flip-flops, a bottle of water, a lollipop and a condom. Any observations?'

'Why flip-flops?'

'It stops women falling off their high heels and breaking their ankles, sir.'

'I see. Are you sure about the lollipops? Couldn't someone poke their eye out? I think we should run this by elf'n'safety.'

'Already done that, guv. It was them what came up with bunging in condoms – part of the safe sex outreach initiative we're running outside the public toilets behind the bus park, in tandem with the cottage hospital.'

'Surely if they're too drunk to stand up, they're too drunk to have sex?'

'Can't be too careful, chief. But we are taking the additional precaution of including consent forms in the goody bags we give to men.'

'Why's that?'

'It comes direct from the Home Secretary, sir. She has just released new guidelines defining any act of sexual intercourse as rape, unless permission has been obtained in triplicate and been witnessed by a serving police officer, magistrate or lawyer acting on behalf of the English Collective of Prostitutes.'

'But didn't she also say that if a woman was too drunk to know what she was signing, she couldn't be considered to be giving her consent?'

'Very true, sir. And that means we can meet the government's target of a 500 per cent increase in rape convictions.'

*

As I concluded, it could only be a matter of time before cops are sent out on the beat wearing flashing Santa hats and police started making drunks a nice cup of coffee and getting them a cab home. Inevitably, I didn't have long to wait for further developments.

A *Daily Mail* reader in West Somerset spotted a uniformed officer complete with flashing fairy lights on his helmet.

And it got worse. In North Wales, our old friend the Mad Mullah was even including personal attack alarms in the goody bags.

They hadn't yet got round to taking drunks home and making them coffee, but some forces were handing out taxi vouchers and free bus ride vouchers.

In Bolton, they were even giving revellers children's bubbleblowing kits to try to stop them kicking each other's heads in.

But even in my wildest imagination I couldn't have come up with Newcastle under Lyme laying on fire-eaters, balloon-modelling artistes and jugglers to distract drunks from getting involved in booze-fuelled violence.

Which left me wondering: what if it puts ideas in their heads?

To the best of my knowledge, it hasn't happened yet, but it can't be long before bobbies are sent out on the beat with fire extinguishers and buckets of sand to put out drunks gargling flaming sambucas while trying to make inflatable giraffes out of the condoms in their goody bags.

Celebrating Perversity

Three soppy Sheffield policewomen dressed in burqas and went out shopping in the city centre.

They spent a whole day swathed from head to foot with only slits for their eyes. One of them, Sergeant Deb Leonard, said: 'I have gained an appreciation and understanding of what Muslim females experience when they walk out in public in clothing appropriate to their beliefs.'

A bit like going to a fancy dress party in a pillar box, I would imagine. According to Sheffield's police magazine: 'The exercise is just one of many activities South Yorkshire Police has planned with communities and ethnic minority leaders to secure strong relationships, celebrate diversity and encourage integration.'

Leave aside the fact that most reasonable people think the burqa has no place on the streets of Britain, being an oppressive symbol of political and religious fundamentalism.

This patronising stunt was the clearest evidence yet that some sections of the police force have gone stark, staring bonkers in the name of 'celebrating diversity'.

We've got a Black Police Association, a Gay Police Association, a Muslim Police Association, even a Pagan Police Association.

The Home Office agreed to the establishment of a support group for officers who practise paganism and witchcraft. Druids and Wicca worshippers are also welcome to join.

A spokesman said: 'The government wants a police service that reflects the diverse communities it serves. It is down to individual forces to make reasonable adjustments to accommodate the religion or beliefs of individual officers.'

Hertfordshire PC Andy Pardy, who says he is a heathen and worships Norse gods, is granted eight pagan holidays a year, including Hallowe'en and the summer solstice.

You can't miss him. He's the one with the horns on his helmet, seconded to the raping and pillaging squad.

Superintendent Simon Hawkins, who styles himself Hertfordshire's 'champion for faith', said: 'While balancing operational needs, the force's religion and beliefs policy gives all staff the choice of re-allocating the traditional Christian Bank Holiday festivals to suit their personal faith.'

In Staffordshire, PC Andy Hill founded the Pagan Police Group UK and has a website dedicated to all Wicca-related policing matters. It offers spells tailored to help officers win promotion and cure those off work with a bad back.

Imagine the next sergeants' exam. While most of the candidates are sitting in the waiting room doing some last-minute swotting up on the Police and Criminal Evidence Act, there's a Plod in the car park dancing naked round a fire and strangling a chicken.

Constable Hill insisted: 'Wiccan has always been a bit of a taboo religion, there are lots of misconceptions about it.

'This is nothing to do with black magic or devil worshipping. Witchcraft is not the hocus-pocus, puff of smoke, turning people into frogs stuff you see on television.'

That's reassuring to know, otherwise the Mad Mullah of the Traffic Taliban would have had witch doctors hiding behind bushes, turning motorists into pumpkins.

In Strathclyde, ten officers claim to be Jedis, which is hardly surprising since Sauchiehall Street is swarming with spacemen at chucking-out time on a Saturday night. But are these *Star Wars* fanatics going to get their own Home Office-backed staff association, too, with time off to celebrate Obe-Wan Kenobi's birthday?

Freedom of religion is one of the basic principles of a liberal society, provided it doesn't run to human sacrifices. But it doesn't belong in the workplace.

Why the hell should any police force appoint a 'champion of faith'? It's not an ecumenical college.

Police officers should be defined by the uniform they wear, not the colour of their skin or their religious beliefs. There shouldn't be a Black Police Association, or a Gay Police Association, or any other race-, sex- or faith-based organisation within an organisation.

All these groups do is foster a culture of division, permanent unrest and grasping opportunism. Stand by for a PC demanding thousands of pounds in compensation after claiming he was passed over for promotion because he's a shaman.

I can't wait for the first annual dinner of the Pagan Police Association, guest speaker Colin Stagg – the self-proclaimed Wicca man fitted up for the murder of Rachel Nickell on Wimbledon Common.

We'll have defendants claiming in court that they only confessed because the investigating detective threatened to turn them into a frog.

How long before some officer decides it is his inalienable yuman rite to wear a goat's head on duty?

All this came to light in the same week in which it was announced that burglaries were on the increase for the first time in six years. Don't be surprised in future if victims are offered a sprig of holly and a quick spell to ward off evil spirits, along with a note for the insurance.

*

There's no limit to this nonsense. The Scottish branch of ACPO, the chief police officers' club, issued a 140-page 'pocket-sized' guide to diversity. More than seven thousand copies were distributed to the troops, at a cost to taxpayers of £4,500.

Officers are warned not to call women 'hen' or 'love' or to refer to police stations as being 'unmanned' – just in case feminists take offence.

The expressions 'policeman' and 'manpower' are also banned, as is referring to the chaps as 'guys'. It's also unwise, apparently, to handle a Hindu statue, touch the head of a Buddhist monk or telephone an orthodox Jew on the Sabbath.

Chairman of the Scottish police diversity committee is Ian Latimer, chief constable of the Northern Constabulary, which covers the Highlands and Islands – that well-known melting pot of multiculturalism. Just how many Buddhists are there in Cromarty?

Maybe I missed that episode of *Hamish Macbeth*, but how often do rural Scottish policemen find themselves called upon to search Hindu statues for hidden contraband, or pat Buddhists on the head.

Admittedly, there are quite a lot of fat, bald blokes wandering round Glasgow who look a bit like Buddha in a bad light, though the Rab C. Nesbitt bandage tends to be a bit of a giveaway and you don't get many Buddhist monks swigging bottles of Buckfast by the neck.

Oh, and here's one I never knew. 'Many people celebrate the St Patrick's Day traditions by drinking green beer, wearing green and generally celebrating their Irish heritage.'

So if you happen to be out on the beat in Glasgow on St Paddy's Day and you see a short, bald, fat guy coming out of the ladies' toilet, wearing a taffeta tutu, waving a stolen Hindu statue and singing 'The Fields Of Athenry', best give him a wide berth. Whatever you do, don't pat him on the head.

Officers are also reminded: 'A transgender person is not breaking the law by using the opposite gender toilet facilities from the gender they were labelled at birth.'

*

On Humberside, five hundred cops and civilian staff were sent on a retraining course to learn how to treat an officer who has had a sex change. Officers were taken off the beat to be taught the correct way to react to someone who has had 'gender reassignment' surgery.

Chief Superintendent Kevin Sharp said it was their duty to help the forty-two-year-old married constable become a WPC.

I'm sure this came as a great reassurance to residents of a police division which has a crime rate double the national average.

*

Which bring us on neatly to the National Trans Police Association. According to its website: 'The NTPA exists primarily to provide support to serving and retired Police Officers, Police Staff and Special Constables with any gender identity issue including, but not exclusively, Trans Men, Trans Women, people who identity as Transgender, Androgyne or Intersex.

'Also the NTPA will give support to people who identify as Cross Dressers. The NTPA further aims to provide support to all serving and retired police officers, police staff and special constables who are dealing with people with a gender identity issue whether that person is a colleague, family member or a member of the public involved in a police matter.'

Note the *'but not exclusively'*. You might have thought that any outfit encompassing transgendered, androgyne and intersexuals had pretty much covered the waterfront.

The roll call of those eligible sounds like a contestant signing off after winning Ken Bruce's Popmaster, rattling through a list of names before adding breathlessly 'and anyone else who knows me'.

The criteria are so widely drawn that, theoretically, they could also include centaurs, who are currently under-represented in the ranks of the Old Bill. They would be welcomed into the mounted branch and could cut costs by 50 per cent by saving on the need for both an officer and a horse.

If the legendary band Half Man Half Biscuit ever decide to turn their backs on the rock and roll lifestyle a whole new career in law enforcement awaits.

The NTPA made its public debut at the Sparkle 09 festival in Manchester's Gay Village, where it set up a mobile police station handing out leaflets and balloons. There are some very fetching photos on its website.

Curiously, the events co-ordinator for the NTPA is called Bernie Clifton. Could this be the same Bernie Clifton who made his name as a comedian by dressing up as an ostrich? I'm assuming it's not him, but you never know.

Actually, if it is the same Bernie Clifton he will probably soon have his own association for people who like to dress up as ostriches.

There appears to be no limit to the number of obscure sub-categories the police can split themselves into. The National Trans Police Association is already recognised and supported by both ACPO and the National Policing Improvement Agency. An application for Home Office funding is sure to follow and is almost certain to be granted.

It can only be a matter of time before a transsexual officer sues for discrimination after being turned down for promotion or demands that the police fund his gender reassignment surgery.

For the record, I have no more objection to tranvestites forming a club than I do to philatelic societies. But it should be done in their own time and not at public expense.

The police need to be reminded that their job is to prevent crime, maintain public order and catch villains. Full stop.

Recruitment and promotion should be solely on the basis of ability, not race, religion, gender or sexual proclivity. Everyone should be treated equally. There should be no place for officially recognised, politically motivated, single-issue lobby groups.

Never mind burqas. At this rate it won't be long before a cross-dressing copper complains that his stockings and suspenders are chafing under his blue serge uniform and insists on being allowed to go on patrol in a leather miniskirt and an Amy Winehouse wig.

This Little Piggy

There are some stories which are so preposterous on so many levels that it is difficult to know where to start. Take the case of the Muslim chef who sued the police for religious discrimination after being asked to cook sausages. Hasanali Khoja accused Scotland Yard of breaking an agreement that he did not have to handle pork.

It was reported that this deal was done when he was appointed as catering manager at Hendon Police College in 2005. Whoever heard of a chef being excused pork?

Apparently, the arrangement worked quite well until he was transferred to a nick in west London, where he was expected to prepare the speciality of the house – the '999 breakfast', which includes bacon, sausages and black pudding.

At this request, Mr Khoja had a fit of the vapours. 'The Met has shown no sensitivity towards my religion. Their response has been ill-thought and discriminatory. No Muslim in my position should have to face such harassment,' he complained.

'I never enrolled to cook pork. I refused to do it. I never did it and I never would.'

Naturally, he expected a large sum of money by way of com-pen-say-shun – an action supported by the usual bunch of pro-fessional troublemakers at the Muslim Police Association.

His lawyer, Khalid Sofi, said: 'He has genuine and strong religious beliefs and expects that they will be accommodated.'

Of course he does.

What astonishes me is that he ever applied for a job cooking for policemen in the first place. What, precisely, did he think they serve up in a police canteen – vegetarian samosas?

The Old Bill marches on its stomach and the Full English is a staple of a policeman's diet. Where would Inspector Jack Frost be without his supply of sausage sarnies?

If Mr Khoja objected to cooking bacon and bangers he should have got himself a job in an Indian restaurant. The curry trade is always crying out for decent chefs, which is why it has to import so many from the sub-continent.

As it happens, much as I love a good fry-up I can't stand the smell of roast pork. So my wife cooks it for herself when I'm out for dinner. For that reason, though, I wouldn't apply for a job as a chef in a restaurant famous for its barbecued pig's trotters.

Yes, I know that they could have asked someone else to cook the bacon and sausages, but why should they?

When Mr Khoja was interviewed at Hendon, he should have been told in no uncertain terms that the job included cooking pork products. If he had a fundamental objection, he should go and work somewhere else.

Hiring a chef who won't cook sausages to work in a police canteen is like hiring a lifeguard who can't swim.

Typically, I would imagine, the police were so terrified of being accused of 'racism' that they took him on regardless.

Then again, he should never have considered taking a job which would bring him into contact with 'unclean' meat.

Initially, the Met capitulated and offered an informal agreement that he wouldn't have to handle pork. But that wasn't good enough for him and he was suspended on full pay pending an industrial tribunal.

So for the best part of a year, taxpayers had to pick up his wages and the bill for legal aid while he pursued his claim.

Eventually, the case was thrown out. But why did this crazy business have to wait a full twelve months to be heard? It shouldn't have taken more than five minutes to resolve. Worst case, the Old Bill paid up his notice period and sent him away to look for another job.

And why were the Muslim Police Association involved? Mr Khoja isn't a policeman. Come to that, there shouldn't be a Muslim Police Association. But, then again, I'm not surprised. This is about political leverage, about who runs the police – senior management or the racially motivated awkward squad.

At a wider level, it's just another example of the concerted campaign to impose a Muslim veto on public life in Britain.

We've already had supermarkets bowing to pressure from Muslim checkout staff who refuse to sell alcohol. They should all be sacked. If you don't want to sell booze, don't get a job in an off-licence.

Then there was the case of the forklift truck driver who claimed it was religious discrimination to be asked to shift pallets of wine and beer from one side of the warehouse to the other. He wasn't being forced to drink it, for heaven's sake.

And plenty of Muslim shopkeepers happily stock alcohol – and sausages, bacon and pork scratchings, come to that – without feeling it compromises their religious beliefs in any way.

Since 9/11 the authorities have been at pains to appease militant Islam. And once again, the police have been leading the pack.

Take the story of the Muslim constable who was excused duty outside the Israeli Embassy in London.

PC Alexander Omar Basha refused to stand guard in protest at Israel killing his brother Muslims in the recent war in Lebanon.

Instead of disciplining Basha for failing to obey orders, his bosses in the Diplomatic Protection Group caved in and agreed to move him.

If they'd stood up to PC Basha they'd have been accused of racism and 'Islamophobia' and would be looking at a six-figure compensation claim.

PC Basha must have known when he joined the Diplomatic Protection Group that his duties could well bring him into contact with the Israeli Embassy and no doubt any number of other regimes which he might find unpalatable.

He didn't have to join the DPG. He could have chosen a career path which involved him doing nothing more controversial than helping old ladies across the road out at Elstree.

Would he also refuse to stand guard outside the American Embassy in protest at Muslim deaths in Iraq and Afghanistan?

Would he consider himself justified in declining sentry duty outside Number 10 Downing Street because he objected to Tony

Blair ordering British troops into action to remove Saddam Hussein and the Taliban?

Given that he took part in Stop The War protests in Trafalgar Square, I think we can take that as a 'yes'.

So does that mean that any Jewish police officer would be justified in refusing to guard the Lebanese, or Syrian, or Iranian embassies?

Or would he be allowed to opt out of investigating an attack on a mosque because PC Basha's brother Muslims are killing Jews in Israel?

Where will it all end?

I shouldn't have thought many members of the old RUC are over the moon about having to provide protection for Gerry Adams and Martin McGuinness.

It can't be much fun, either, for coppers who have to babysit paedophiles in safe houses – especially if they've got young children of their own.

How do you think those Metropolitan Police officers, from a variety of religious backgrounds, felt about being assigned to provide a police escort for the Disciples of Death marching through London calling for the murder of all infidels and praising the 7/7 homicide bombers?

Nor can I imagine that too many Catholic policemen were that thrilled about having a gang of Muslim rabble-rousers bouncing up and down outside Westminster Cathedral and demanding the beheading of the Pope.

If, instead of turning the other cheek, the congregation had turned out of the cathedral and decided to kick seven sacks out of the demonstrators, would the police have been justified on moral grounds in letting them get on with it?

Furthermore, would any devout Christian be excused duty at chucking-out time at a gay bar because of his sincerely held opposition to homosexuality?

It would be career suicide. PC Basha should have been ordered to report for duty outside the Israeli Embassy first thing the following morning. If he refused, he should have been booted out of the force.

There is no place in Britain for pick'n'mix policing based on personal prejudice. Nor should there be any special treatment for any religious or racial group.

But it's not just the sensibilities of chefs and diplomatic protection officers which have to be taken into consideration. The police even go out of their way not to offend criminals who happen to be Muslims.

Some bright spark in Luton came up with a plan to make sniffer dogs wear leather bootees when they search for explosives in the homes of Muslim terror suspects.

The ever-vigilant diversity branch feared Muslims would be offended by having 'unclean' animals in their houses.

And, in Dundee, police apologised to local Muslims for a crime prevention leaflet featuring a dog in a peaked cap on the grounds that some followers of the Islamic faith may find dogs 'unclean' and therefore culturally offensive.

Meanwhile on *Woman's Hour*, I listened in amazement as a senior female officer from Scotland Yard explained that there were no barriers to women being used in specialist weapons units, bar one.

'Young black males and Muslim males don't react well to being told what to do by a woman,' she said. 'So we adapt and overcome and use a male officer.'

So that's all right, then.

What happens if a female member of SO19 confronts an Islamic suicide bomber about to blow himself up on the Tube?

Does she shout: 'Armed police! Put your hands on your head and get down on your knees NOW!'?

Or does she say: 'I'm so sorry to trouble you, sir, but would you mind awfully not detonating your device until I have had the opportunity to summon a male officer who will be able to arrest you in a manner appropriate to your cultural sensitivities'?

Bacon sandwich, anyone?

War on Terror

Some years ago, in the wake of the Afghan hijack fiasco at Stansted, I invented a spoof game show called 'Asylum!'.

Anyone could play provided they had no links to Britain. International terrorists were especially welcome. All you had to do to win was find your way here and remember the magic word 'asylum'.

Prizes included a council house, lavish benefits and lashings of legal aid.

It was supposed to be a joke but, as always, was based on fact. I can remember writing at the time that none of the hijackers would be deported and they'd all end up living here permanently, courtesy of the mug British taxpayer.

That's exactly what happened. The Afghans took their place among a motley crew of foreign undesirables granted refuge in Britain.

Top of the list was Abu Qatada, described as Osama bin Laden's European ambassador.

He's been shacked up in west London since 1993, when he arrived from his native Jordan on a false passport. Since then he's cost us £50,000 a year in benefit payments and more than £1.5 million in lawyers' fees.

After 9/11, the government woke up to the enemy within. Tony Blair announced that 'the game has changed'. No longer would we play host to Islamist headbangers, dedicated to our destruction.

Britain's reputation as a soft touch was over. The preachers of hate were to be rounded up and kicked out, we were promised.

Blair knew perfectly well that was never going to happen, thanks to Labour's embrace of the European yuman rites act, which he once called his proudest achievement in politics.

And, despite a raft of grandstanding 'anti-terror' measures,

Qatada is still here, along with a roll call of psychopaths from across the globe.

In 2009, after a drawn-out legal battle, the Law Lords ruled finally that Qatada could be returned to Jordan, where he has been convicted *in absentia* of terrorism offences. But that's not going to happen any time soon, either. The appeals process isn't exhausted by any means and will drag on for years, fuelled by a bottomless well of legal aid.

To add insult to injury, a panel of European judges awarded Qatada £2,500 in damages for the brief period he spent in Belmarsh prison after 9/11.

Another ten foreign terror suspects held at the same time also received payouts ranging from £1,500 to £3,400 each. They include a variety of North Africans with links to al-Qaeda and other terror groups. Most, like Qatada, entered on false passports. They should have been deported instantly.

Even after they were jailed as a threat to national security, they were all free to leave the country voluntarily at any time. They chose to remain in prison and fight expulsion through the courts. Eventually, they were released under 'control orders'.

And until Britain repeals the pernicious yuman rites act, here they'll stay, indefinitely.

The 'rights' of foreign terrorists will continue to trump the rights of law-abiding British citizens, who will be forced to carry on picking up the bill for their expensive lawyers and welfare benefits.

We're not even allowed, 'for legal reasons', to know the names of eight of the men we have been ordered to pay compensation. So who are we supposed to make out the cheque to, then?

Why the hell did the government expend so much time and political capital on securing the release of the so-called 'British residents' from Guantánamo Bay?

As I pointed out the previous August, when this preposterous Free The Gitmo Gang campaign began, they're not British citizens. They're not even British residents, just people who lived here for a while. When they had their collars felt, they were 'resident' somewhere else.

The three who were heading 'home' were actually resident in Afghanistan, Pakistan and Africa when they were arrested on terrorism charges.

If they were so relieved about finding sanctuary in Britain after claiming their lives were in danger, why didn't they stay here?

One of them converted to Islam and moved to Pakistan after 9/11. Another said he left Birmingham to look for work in Afghanistan. As you do. What sort of lunatic thinks he stands more of a chance of finding a job in Taliban country than Tamworth, unless he's a beheading specialist or skilled at pushing brick walls on adulterous women?

The soppy Liberal MP Sarah Teather worked herself up into a lather of self-righteous indignation over the detention of her 'constituent', Jamil el-Banna, who was linked to Osama bin Laden's European 'ambassador', on the grounds that he lived for a brief period in Brent. El-Banna is a Jordanian who was picked up in the Gambia.

Given the choice between the CIA and some dopey bird from what used to be the SDP, I'm with the boys from Langley, Virginia, every time.

Teather rejoiced on his release: 'His family are very excited and we all have our fingers crossed that he will be home to spend Eid with his family.'

These men are about as British as I am French on the strength of spending a long weekend in St Tropez. It is beyond me what any of this has got to do with either the LibDem MP for a scruffy part of north London or the British Foreign Office.

Well, I can see what's in it for soppy Sarah. She needs the Muslim vote to hold on to her seat and there are no limits to the depths to which opportunist politicians are prepared to abase themselves in cynical pursuit of popularity.

But the Foreign Office? Why did the government spend £100,000 chartering a private plane to fly the three Gitmo 'residents' back to Britain?

Here, the dead of 7/7 have been swept under the carpet while the caring, sharing, multi-culti 'liberals' concentrate on beating up

Plod over the shooting of an immigrant who was in the wrong place at the wrong time.

Then there was Binyam Mohammed, an Ethiopian citizen who was granted leave to live in Britain. He worked for a while as a janitor and in 2001 went to Pakistan 'to resolve some personal issues'. (At least he didn't claim to be on a computer course or attending a wedding.)

After that, he decided he'd rather live in Afghanistan. Shortly after 9/11, he was arrested at Karachi Airport carrying a false passport, trying to board a plane for London. He ended up at Guantánamo Bay.

Britain moved heaven and earth to bring him 'home'. Yet he hadn't lived here for eight years and left of his own free will. By no stretch of the imagination is he a British 'resident', let alone a British citizen.

We've got enough problems without working ourselves into a lather over the fate of an Ethiopian who was resident in Afghanistan when he was arrested in Pakistan.

In the case of Binyam Mohammed, what we were looking at is extraordinary rendition in reverse.

Instead of flying terror suspects abroad to be tortured, we're flying them here to be pampered. He touched down in a private Gulfstream jet, accompanied by the kind of entourage you normally associate with Madonna.

Why the hell should we care what happens to any of them?

Now we're going to have to house them, feed them, ply them with benefits and spend a small fortune on round-the-clock surveillance. It's not as if the anti-terror boys haven't got anything better to do.

Taken to its logical conclusion, the definition of British 'resident' would also apply to Osama bin Laden. After all, he lived in London for a few years before moving to Afghanistan. Maybe we should offer to bring him 'home' too.

And if bin Laden was discovered living above a kebab shop in Finsbury Park he'd be given indefinite leave to stay, showered with benefits and afforded access to the best yuman rites lawyers tax-payers' money could buy.

If we can't even deport Abu Qatada, because he wouldn't face a fair trial, what chance would we stand with bin Laden?

Welcome to London, twinned with the Hotel California. You can check in any time you like – but you can never leave.

*

One of the terrorists in the 1980 Iranian Embassy siege in London, who held hostage twenty-six people and murdered two of them, was released from prison in 2009 and was allowed to remain in Britain, living on benefits of £1,000 a month.

*

The 2007 case of Samina Malik, the so-called 'lyrical terrorist', turned into a *cause célèbre*. According to some sections of the media, this woman was a modern-day Joan of Arc.

Malik was the first woman convicted at the Old Bailey of terrorism-related offences but escaped with a paltry nine-month suspended sentence. Is it any wonder Osama bin Laden thinks we don't have the stomach for the fight?

Most comment centred upon a book of her poetry in which she fantasises about beheadings. It was claimed she's a victim of thought crime, persecuted for what she thinks, not what she has done, or was intending to do.

Cue Dr Abdul Bari, the Spike Milligan-lookalike 'secretary-general' of the Muslim Council of Britain, who protested she has been criminalised merely for harbouring 'silly thoughts' and warned ominously of the serious consequences for the government's plans to win 'hearts and minds' and persuade young Muslims to reject the overtures of terrorists.

Malik found enthusiastic supporters in the press and the BBC. A gormless bird in *The Times* argued that her conviction was an 'affront to society'.

Another *Times* columnist, the admirable Matthew Parris, equated her to the students who demonstrated in 1968 against the

Vietnam War and suggested that she has been singled out for victimisation because of her faith and skin colour.

If writing leaden poems was all the Old Bill had on her I'd have been inclined to agree. But there was more, much more.

The BBC sent a reporter to the street where she lives in Southall to solicit local opinion. Inconveniently, and instructively, they found not all her neighbours shared the bien pensant view of a misguided innocent falling foul of a heavy-handed police state.

Malik was described on the BBC as a shop assistant from west London. Which is true, up to a point. But that's a bit like describing the failed 21 July suicide bombers as 'commuters'.

What they didn't mention was that she worked at Heathrow Airport, in WH Smith.

Anyone who has flown out of Heathrow, or any other British airport, recently will have been seriously inconvenienced by draconian security measures imposed after an Islamist plot to blow up transatlantic airliners was thwarted last year.

Millions of travellers face interminable queues and body searches. Woe betide anyone who cracks a joke going through the screening process. Prominent posters warn that any passenger talking about carrying a bomb, knife or any other weapon – even in jest – will be arrested and prosecuted to the fullest extent of the law.

On the back of a till roll, Malik had written that 'the desire within me increases every day to go for martyrdom'.

Would you take the risk?

Imagine if the police had ignored it, or dismissed this as the ramblings of a 'silly girl'. And then a couple of days later she'd made fantasy a reality, walked into the crowded terminal with a couple of pounds of Semtex and a box of two-inch nails in her handbag, lit the blue touchpaper and blown herself and God knows how many holidaymakers and airport workers to kingdom come.

Still think this was about free speech? Well, it wasn't just poetry. She was also found to be in possession of seditious material – including *The Al-Qaeda Manual*, *The Terrorist's Handbook*, *The Mujahideen Poisons Handbook*, a manual for a Dragunov sniper rifle, a firearms and RPG handbook, and a guide entitled *How to Win Hand-to-Hand Fighting*.

You can't pick up any of those choice publications alongside your *Daily Mail* on the racks of WH Smith, Heathrow.

Yet still her apologists bleated that she was a hapless victim of a racist witch-hunt. Matthew Parris says we all 'think and say silly things when we are young'.

True. But there's a world of difference between trust-fund LSE students wearing tie-dyed Che Guevara T-shirts and shouting 'Ho, Ho, Ho Chi Min' in Grosvenor Square forty years ago, before heading off back to the nearest boozer, and the clear and present danger we're facing today.

Plus, she's not a teenager, she's twenty-three-years old. I don't know what you were up to at twenty-three, but I was married with a two-year-old daughter and on to my third mortgage.

Malik says she only adopted the name the 'lyrical terrorist' and wrote the poems about beheading to attract men.

The kind of men who would be turned on by a woman who fantasises about beheading and lines her bookshelves with al-Qaeda literature are precisely those most likely to turn themselves into a human Hiroshima at Terminal 4.

Even if she was simply a silly slip of a girl on the pull, she only has herself to blame. After the terror attacks on our own soil, not to mention 9/11 or Madrid, we have to take all threats seriously.

There are said to be thousands of people living among us who want to kill us and destroy our way of life.

If Malik isn't one of them, then she at least gives the impression of being more than willing to help them out when they're busy.

Our fellow citizens are being wiped out on the streets of London by fanatics who buy in to precisely this kind of dangerous fanaticism.

There's nothing sophisticated about the useful idiots who rallied to support her. Save your sympathy for the victims of terrorism and their relatives. Stupidity and ignorance are no defence, even if you believe her. Which we do at our peril.

Joan of Arc, she ain't.

You'll Find It Under 'Jihad', Sir

Borrowed any good books from your local public library lately? I'm told *Women Who Deserve to Go to Hell* is especially popular in the London Borough of Tower Hamlets.

It may not have been shortlisted for the Whitbread Prize, but it apparently flies off the shelves in east London.

The crazy guys at Hibt ut-Tahrir are behind *Funds In The Khilafah State*, which contains a handy guide for Muslims on shedding the blood and seizing the property of apostates.

That, too, found its way into the public libraries of Tower Hamlets, where you can also lay your hands on books by Abdullah al-Faisal and Abu Hamza, aka Captain Hook.

Al-Faisal specialises in preaching death to Jews, Hindus and all Westerners and encourages young Muslim boys to learn how to make bombs, fire guns, fly aeroplanes and use missiles to murder 'unbelievers'.

In his seminal *Natural Instincts*, he writes: 'The kafirs [unbelievers] are the henchmen of the Shaitaan [the devil]. The only language these kafirs respect is jihad [holy war].'

Captain Hook, an al-Qaeda recruiting sergeant, is doing a seven-year stretch in Belmarsh after being found guilty of eleven counts of incitement to murder and racial hatred.

Hitherto, his literary achievements have gone largely unheralded, unless you include a number of pamphlets he has published for the benefit of wannabe suicide bombers.

Not everyone's choice of bedtime reading, granted. But Tower Hamlets library committee deemed both authors worthy of sufficient merit to be put on public display.

Call me old-fashioned, but not so long ago the only mention of Captain Hook you'd find in the library was in a dog-eared copy of *Peter Pan*, in the children's section.

I'd love to have been in the meeting at which the librarians decided to stock these books.

> Right, we've got to get that new Ian McEwan and the Sebastian Faulks. Oh, and the Monica Ali, she's very popular with our borrowers in the Brick Lane branch. The *Guardian* gave her four stars on Saturday.
>
> How about Captain Hook? No, not the J. M. Barrie version, that mullah from Finsbury Park. What's it called? *The Martyrs' Guide to Throat-Slitting*, I think it is. It was Pick of the Week in the *Independent on Sunday*.
>
> We had a couple of young chaps in yesterday asking for it. You know, those quiet lads with the beards and the rucksacks who spent all afternoon online, downloading bomb-making instructions. I remember because the copier packed up and they said they'd be back today.

*

It's not just Tower Hamlets, either. A report from the think-tank the Centre for Social Cohesion claims that some libraries are becoming 'saturated with extreme Islamist books'.

Many councils, including Birmingham, Leicester, Ealing and Blackburn, are happy to spend taxpayers' money on this seditious poison.

The report says: 'Many of these books glorify acts of terrorism, incite violence against anyone who rejects jihadist ideologues and endorse violence and discrimination against women.'

I wonder what the committed feminists on these councils' equality committees make of *Women Who Deserve to Go to Hell*.

Other titles include forty books by Hassan Banna, of the violent Muslim Brotherhood, and Sayyid Qutb, who is said to have been a major influence on Osama bin Laden.

Steve Rigby, of Blackburn Council, said: 'Librarians do not act as censors where titles are freely available.'

Would the same attitude apply to a book which, for instance, called for holy war against Muslims, or described members of any other ethnic or religious minority as 'filthy kafirs' who should be killed?

The ubiquitous Mr Bean lookalike Inayat Bunglawala, of the Muslim Council, said it was right that public money should be spent on these books.

> These are authors who are widely read in the Muslim world and it is not surprising that they are stocked in areas where there happens to be the highest concentration of Muslims.
>
> It does not necessarily mean you agree with them. It is part of a free society.

Pity that tolerance doesn't extend to Salman Rushdie's *The Satanic Verses*, or Danish cartoons of the Prophet Mohammed.

Remember those 'Free Speech: Go To Hell' posters waved by Muslim beheading enthusiasts on the streets of London?

At a time when the government is supposed to be 'reaching out' to young Muslims to prevent them becoming radicalised, local councils are spending taxpayers' money putting into public libraries books by convicted terrorists which advocate death, destruction and holy war and preach violence against women and 'kafirs'.

If you're late bringing them back, do they chop your hands off?

Ostrich Farms for Illegals

After abandoning all border controls for ten years, Labour decided to spend £36 million bribing illegal immigrants to go home.

Which is how British taxpayers ended up subsidising an ostrich farm in Iran.

Failed asylum seekers were given grants of £4,000 each to help them set up businesses in their country of origin.

As well as the aforementioned Iranian ostrich farm, we are also bankrolling a beauty salon in Zimbabwe, a car dealership in Kenya, an Islamic dress shop in Sudan, a ferry in the Democratic Republic of Congo, a hotel in Nepal, a shoe factory in China, a market stall in Jamaica and an internet café in Equador.

Oh, I nearly forgot the fish farm in Angola and the Albanian vineyard.

A Sunday newspaper reporter turned up at the Home Office-funded International Organisation of Migration posing as a bogus refugee from India.

He said had been living here illegally for eleven years and had most recently been making a living selling drugs. He told his case officer that he wanted to return to India to open a travel agency to help more illegal immigrants come to Britain.

Despite his admission of criminality and the dubious nature of his alleged enterprise – which would actually make illegal immigration worse – the official drew him up a business plan and promised him a grant of £4,000, enough for an airline ticket, rent, a car, office equipment and three months' money for two members of staff.

More than 25,000 people have taken advantage of this ludicrous scheme. Why wouldn't they, especially when there's nothing to stop them returning to Britain when the money runs out?

With warped logic, the Home Office tried to justify this lunacy by claiming it works out cheaper than forced deportation, which costs £11,000 a head.

Where do they get that figure from? How much can a pair of handcuffs and a one-way goat class ticket cost?

One lucky recipient of the government's largesse is a thirty-one-year-old Kosovan, Valent Xhigolli, who was smuggled here from Albania. After being turned down for asylum, he shacked up in a bedsit in Wembley, living on benefits.

Mr Xhigolli is now the proud owner of a car workshop in Kosovo, courtesy of the mug British taxpayer. He arrived in the back of a lorry and left on a gravy train.

Then there's the thirty-year-old Armenian who came here illegally but after three years decided he was homesick. 'I realised that London was not for me. I felt like an alien,' he grumbled.

You and me both, pal. The difference is that if I applied for a government grant to go and open a beach bar in Barbados, I'd be told to take a running jump . . .

We bought him a farm.

There couldn't be a more graphic illustration of the extent to which those in charge of what passes for our immigration system have lost all touch with reality.

They don't have the faintest idea how many people are living here illegally, who or where they are. But they are willing to write out a blank cheque to encourage them to go home.

The scheme is being advertised in foreign language newspapers. There's nothing to prevent anyone turning up on a day trip to London, claiming to have been here for years and volunteering to go home in exchange for a grant to open a tattoo parlour in Tirana.

It defies belief, even in the Looking Glass world of New Labour.

How many British citizens could use a nice little start-up grant to escape their mundane jobs and set themselves up in business?

While NHS patients are being denied life-saving drugs on the grounds they're too expensive, the government is playing Father Christmas throwing money at hairdressing salons in Harare.

Bog Standard

While filming a documentary for Channel 4 in 2007, I found myself in Stamford Hill, north-east London, when I felt the call of nature. Fortunately, there was a spanking new superloo at the cross-roads.

The first cubicle I came to was a unisex/disabled toilet, but by the time I realised I'd already put my 20p in the slot. As I turned the handle to open the door, I felt some resistance. It must be stuck, I figured, and gave it a hefty tug.

'No, no. Go, go,' shouted a heavily accented voice within. Maybe I'd disturbed an unfortune wheelchair user in full flow. The door opened to reveal not one, but two men inside, both of whom appeared to be of Eastern European origin.

There were clothes draped over the sink, sleeping bags on the floor and cartons of food propped up against the toilet bowl. 'You go, you go,' they yelled at me.

It was only after beating a hasty retreat to another, vacant cubicle that it dawned on me. They were living there.

Then I vaguely remembered reading a story in the *Mail* a few weeks earlier about Polish builders using a superloo in Hackney as a makeshift dormitory.

Since Stamford Hill falls within the London Borough of Hackney, this must be the place.

Local residents reported seeing fights break out among Eastern European immigrants over the two disabled toilets in the block, which measure 6 foot 8 inches by 4 foot 10 inches, capable of accommodating at a pinch two people sleeping side by side.

Those who didn't cop a disabled cubicle had to settle for a standard toilet, which is only 3 foot 10 inches by 2 foot 6 inches and would involve sleeping sitting up.

A shopkeeper was quoted as saying: 'People are turning up with rucksacks and sleeping bags and they get nice accommodation fully maintained and with a bathroom for just 20p a night.

'You can see cardboard on the floor in the morning where they have been making their bed.

'Every morning the cleaners have to try and drag them out and this has been going on since the toilets were built three months ago.'

Hackney Council said: "We do see this as a problem. They are stopping legitimate users from getting into the toilets and the cleaners can't do their job.'

When I first came across this story, I assumed that maybe it was one of those urban myths which do the rounds – like that report about immigrants killing swans and carp from local lakes for their supper.

Or it was a one-off which had been picked up by an enterprising stringer and passed on to Fleet Street.

If I hadn't stumbled across it myself, I would have forgotten all about it. Little surprises me these days.

But I can't be the only person either caught short or 20p out of pocket. Maybe I should apply to the Town Hall for a refund.

The council may see it as a problem, but they clearly haven't bothered doing anything about it. And where are the police? Don't we still have laws on vagrancy and trespass? Is it now official policy to turn a blind eye to public conveniences being used as transit camps?

I mean, I've heard of cottaging but this is ridiculous. Something must have got lost in translation between Gdansk and Stamford Hill.

When these immigrants set out to build a new life in England, did they really think they'd end up living in a loo with a view?

Clearly, the authorities are in no hurry to move them on. At least if they are Polish the plumbing will be kept in good working order at a very reasonable price. Perhaps that's the deal – they can live in Trap Three provided they agree to fix dripping taps and unblock the U-bends.

But at what stage do squatters rights kick in? How long before they apply for permanent tenure, like that bunch of layabouts who occupied an empty £10 million mansion in Hampstead?

Presumably, we can then start charging them council tax. Government inspectors can visit to check whether or not they have made any improvements, such as building a conservatory or putting in a Jacuzzi.

If this catches on, we'll soon have all our public toilets festooned with thatched roofs, stone cladding, double glazing and satellite dishes. The BBC will dispatch that Laurence bloke with the flamboyant cuffs to do a makeover show, live from the disabled khazi on the A10.

It's easy to laugh about it – otherwise you'd slash your wrists – but at every level, whichever way you look at it, this is total madness, last days of Pompeii stuff.

If ever anything illustrated graphically the complete absence of 'joined-up thinking' this is it.

When Labour recklessly tore up our border controls, did anyone think we'd end up with immigrants living not just ten to a room, but two to a loo?

Meanwhile ministers cackle on about 'cultural capital', 'cohesion' and 'diversity packs' and order councils to put up taxes to find £50 million for English lessons for migrants – so at least they'll be able to understand 'Gentlemen, Lift The Seat' and 'Now Please Wash Your Hands' before they settle down in their sleeping bags for the night.

I guess this is what Labour means by 'bog standard'.

Intermission

The Environment Agency announced in April 2007 that fishing is horribly white, male and middle-aged. It decided to spend £100,000 a year to attract more women and ethnic minorities to the riverbank.

To demonstrate the government's commitment to diversity, a pilot scheme was launched in Swansea, which involved taking Muslim women and children to a lake and teaching them to fish for trout.

It was headed by Nica Prichard, the president of the International Ladies' Fly Fishing Association. She said, 'A couple of hours out in the countryside and you come back a new woman. If you could just see their faces when we're teaching them, you'd know we're really on to something.'

They're Muslims, pet. They're not handicapped.

What struck me about the accompanying picture of these women was that they were forced to wear goggles over their head-scarves on the insistence of elf'n'safety officials.

*

Omed Aziz, a blind Iraqi immigrant, was convicted of dangerous driving in the West Midlands.

Aziz was behind the wheel and being given instructions by his front seat passenger. He was stopped when police saw the car swerving all over the road.

PC Stuart Edge told Warley magistrates: 'He removed his dark glasses and I could clearly see he was blind because he had no eyes.'

Aziz was given a three-month suspended prison sentence, had his licence endorsed, was disqualified from driving for three years and ordered to take an extended driving test.

Run that past me again. How do you endorse the licence of someone who doesn't have one? And why only disqualify him from driving for three years?

He's not only blind, he hasn't got any eyes. How is he supposed to take an extended driving test when his ban expires?

Were they expecting optical surgery to make such leaps and bounds in the intervening thirty-six months that he will qualify for eye-transplant surgery on the NHS and be back behind the wheel in no time?

Meanwhile, Aziz will continue living here on benefits. Guess who's really being taken for a ride.

*

In Stockport, Greater Manchester, a witches' coven was banned from booking a church hall for a Hallowe'en party.

Sandra Davis, aka Amethyst Selmeselene, the high priestess of the Crystal Cauldron group, claimed they were victims of religious persecution.

Mrs Davis, who gave up her job with a fork-lift truck company to become a full-time witch, could not hide her disappointment. 'It makes you think that there is still a little bit of the attitude from the past of Catholics wanting to burn witches,' she complained.

She said they had chosen the hall for its excellent facilities, including disabled access. I'd assumed they'd be arriving on broomsticks, not in wheelchairs.

*

Watching Spurs implode at Stoke on TV one Sunday, my eye was drawn to an advertising hoarding behind the corner flag.

It read: 'Chlamydia Test'.

Call me old-fashioned, but I can remember when football ground advertising consisted of nothing more controversial than Brylcreem.

*

The Animal Health agency, a government-funded body, suffered a serious attack of mad cow disease.

Officials decided that 1,700 government vets working to prevent the spread of bovine tuberculosis were under so much stress they needed help relaxing and learning to work as a team.

So they were sent on away days, where they were taught to play the bongos.

One vet said: 'Farmers are under stress, cattle are being slaughtered, sick badgers are suffering enormously and disease is spreading to domestic animals. And what are we doing? Banging drums.'

Still, it should come in handy if they ever find themselves working in a remote area with no mobile phone service. They can always try communicating by jungle drum.

It shouldn't happen to a vet.

*

A pregnant woman was thrown out of a pub for ordering a second glass of lager because the bar staff said she was harming her unborn baby.

*

A mechanic who cut his finger repairing a police car was awarded £400,000 damages by Scotland Yard.

*

A man in a wheelchair sued MI5 after being turned down for a job as a secret agent.

*

A vicar in Sussex took down a statue of Christ on the cross because he thought it was 'too scary' and could frighten children.

The Rev. Ewen Souter said it could 'put people off'. Oh, ye of little faith.

At this rate, churches will soon stop teaching about how Jesus turned water into wine in case it encourages binge-drinking.

And there'll be no lesson on the Last Supper, or the loaves and fishes, without a statutory reminder to eat your five portions of fruit and veg every day.

Heaven help us.

*

Rent-a-quote Scottish Nationalist MSP Michael Matheson wants the hokey-cokey classified as a 'hate crime'.

He says the popular party song and dance has anti-papist roots and is therefore sectarian.

Matheson is demanding that anyone performing it is arrested. All this idiocy will achieve is that, at the next Old Firm game, thousands of Rangers fans will be putting their right foot in, their right foot out, in, out, in, out and shaking it all about.

*

A lorry driver from Hartlepool appeared in court charged with arson for holding a bonfire – on Bonfire Night.

Brett Duxfield, thirty-nine, was thrown into the cells for ten hours and had his fingerprints and DNA taken when the fireworks party on the village green at Elwick was raided by fourteen police officers.

Even though the bonfire has been lit every year since 1994, some killjoy on the parish council invoked a 130-year-old by-law against rowdy behaviour and called in the Plod.

Instead of telling the complainant to get lost, the Old Bill steamed in mob-handed. Where's Guy Fawkes when you need him?

*

A coach driver was fined £70 after stopping for one minute in Oxford High Street to help a disabled passenger get on board.

He was taking a group of people from Bath to Oxford for a Christmas shopping trip and was driving a bus with a wheelchair lift, specially designed to comply with the Disability Discrimination Act.

The driver was helping a severely disabled man and his carer use the lift when a warden approached and issued him with a fixed penalty notice for contravening 'no loading' restrictions.

He had pulled up at the side of the road to save the female carer having to push the wheelchair half a mile uphill to the coach station. This cut no ice with the warden, despite Oxford Council boasting that it is opposed to any form of discrimination. Rules is rules.

The incident occurred during Disability Awareness Week.

*

Mounted police had to be called in to break up crowd trouble at the opening of a new Primark shop, in London's Oxford Street.

Apparently, a rumour had swept town that everything was on sale for just £1. The Primark stampede was right up there with the Great Ikea Riot of 2005, when someone was stabbed in a dispute over a cut-price sofa at the opening of a new store on the North Circular Road.

Shopping and stabbing – two of our great national pastimes.

*

A Pakistani woman applied for asylum in Britain after claiming she was 'too tall' to be deported.

Zaynab Bibi is 7 foot 2 inches tall and alleged she would be persecuted over her height if she was forced to return home.

She lived on benefits in a council flat in Stockport, for which she paid no rent or council tax.

Through an interpreter she explained that she wanted to stay in Britain to receive free treatment for diabetes because private health care in Pakistan is too expensive.

So that's all right, then.

*

Lambeth Council spent £90,000 on foot massages for young tear-aways.

Reflexologists were sent into schools to 'calm aggressive feelings, improve listening skills, concentration and focus'.

Coming soon: manicures for muggers, botox for burglars and pedicures for paedophiles.

*

Wigan Council has appointed something called a Reassurance Officer. Like Harry Enfield's Scousers, Kate Watts's job is tell people to 'calm down'.

She said: 'I have lived in Wigan all my life and know what a great place it is. Fear of crime in the borough far outstrips people's actual

experience of crime and it's my job to put those few bad things into perspective.

'We're going to be tough on fear of crime and tough on the causes
of fear of crime.'

Kate, who used to work in the libraries department, added: 'It's a
really exciting job and I'm thrilled to have got it.'

It's certainly reassuring to know that there's so little wrong with
Wigan that the council has nothing better to do with its money than hire
a woman to emulate The Card, Arnold Bennett's fictional character
whose role in life was the great cause of cheering people up.

Perhaps they could kit her out in a Home Guard uniform and she
could frolic around town shouting 'Don't panic!'

*

Cheltenham Council came up with a plan to paint coloured rings
round dog messes on the pavement.

Wardens have been ordered to draw a red circle round a newly
laid mess. If it's still there a week later, a second, yellow, ring is
added.

By the end of the third week, a further white circle is sprayed
on the outside.

Council officials say this will act as a deterrent and encourage
dog owners to scoop the poop and take it home with them.
There's nothing more unpleasant than stepping in a pile of dog
dump. But this deranged plan borders on mental illness.

What did you do at work today, Daddy?

I painted a little red circle around some doggy droppings, son.

As one Cheltenham resident said: 'These people need their
heads examined.'

Instead of a paint gun, it would be a darn sight easier – and
more hygienic – to issue the wardens with a power washer.

No one is condoning inconsiderate dog owners. But it's the
council's job to keep the streets clean, not turn them into an al
fresco, multi-coloured excrement exhibition.

Who's running Cheltenham Council – Gilbert and George?

I've heard of crop circles, but this is ridiculous.

*

Bread is killing seven thousand people a year, according to one alarmist health scare.

No, it's not. But that's how many lives could be saved if supermarket loaves contained less salt, say 'experts'.

Nine slices a day will put you over the recommended daily intake of salt, they insist. Who do you know who eats nine slices of bread a day?

You'd have to have sandwiches for breakfast, lunch, afternoon tea and dinner to get anywhere near that.

And you'd still have to find room for an extra slice of toast before you go to bed.

Still, that won't stop the hysteria. Stand by for random bread tests outside Tesco and an expensive advertising campaign aimed at convincing us that Bread Kills!

*

Brighton Council advertised for a Researcher/Interpreter (The Rules of Attraction).

'Brighton & Hove Museum is planning a major project exploring human courtship and animal courtship.

'Our city has long played a special role in courtship – from George IV's pleasure palace to the dirty weekend, from rutting to reproduction.'

Experience of flashing/dogging/cottaging preferred but not essential. Full training provided.

The job was advertised on cards in phone boxes. Would suit heavy breather.

*

The elf'n'safety nazis insisted that Reading Football Club has signs facing the crowd, warning: 'PLEASE BE AWARE OF FLYING FOOTBALLS.'

*

The organisers of the World Pie-Eating Championship in Wigan have changed the rules to comply with healthy eating guidelines.

The winner will now be the contestant who eats one meat pie in the fastest time, not eats the most pies in the time allotted.

Surely the whole point of such a contest is that it doesn't conform to healthy eating guidelines?

The organisers have also introduced a vegetarian alternative.

Why?

If there were a World Vegetarian Pie-Eating Championship, they wouldn't allow a steak and kidney pie anywhere near the event.

The logical conclusion of this madness is that, next year, bulimics will be allowed to take part, too. The winner will be the person who brings it all back up quickest.

*

Lee Kildare, a dwarf who was recruited by a gang of burglars to squeeze into tight spaces, was apprehended by police who saw his head sticking out of a hole in the front door of a house he was robbing.

Just as well he was caught in the act. They'd have had a hell of a job arranging an identity parade.

It would seem the 'diversity' agenda is making it difficult for dwarfs to pursue their traditional avenues of employment, so it's hardly surprising Lee Kildare turned to crime.

Mercifully, they didn't send him to prison. A smart move, all things considered.

If he can break into houses through the cat flap, he wouldn't have much difficulty breaking out of jail.

*

In 2007, in what the *Observer* called a 'boundary-breaking' documentary, a team of disabled men got their kit off for the cameras.

The programme was promoted with the tagline: 'They might not have legs, but do they have the balls'.

It was supposed to be a serious film which challenges preconceptions about the sexuality of disabled people.

Of course it was.

Oh, by the way, they call themselves The Crippendales.

*

A town band was told that it must pay £150 for a licence if it wanted to play 'Jingle Bells' this Christmas. The band, in Callington, Cornwall, raises money every year for a number of charities.

But council officials were unmoved and said because 'Jingle Bells' has no religious content it is not exempt from laws requiring an entertainment licence.

Rules is rules and failure to comply would leave the band liable to a fine of £6,000.

Merry Christmas.

*

The average zebra crossing costs £114,000.

*

The 'prestigious' Turner Prize was won by a man dressed as a bear.

*

A thief in Brixham stole a car without realising there was a 9-stone, 6-foot-high Great Dane fast asleep on the back seat.

He'd only got about 30 yards when he looked in the rear-view mirror and saw Scooby Doo's ugly brother staring at him.

Needless to say, said bold thief dumped the car and legged it.

This reminds me of the tale about the man who parked his Mondeo near Anfield football ground in Liverpool. He was approached by the ubiquitous gang of scallies, offering to mind his car for a fiver. 'No need, boys,' he said. 'My Rottweiler's in the back.'

'Your dog, mister,' came the reply, 'can he put out fires?'

*

A woman who described herself as a 'human pet' and her keeper were thrown off a bus in Yorkshire for being weird.

Tasha Maltby goes round the streets of Dewsbury on a dog lead.

My Geordie mate Black Mike would take one look at her in her absurd 'Goth' outfit and remark:

'Gi' us a stick and I'll kill it.'

When her owner – er, fiancé – Addams Family lookalike Dani Graves tried to take her on to a bus, the driver stopped them, saying: 'We don't let freaks and dogs like you on.'

The couple complained that it was a 'hate crime'.

Tasha says she always behaves like an animal and enjoys having her tummy tickled.

Let's hope she's house-trained. But just as it's their prerogative to play *One Man and His Dog*, so the driver should have the right to decide whom he wants, and doesn't want, on his bus.

What the hell were the bus company doing apologising? 'We take any allegation of discrimination seriously,' said a spokesman, who really should stop reading the Guardian in his tea break.

Where it really ceases to be funny is when we learn that the couple live in a council house, on benefits, spend all day in the pub and plan to start a family. Maybe that should be a litter.

*

Derby City Council refused to reinstate an ancient statue of a wild boar in a local park in case it offends Muslims.

And the Cooper Gallery in Barnsley withdrew a nineteenth-century painting of a monkey in a fez playing a violin because it is 'demeaning to animals and possibly offensive'.

The painting has been hanging in the gallery for more than a hundred years without any complaints.

*

The National Health Service helped a mentally ill woman get a job as a pole dancer.

Dr Rachel Perkins, of St George's Hospital in London, said it was part of a programme to help vulnerable people regain their confidence.

Some might argue that getting your kit off and gyrating in front of a team of braying, drunken City spivs is good for your self-esteem.

But since when did the NHS act as an employment agency for strippers?

Spearmint Rhino – you don't have to be mad to work here, but it helps.

*

According to a report in Her Majesty's *Daily Telegraph:* 'Police are seeking a one-armed, hunchbacked dwarf, who walks with a limp and talks with an Irish accent, in connection with a £10,000 jewellery raid'.

He was seen acting suspiciously outside a home in Wisbey, Bradford, the day before it was burgled.

If he turns out to be gay, too, it's trebles all round. Especially, as it's Bradford, there's a chance he might be half Asian.

Police shouldn't have too difficult a job tracking him down. There can't be that many one-armed, limping, hunchbacked dwarfs with Irish accents hawking ten grand's worth of tom round the pubs of Bradford.

If they do ever find him, they'll have a job getting an identity parade together.

They'll probably give him a grant.

*

A hungry Muslim who killed and ate a swan while fasting during Ramadan was given a two-month prison sentence by magistrates in Llandudno.

When arrested, police officers told Shamsu Miah that the swan was the property of the Queen.

He replied: 'I hate the Queen, I hate this country.'

Firemen in Burqas

Having emasculated and politicised the police, Labour then turned its attention to the fire brigade, which is subject to the same, sometimes worse, excesses of the diversity agenda.

The main business of the fire service these days seems to be social engineering. The government put pressure on all fire brigades to sign up to the 'Diversity Champions' programme being promoted by pressure group Stonewall, run by gay rights bigot Dame Ben Summerskill. Minister Sadiq Khan said he wanted to see 'real cultural change'.

But when it comes to tolerance there's no limit to the intolerance of the diversity nazis.

A group of Strathclyde firemen were suspended from duty and fined for refusing to hand out leaflets at a gay pride rally. The fact that they said it conflicted with their religious beliefs counted for nothing.

Ten men from the Cowcaddens fire station found themselves under investigation after they declined to man an information stall during the Pride Scotia parade in Glasgow. Some refused on grounds of conscience, while others said they were too embarrassed to attend the event in uniform.

The most senior of the dissenters was demoted and the others docked pay and forced to attend compulsory 'awareness' retraining.

It turns out that at a time when public services are short of money, Strathclyde employs not one, but three, full-time diversity officers.

A similar fate befell another fire crew, in Bristol, who disturbed four men having an al-fresco orgy in the bushes next to a public convenience – a practice popularly known as 'dogging'.

Two of the firefighters from Blue Watch were fined £1,000, a third was demoted and a fourth received a written warning. Their 'offence' was to shine a torch on the scene of the debauchery.

All were suspended for three months while an official inquiry took place. That's right – three months. What's to investigate? And how much did it all cost?

I've no idea what the firemen were doing there and you could argue that they should have turned a blind eye.

But what about the men in the bushes – one of whom made an official complaint?

Now if you found yourself in that situation – heaven forfend – once you were disturbed, my guess is you'd leg it with your trousers round your ankles, pulling them up hurriedly as you made good your escape.

They were lucky not to have had a fire hose trained upon them.

Instead they took the intervention of the firemen as a gross intrusion into their divine right to do whatever they like, with whomever they like, wherever the hell they like.

One of them rang the Terence Higgins Trust, who passed the complaint to the Avon Fire Service and set in train this grotesque carnival of madness.

I've always assumed the Terence Higgins Trust was a worthy charity involved in AIDS prevention. Surely having rough sex with three complete strangers you've met in the bushes next to a public toilet is not the wisest way to behave if you wish to avoid catching AIDS. Shouldn't the Trust have simply reminded this chap that he was breaking the law and told him not to be so bloody reckless in future?

Why didn't the fire brigade tell them to get stuffed otherwise they would be reported to the police for gross indecency?

Yet – surprise, surprise – none of the men in the bushes faced any charges. The shame, ignomy and punishment were heaped upon the heads of the firemen.

Avon Fire Service says the crew were disciplined for breaching 'internal policies'. Does the handbook have a section on the correct way to respond when confronted with a dogging situation?

What is the proper etiquette when accidentally stumbling across four half-dressed men in a park going at it like Labradors?

I thought the fire brigade was about putting out fires, cutting people from car crashes and rescuing cats from trees, not conducting witch-hunts.

*

It's not just diversity, either. Fire prevention is one of the few areas of this government's lunatic obsession with elf 'n' safety which it is difficult to mock.

Difficult, mind you, but not impossible.

I could point to the millions spent on producing leaflets in thirteen different languages, or the fact that there's special guidance for gypsies and travellers.

But that would be churlish. It would be a tragedy if a house caught fire because those people who speak only Somali, Hungarian or Tamil didn't realise that cigarettes should always be stubbed out in a proper ashtray, not thrown into a waste-paper basket.

Anything which minimises the chances of our brave firemen and women having to put their lives on the line to save others from the consequences of their own carelessness is surely worth it.

If that involves advising members of the travelling community not to roast hedgehogs over an open flame in their caravan, and to be careful when burning tyres next to a wooden cricket pavilion, then who am I to argue?

Prevention is always better than cure, which is why the government is encouraging us all to take up an offer of a free home fire safety consultation.

Sheila Bushell, from Willesden Green, north-west London, decided to avail herself of this service, for a couple of reasons. It not only confers peace of mind but can also stop your insurance company wriggling out of any claim in the unfortunate event of your home burning down.

She sent me the letter from the London Fire Brigade confirming her appointment. It also contained a warning:

> While our primary aim is to provide you with this valuable service, the Fire Brigade has a legal duty to provide a safe working environment to protect the health of its staff.

To assist us with this, we would therefore ask that if you do smoke, you would do everything possible to provide a smoke free environment when our staff visit you in your home by:

- Refraining from smoking both during the visit and for a period before our staff are due to arrive. We suggest a period of one hour.
- Ventilating your home before the visit to clear any smoke.

If a smoke-free environment cannot be provided, our staff will need to assess the situation before proceeding, which in some instances may result in the visit being postponed.

What, Sheila wondered, would happen if her house was actually on fire? Would the firemen refuse to put it out if they arrived to find her puffing on a Silk Cut to calm her nerves while her earthy possessions went up in flames?

As it happens, Sheila doesn't smoke. But she was struck by the absurdity of it all and the impertinence of being told what she could and couldn't do in her own home.

We're talking about an organisation which rushes into burning buildings for a living, yet refuses to enter any premises to conduct a routine inspection if there is evidence that someone had been smoking in there less than an hour previously.

Are they really suggesting that firemen are more at risk from inhaling the lingering fumes of a small cheroot than saving someone from the eighteenth floor of a towering inferno?

Rather than leave it there, I called Sheila to ask her what happened when the inspector turned up. 'It was absolutely hilarious,' she told me.

She was expecting a man in a van with a clipboard. Instead, a fire engine arrived and *three* firemen got out.

'I couldn't have wished for a better response if I'd dialled 999,' she said. The neighbours came into the street, wondering what was going on.

Bearing in mind the letter she had received, Sheila asked if they wanted to test for the presence of cigarette smoke before they crossed her threshold. Perhaps they had brought a canary in a cage for this very purpose.

The firemen simply blanked her. She told them she'd only expected one person. 'Are the other two of you here to hold the ladder?' she asked.

Oh no, madam, they said, they don't use ladders any more. Elf'n'safety, you understand.

Instead they produced something which resembled a broom handle with a sort of grabbing device on the end and began to prod her ceiling-mounted smoke detector.

When it wouldn't budge, Sheila offered them her kitchen steps. After conferring they agreed that would probably be OK.

Two of them secured the steps while the other climbed to dizzy height of the second rung. One of the officers then asked Sheila to stop talking because it could cause a distraction.

Sheila started laughing. At this, the intrepid climber gave up his ascent and came back down to earth. Better safe than sorry.

And that, bar the usual form-filling, was that. They got back in their fire engine and drove off.

Sheila told me: 'Please don't think I'm denigrating the firemen. I have nothing but admiration for them.

'But I despair at the ludicrous, absurd, petty regulations which cover the way they are supposed to do their job. You couldn't make it up.'

I couldn't have put it better myself, Sheila.

There's no smoke without fire, they used to say. But these days, it seems, where there's smoke, there's no firemen.

*

After I wrote about Sheila's experience of fire prevention, I was inundated with e-mails and letters from firemen drawing my attention to the damage the Guardianistas have done to their once-proud service.

One watch commander from the Home Counties – I shan't identify him lest he becomes the victim of the usual witch-hunt – told me that the ban on ladders and refusal to visit premises where someone has been smoking up to an hour previously isn't even the half of it.

For a start, they have to go round team-handed to ward off allegations of sexual harrassment from bored housewives.

If the householder is a member of an ethnic minority, they have to take a fireman from an ethnic background. It doesn't matter which, just so long as he's not white.

Theoretically, a Red Indian would do, even if the householder was an Eskimo.

Ladders are on the way out, too, not just for inspecting smoke alarms. There's a move to fit cherry pickers to fire engines and firemen are not allowed to work at height without a harness.

The commander said that they're banned from practising the 'fireman's lift', even with dummies, in case someone gets hurt. They're certainly not allowed to carry anyone down a ladder.

Nor can they use real smoke for training exercises – and some councils have even banned artificial smoke.

Every single piece of equipment is plastered with idiotic instructions on how to use it and comprehensive elf'n'safety warnings. Oh, and they can't rescue cats from trees, because they might fall out and hurt themselves.

It can only be a matter of time before they're banned altogether from putting out fires.

*

Meanwhile, the political indoctrination continues apace. Back in Scotland, where those firemen were suspended, fined and sent for re-education for refusing to attend a Gay Pride rally, officers are all being sent on a compulsory 'Getting Along With Islam' course.

That should come in handy next time they're called upon to inspect a gay Muslim's smoke alarm.

In fact, if they are called upon to inspect a gay Muslim's fire alarm, they may in future be able to send a Muslim officer. And a female Muslim officer at that.

(Come to think of it, though, that probably wouldn't ever happen, since the Koran considers homosexuality a mortal sin. And I wonder what would happen if a devout Muslim firemen refused to attend a Gay Pride rally.)

Anyway, in 2009, at a press conference in Lincoln, the fire brigade unveiled a new uniform, including full-length skirts, hijab headscarfs and long-sleeved shirts for Muslim women recruits.

Mike Thomas, Chief Fire Officer for Lincolnshire, said the uniforms would help dispel the 'traditional image of the hunky, British, white, male, firefighter'.

There are no better positive role models than women and ethnic recruits in these uniforms, and hopefully they will encourage people to join.

Jagtar Singh, spokesman for the Asian Fire Service Association, said: 'We are pleased to note that the fire service is now taking seriously the issues of culture and religious belief when purchasing corporate and protective clothing for firefighters.'

Maybe that's why they won't climb ladders any more. You try getting up a ladder wearing a burqa.

*

And just when I thought firemen in burqas was as about as ridiculous as it gets, news reached me of the formation of, wait for it, the National Disabled Fire Association.

I wonder where they stand on ladders, so to speak.

*

Perhaps the most ludicrous example of the obsession with diversity came from the Isles of Scilly, where the fire service was accused of ignoring the government's quota requirements because it doesn't have any black recruits. A spokesman for the local council said the fire service did have one woman member of staff, but admitted there was no one from an ethnic minority background. He added: 'The council has no problem with ethnic inclusion, but we have no ethnics to include.'

The G&T Community

Labour's obsession with diversity has led to Britain being broken down into more racial and ethnic sub-categories than apartheid South Africa. In creating ever more dependent client groups, the government even designated so-called 'travellers' as a vulnerable minority, to be showered with benefits and special treatment.

Since they managed to get themselves classified as an homogenous, oppressed ethnic group, they have been entitled to all the rights, privileges and lavish welfare benefits that entails.

Once again, the police have embraced the new policy with excessive zeal. Let me introduce you to PC Mick Leighfield, Wiltshire Police's official Race and Community Relations Officer in the Salisbury area.

Mick, who made his name in the arena of gay men's health, turned his attention to the burning issue of the 'G&T community' and road safety.

At first glance, I assumed this was something to do with random breath-testing of people driving their Jaguar XJ6s home from the local golf club after a couple of large ones.

The 'G&T community' conjures up visions of a bunch of Leslie Phillips types in cravats and blazers, ogling barmaids.

Ding, dong.

But, no, it stand for the 'gypsy & traveller' community, a group with whom Mick was anxious to break down barriers.

There have long been concerns about members of the G&T community driving around in untaxed vehicles, without licences, road tax or insurance.

Mick e-mailed his colleagues in the Wiltshire Constabulary, with this warning: 'I know all the stereotypes that some of you may have of this community and I don't want to hear those obviously.'

Perish the thought.

The problem, Mick explained at a meeting of the Salisbury Diversity Forum was that: 'Many of the G&T community are unable to read or write. This has the effect that they are not able to read things like the Highway Code, insurance forms, driving licence applications etc. 'This is one reason as to why some of them have no documents or have never past [sic] their driving test.'

Mick's solution was that, rather than nicking them, the police should explore ways of helping them to pass their driving test and become 'road legal'.

And when they've done that, perhaps they could offer free eye tests to members of the Gypsy & Tarmacking community to find out how many of them are colour blind.

That must be why so many of them don't know the difference between regular derv and agricultural red diesel.

Maybe Mick could also offer crash courses in map reading, so that members of the G&T community don't find themselves accidentally parking their caravans illegally on other people's land.

Elsewhere, Warwickshire Police held a picnic and a day of festivities for the 'travelling community' at their Leek Wootton headquarters.

The manicured lawns of the country house HQ played host to a traditional Roma band, story-telling and even a 'graffiti project'. I hope they remembered to lock up their lawn mowers.

The beanfeast was designed to improve relations with the gypsies after armed response units were called to a recent horse fair in Kenilworth following reports that revellers were firing guns and shoplifting.

When was the last time the police threw a party for long-suffering, law-abiding local taxpayers?

That's the real problem. While I'm sure that most travellers of whatever denomination lead blameless lives, it is beyond doubt that others are a downright nuisance. Yet official Britain constantly makes excuses for those who flout the law and indulge in anti-social behaviour.

It's no wonder people get incensed. There's a world of

difference between treating everyone fairly and singling out certain groups for special treatment.

When I suggested in jest that they start offering free eye tests to members of the Gypsy & Tarmacking Community, I was unaware that the NHS was soon to unveil a plan to give priority to gypsies in hospitals and GP surgeries.

Now I can understand that this policy may have arisen from the most noble of intentions. If someone with a sick child is passing through town they shouldn't be refused treatment simply because they don't have a fixed address.

But this has nothing to do with the milk of human kindness and owes everything to the venomous bile of the 'diversity' industry, which takes sadistic pleasure in persecuting the taxpaying majority.

Under the NHS edict, gypsies are allocated a full twenty minutes with a doctor and allowed to bring their extended family into the waiting room. The average length of a normal appointment, always assuming you can get one, is between five and ten minutes.

A Department of Health statement said it was 'fast-tracking' what it calls 'members of the mobile community' because they have difficulty accessing services.

The '*mobile community*'? That's a new one on me. Is it because they all have top-of-the-range mobile phones?

Apparently: 'If members of the mobile community are not seen quickly, the opportunity could be lost as they move on or are moved on.'

Run that by me again. If the opportunity is lost, they can't have been that sick in the first place.

Groups covered by the preferential NHS treament policy include Scottish gypsies, Welsh gypsies, circus performers, fairground folk, New Age travellers and bargees.

I'd love to have been a fly on the wall at that meeting. You can just imagine them all sitting round, sipping their Fair Trade coffee and nibbling their ethically sourced mung bean snacks, when someone pipes up: 'What are we going to do about the bargees?'

The actual numbers of proper raggle-taggle, Romany gypsies

in Britain is minute. Most of these 'travellers' are Irish tinkers, run out of Ireland; itinerant scrap-metal merchants; scruffy hippies left over from the 1983 Glastonbury Festival; or dubious waifs and strays from Eastern Europe doing a bit of freelance begging. Yet they are classified as an homogenous victim group and also seem to be exempt from the clutches of the Inland Revenue and, especially, the planning laws.

Hardly a week goes by without some poor sap having to demolish a house or barn conversion which has been built without permission two feet too close to the road or in an area of natural beauty.

Yet opportunist 'travellers' can Tarmac over the Green Belt during a Bank Holiday weekend and, in utter contravention of planning regulations, set up an illegal caravan park and stay there for life.

One of the most striking aspects of the 'mobile community' is that they tend not to go anywhere. Once they drop anchor, legally or otherwise, they tend to stay put.

South Cambridgeshire residents were furious to discover that their local council intended to spend £500,000 on a sound-proof wall to protect a gypsy camp alongside the A14 from being subjected to road noise and 'abuse' from passing motorists.

Families on the Blackwell site, at Milton, complained about the constant rumble of traffic and also claim their lives are made a misery by cars and lorries beeping horns, flashing their lights and shouting obscenities.

Given that traffic roars by at 70mph, I'd have thought it highly unlikely that anyone would be able to hear any drive-by shouting.

Councillor Nick Wright said Blackwell has become a 'very uncomfortable place to live' since the homes don't have double-glazing or sound-proofing. Give it time – the grant application is probably in the post. He added, 'They are entitled to their privacy.'

No doubt these residents live a law-abiding existence, pay their taxes on time and never ask for a penny in benefits. But down the road in Cottenham, an extended family of Irish tinkers moved on to private land at Smithy Fen five years ago and have up to now resisted all attempts to move them on.

Locals complained of increased noise, litter, crime and intimidation, to say nothing of loss of privacy. Cottenham has become a very uncomfortable place to live, too.

It's a pity South Cambridgeshire Council didn't spend £500,000 on a wall to stop this illegal camp being set up in the first place.

Over the border in Bedfordshire, even the police were told they couldn't object to the siting of a gypsy camp because it would be 'racist'.

There have even been instances of mobile benefit offices being set up at illegal camps to spare travellers the inconvenience of having to travel into town to sign on.

A whole taxpayer-funded industry is dedicated to pandering to the needs of travellers.

As Irish tinkers demonstrated in Basildon, Essex, against a long-overdue order to evict them from Europe's largest illegal settlement, it was revealed that £4.7 million of lottery money has been spent helping travellers to subvert the planning laws.

None of this would be necessary if Britain simply followed the example of Ireland and made the occupation of private land a criminal, not civil, offence. But that's not how it works when you are dedicated to celebrating diversity.

And after a decade of denial, the government was forced to admit the truth. Communities Secretary Shahid Malik conceded that planning laws are deliberately biased in favour of gypsies and travellers.

He confessed that travelling families are treated differently from 'the settled community' as a matter of official policy.

'Fairness is what the Department for Communities and Local Government and the Government are all about; but fairness does not mean treating people equally; it means addressing the different needs of different people.'

So there you have it. In New Labour's La-La Land, some are more equal than others and fairness does not mean treating people fairly.

Large G&T, anyone?

The government also spent £70,000 on a gypsy history month, inviting us to 'celebrate the richness that gypsy, Roma and travellers communities bring to our everyday lives'.

As part of the propaganda drive, the government put out a booklet which claims a number of well-known celebrities have gypsy origins: Michael Caine, for example.

Not a lot of people know that. Including Michael Caine.

My favourite was Elvis Presley, who is said to be descended from German gypsies.

Presley sounds more Irish to me. But it got me wondering what 'Heartbreak Hotel' would have sounded like had Elvis been alive today:

> 'Well since I came to England
> I've found a new place to dwell
> It's an illegal site in Cambridgeshire
> I get benefits as well . . .'

Wanted for Hate Crimes

Not content with introducing more than 3,500 new laws, Labour invented a whole exciting new category of offences called 'hate crimes'.

The Home Office definition of a 'hate crime' is: 'Any incident . . . which is perceived by the victim *or any other person* [my italics] as being motivated by prejudice or hate.'

While he wasn't actually prosecuted, unlike two South Coast pensioners who protested against a Gay Pride rally, Prince Charles found himself in big trouble for referring to his polo partner as 'Sooty' – even though the gentleman in question has no problem with his nickname.

The fact that no offence was either intended or taken would not have been enough to stop him being charged, provided someone – anyone – made a complaint. This puts the power of prosecution in the hands of any self-righteous, malevolent, mischief-maker, of which we have no shortage.

I couldn't help wondering how long it would be before the 'hate crimes' vigilantes widened their net still further.

For instance, one phone call to Kent Police could have closed down Margate's Winter Gardens. The attractions for the 2009 season at the seaside theatre featured not only 4 Poofs and a Piano, but also *Sooty in Space*.

In my capacity as a gay icon, I once worked with 4 Poofs and a Piano, Jonathan Ross's house band. I've still got the T-shirt to prove it.

They turned up on one of my old TV shows after they were refused permission to register the name 4 Poofs and a Piano as a trademark. The authorities said that someone could find the name offensive.

The 4 Poofs protested that, given they were the poofs in question, no one could possibly take offence. If that's what they chose to call themselves, what was the problem?

None of this cut any ice with the Trademark Taliban, who continued to insist that 'poofs' was intrinsically insulting and therefore could not receive official endorsement.

As for *Sooty in Space*, the possibilities for prosecution were twofold, both racist and homophobic. Not only is 'Sooty' considered to be an outrageous racial slur, but Sooty himself spends the entire show with someone's hand up his backside.

One phone call to the Old Bill from the Margate branch of Stonewall and it would be: 'Izzy-wizzy, let's get busy!'

I logged on to the Kent Police website and clicked 'diversity'. The only difficulty would be knowing which branch to complain to. You're spoiled for choice.

There's the Lesbian, Gay, Bisexual and Transgender Action Group, which gives lesbians, gays and bisexuals an 'influential voice that will be listened to' and guarantees 'a dynamic forum for positive action'.

This isn't to be confused with either the Gay and Transgender Action Group or the Kent Police Gay and Lesbian Support Group.

If they don't take your complaint seriously, you could always ring the Kent Homophobic and Transphobic Reporting Line on freefone 0800 328 9162.

Be assured: 'We know in Kent that homophobic crime is still going unreported. This needs to change!'

Then there's always the Hate Crime Action Group, the Minority Ethnic Action Group and the Fairness Action Group, all of which come under the umbrella of the Diversity and Fairness Strategy Board, part of the new Citizen Focus Performance Gold Group, chaired by a deputy chief constable.

They all have to justify their existence somehow. Which is why they are urging you to report any potential 'hate crime', however trivial. Between them, they should be able to cobble together some kind of charge that will stick and ensure that Sooty and the 4 Poofs are banged up in Maidstone nick for the next ten years.

I dread to think what all this is costing, both in terms of hard cash and the monumental waste of police time, sitting around in committee meetings, talking bollocks and ticking boxes. And this madness isn't just confined to Kent, it's replicated in every police force across the country, in triplicate. (I hesitate to say 'in spades'.)

Sooty may have got away with it for now, but Basil Brush wasn't so lucky. In 2008, he found himself being investigated by the Old Bill after being put in the frame by someone called Joseph Jones, who styles himself vice-chairman of the Southern England Romany Gipsy & Irish Traveller Network.

Jojo took extreme offence at the 'racist and offensive' nature of an episode broadcast on the children's digital channel CBBC.

In the programme, Basil's friend Mr Stephen falls under a gypsy's spell which makes him attractive to women – no mean feat, by all accounts, if the rumours about most of the other male presenters of children's TV programmes are anything to go by.

Basil's neighbour, Dame Rosie Fortune, tries to sell him pegs and lucky heather and offers to read his palm. Basil's having none of it.

He says: 'I went to a fortune-teller once and he said I was going on a long journey. He stole my wallet and I had to walk all the way home.'

Boom, and indeed, boom!

Jojo complained: 'This sort of thing happens quite regularly and we are fed up with making complaints about stereotypical comments made about us.

'When a comedian makes a joke on TV about pikeys or gippos, there's no comeback.'

These days I watch very little on TV, apart from sport and reruns of *New Tricks*, *The Sweeney*, *Minder* and *Hill Street Blues* but I can't recall hearing many 'gippo' jokes.

There's no show without Punch (which in some places there isn't, because councils have banned Punch and Judy for being too violent and no doubt in breach of numerous elf'n'safety directives).

Following Jojo's complaint, police officers were said to be studying the offending episode for evidence.

I still can't believe I've just written that sentence. Police officers in Northamptonshire were sitting around staring at a video of a glove puppet to see whether they can bring a charge of 'racism' against him.

I was looking forward to the press conference and 'Wanted' poster:

We are anxious to interview Mr Brush in relation to allegations made under the Race Relations Act 1976. He was last seen wearing a furry coat and sporting a bushy tail.

When soul legend Clarence Carter recorded 'Looking For A Fox', he couldn't have imagined that it would one day become the official theme tune of the Northamptonshire Constabulary.

Clearly they have no more sense of the ridiculous than the complainant. How did Jojo come to hear about this shocking smear against sensitive, law-abiding members of the diddicoy community?

It was first shown six years ago and has been repeated eight times since. It's also available on a DVD called *Basil Unleashed*. So why complain, if not to make mischief? And more to the point, why didn't the Old Bill simply tell Jojo to go away and stop wasting their time?

One of Jojo's complaints centred on the fact that gypsies no longer sell lucky heather and pegs for a living.

Actually, if Basil really wanted to be bang up to date, he'd have Dame Rosie Fortune moving her caravan illegally on to land which doesn't belong to her and living on benefits, while supplementing her income stealing lawnmowers, dealing in scrap metal and Tarmacking drives; running her brand new Toyota Land Cruiser on cut-price agricultural diesel; and taking six-month holidays in Goa with her latest boyfriend and eight children.

But if Basil Brush can fall foul of the 'hate crimes' brigade, where will it all end?

Will Northants social services take Andy Pandy into care because he's forced to live in a box with two other puppets?

Will Pugh, Pugh, Barney McGrew, Cuthbert, Dibble and Grub be prosecuted for operating an all-white recruitment policy at Trumpton Fire Station?

Remember this the next time some chief constable complains about 'lack of resources' and says he can't afford to put bobbies on the beat or investigate domestic burglaries.

What's that, Sooty?

Bye, bye, everybody. Bye, bye.

Good Evening,
I'm from Ethnics

At last I've cracked it. I'm now officially an ethnic minority. I suppose it was only a matter of time before they got round to Essex boys.

Up until fairly recently, those of us born in God's Own County have been denied the protection of the race relations industry.

We've been fair game for every smear and insult going. As I wrote in my book *You Couldn't Make It Up* fourteen years ago: 'I was born white, male and in Essex. In 20 years' time any baby answering that description will be found in the bullrushes.

'I'm assumed to be racist, sexist and philistine.' (I don't think they'd invented 'homophobia' or 'Islamophobia' back then.)

Along with Old Etonians, white men from Essex are about the only section of society it is acceptable – nay, even compulsory – to vilify.

Not any more, though. I hadn't realised we'd made protected species status until I read the story of the Irish Catholic who was forced to resign his editorship of his village magazine after being branded 'racist' by the Obergruppenführer of the Cornwall Panzer Division of the Diversity Nazis.

His crime? Telling Irish jokes. More of that later.

But buried away down the page was the revelation that this wasn't the first time he'd fallen foul of the equality gestapo.

Denis Lusby, a shopkeeper from St Breward, near Bodmin, had earlier been reprimanded for including a couple of feeble Essex girl jokes in his fifty-six-page monthly.

Ginny Harrison-White, the humourless madwoman who runs Cornwall's race police, complained that the jokes could cause offence to people from Essex who may have settled in the West Country.

Thus, natives of Essex have taken their place on the list of persecuted persons, presumably just after Eritreans and Eskimos (although I've got a vague notion that you can't call Eskimos 'Eskimos' any more, either).

Now it is undoubtedly true that some Essex jokes, especially Essex girl jokes, are indeed offensive, sexist and downright disgusting.

I should know – I wrote most of them, along with my old friend Mitch Symons. Between us, under the pseudonyms Ray Leigh and Brent Wood, we knocked out about 250 of them in three or four days in Mitch's office above a burger bar in Chiswick, including a learned introduction from Professor Theydon Bois, principal of the Romford Library of Video.

It was one of the best tickles of both our otherwise undistinguished literary careers.

If not money for old rope, then *The Official Essex Girl Joke Book* was certainly money for old jokes, some of which had been doing the rounds in different forms for donkey's years.

I seem to remember we sold well over 100,000 copies in about a fortnight before the Christmas of 1991. The bookshops of Essex did a roaring trade.

We didn't get a single complaint, although a few of the dopey birds at the publishers affected faux feminist outrage at the whole concept.

Now we have an entire industry devoted to taking offence on behalf of other people. So it makes sense that Essex boys and girls have been designated worthy of special protection.

Yet I'd never have discovered this had it not been for Cornwall's answer to Millie Tant hounding the unfortunate Mr Lusby.

She said the Irish jokes were deeply insulting to members of the 'travelling community' with whom she works.

In the unlikely event of any member of the 'travelling community' subscribing to Mr Lusby's magazine would they really have been incensed by a couple of lame gags – any more than people in Ilford were likely to take to the streets over the one about the difference between an Essex girl and a walrus? (Don't ask.)

Why does Cornwall even need a diversity and equality unit,

other than to put otherwise unemployable Guardianistas on the payroll?

Last time I looked, Cornwall wasn't exactly a crucible of multi-culturalism. I don't suppose Sloane Rangers surfing at Rock count as an oppressed minority, but you never know. Does Ginny also do piskies, as well as gypsies?

I wonder if she's ever seen *Hell's Kitchen* on TV. If so, she would almost certainly have been appalled at Marco Pierre White's deployment of the word 'pikey' – an alternative term used occasionally to describe members of the diddicoy community.

The problem ITV faced was that if they kicked Marco, the host, off the show, there wouldn't have been a show, so he got away with it.

Mere contestant Jim Davidson, on the other hand, could be relied upon to Act As Known. He was shown the door for uttering the word 'shirtlifter' which upset one sensitive homosexual, who apparently was once on *Big Brother*.

So they got a 'homophobia' row rather than a race row. Trebles all round.

That's what Jimbo was there for. It's why they would have paid him six figures towards his serial alimony commitments.

As it happens, that could have been me. They asked me to be on *Hell's Kitchen*, presumably so that I could be presented as the three-headed BNP/racist/sexist/Little Englander/homophobe car-icature of left-wing media-page fame.

As I was not born in Essex yesterday, it was an offer I felt able to graciously decline.

So please spare us the mock horror. Jimbo did precisely what the script required, just as the preposterous Jade Goody delivered on *Big Brother*.

Put a thick pig in lipstick in a goldfish bowl with a sophisticat-ed Bollywood actress and it's only a matter of time before she blurts out the P-word.

Some racial abuse is acceptable, however. Complaints about Trevor McDonald describing Bernard Manning as a 'fat white bastard' on a comedy show were rightly rejected, probably on grounds of factual accuracy.

But they should never even have been entertained in the first place. Anyone with nothing better to do than ring up and complain about a light-hearted, probably scripted, aside from the charming Trevor should be sectioned under the Mental Health Act.

Some people get away with the most appalling abuse. If you're left-wing enough, it is assumed that you can't possibly be racist.

But the former London Mayor Ken Livingstone could be accused of anti-Semitic hatred over remarks he made to a Jewish reporter, and telling a couple of developers to push off back to Iran, and walk away scot-free.

Livingstone's most disgusting barb was directed at Trevor Phillips, of the Commission for Racial Equality, whom he accused of pandering to the BNP.

To my mind that was as bad as, if not worse than, hurling the N-word at him.

The false accusation of 'racist' thrown about by Livingstone and other leftist thugs, some with their own newspaper columns, is spiteful and can be damaging.

When Boris Johnson challenged Red Ken (successfully), the London Labour Party, in league with the *Guardian*, coated him with hateful smears of 'racism'.

Yet loud-mouthed Muslim rabble-rousers are free to yell 'filthy kafir' and 'infidel' with impunity and Livingstone invited preachers of hate to County Hall as 'honoured guests'.

Even if sticks and stones break our bones, words can still be hurtful. We must sometimes mind our language – but that doesn't mean we need a vast state apparatus of pursed-lipped madwomen to police parish magazines which publish Irish jokes.

Still, no doubt now that I'm an ethnic minority, too, I'll be getting an easier ride in some quarters.

As the Bard of Upminster, Ian Dury, wrote:

> Good evening, I'm from Essex, in case you couldn't tell.
> My given name is Dicky. I come from Billericay.
> And I'm doing very well.

Maybe that should be: Good evening, I'm from Ethnics.

The Last Refuge

Dr Johnson's dictum 'Patriotism is the last refuge of a scoundrel' was never more apposite than when applied to New Labour.

Having spent years trashing any notion of patriotism, especially on the part of the English, the government shamelessly wrapped itself in the flag when it ran on to the rocks over mass immigration.

Instead of denigrating our culture and identity, we should celebrate it, ministers announced. They even dusted off plans to turn the August Bank Holiday weekend into a celebration of 'Britishness'. According to the *Guardian* it 'would allow people permission to celebrate everything they like about the country and help frame the progressive case for controlled immigration'.

In a speech to a left-wing think-tank, the then Home Office minister Liam Byrne said: 'We are not a nation of Alf Garnetts. And in our hearts we know Britain is richer and more interesting because of the contribution that migration brings.'

Labour's researchers have come up with twenty-seven (why not twent-five or thirty?) different ways in which we could celebrate our common cultural identity – including street parties, community work, festivals of food and drink down the local pub and a speech by the Queen.

Warming to his theme, Byrne said: 'What people wanted above all was a space – permission if you like – to celebrate what they like about living in this country.'

'I myself have become convinced that the August Bank Holiday weekend has the virtue of being in the summer and already being a Bank Holiday.'

He's sharp, this boy. It would never have occurred to most of us that August Bank Holiday is a Bank Holiday which falls in the summer.

Can you imagine what a New Labour celebration of

'Britishness' would amount to? I managed to obtain an early draft copy of the blueprint for 'Britain Day' – which is designed to evoke the spirit of a traditional village fête.

*

8am A Full English breakfast of muesli and Fair Trade papaya juice will be served in Mr Papandreaou's Manhattan Deli and Kebab House, next to the Hong Kong and Shanghai Bank in Mandela Crescent.

9am Demonstration of the ancient craft of Tarmacking will be staged by the Cottenham branch of the Irish Tinkers' Co-operative in the driveway of the Mayor's official residence. Lucky heather also available.

10am Bring and buy sale, on the corner of Electric Avenue and Brixton Hill, this year featuring a wide selection of organically grown hallucogenic products from Colombia and Afghanistan at popular prices. Guns will be worn.

11am Assemble at the War Memorial for a minute's silence in honour of all the innocent members of the Taliban and al-Qaeda murdered by British and American aggression. Please note that, on the advice of Inspector Blair, anyone reading out the names of the dead will be arrested.

12 noon Morris dancing. Unfortunately this event has been cancelled on the advice of Health and Safety. Officials were concerned that after a few pints of scrumpy, dancers could fall over and hurt themselves. Miss Flint reminds patrons of the beer tent that they are limited to one unit of alcohol, per person.

1pm Mr Oliver invites you to partake of a traditional ploughman's lunch of turkey twizzlers. Vegetarian option (deep-fried Mars Bars) available at no extra charge. During the luncheon interval, our writer-in-residence, Sir Martin, will read from his Pulitzer Prize-winning romantic short story, *Ode to Tony Blair*.

2pm The three-legged race, won last year by our Lord of the Manor, Lord McCartney and his Lady Wife, has been declared null and void following a stewards' inquiry by the Disability Rights Commission.

3pm Synchronised stabbing. Play-off final between the Streatham Soldjas and the Peckham Pickpocket Posse. Please attach all floral tributes and teddy bears to the nearest lamp post. Correct spelling not essential.

4pm Traditional British afternoon tea, to be served in Mr Starbuck's coffee house, offering a tasty assortment of muffin tops. Warning: may contain nuts.

5pm Grand parade, along the M4 bus lane, led by Mr Prescott's two Jaguars and a traditional British bendy bus, with Mr Tatchell bringing up the rear on the Harvey Milk float. This will be followed by an exciting exhibition of twocking and joyriding by the Blackbird Leys Estate car theft workshop, under the supervision of Mr Clarkson.

6pm Mass picket and candlelit boycott of Mr Cohen's Gentlemen's Outfitters, in Gaza Street, organised by Mr Galloway, the Islington Branch of Hezbollah and the National Union of Journalists.

7pm Village Green Preservation Society Texas-style barbecue, offering several million sheep and cattle carcases left over from the foot and mouth scare, cooked over a bonfire of British fishing boats and memorial benches.

8pm Romanian country dancing, at the traffic lights next to the gas holder on the North Circular Road. Our most recent citizens give a delightful al-fresco performance of skipping in and out of the traffic, washing windscreens.

9pm On the main stage, next to the gallows, Mr Reid, accompanied by the Guantánamo Bay Choir, will perform his ever-popular 'I Belong To Glasgow – And Don't You Forget It, Pal'.

Hecklers will be removed and detained for ninety days without trial.

10pm   Ceremonial ejection of token racist from the Big Brother house, in Shilpa Shetty Boulevard (formerly Goody Street). The organisers regret that, due to lack of funding, the concert of Sir Edward Elgar's music has been cancelled.

11pm   Mr Brown finally arrives on stage, dressed as a pearly king, and proclaims his Britishness, before leading the Haringey African Drummers in a stirring rendition of 'Chim Chim Cherie' and 'Maybe It's Because I'm Not A Londoner'.

12 midnight   Fireworks spectacular. Cheering revellers join hands, set fire to the Union Jack and dance round burning effigies of Tony Blair and George W. Bush. In a stunning finale, four members of the Provisional Wing (Bradford Chapter) of Islamic Jihad celebrate diversity by spontaneously combusting on the last bus home.

*If wet, in Millennium Casino and 24-hour Lap Dancing Bar. Dress code: yellow ribbons.

An A to Z of Modern Britain

One of the bestselling books of 2007 (apart from *Littlejohn's Britain*) was *Life in the United Kingdom: A Journey into Citizenship*. Published by the Home Office, it is a guide for immigrants who wish to apply for British nationality. Figures released yesterday show that 690,000 people moved here last year. Now wonder it's selling so well.

With the Christmas gift market bearing down upon us, I thought it was time to check out the opposition.

The best place to start with official publications is usually at the back. So I headed straight for the glossary, which contains a selection of 'key words and key expressions' for would-be citizens. The italics are mine, the rest is all kosher.

A   is for abusive (*behaviour*), adultery and asylum seekers.

B   is for baron, birth parent, brutality and burglary.

C   is for cannabis, chieftain, civil disobedience, clamp (*as in wheel*), cocaine, colonise, corrupt and Crusades (*wars fought to spread Christianity*).

D   is for degrading (*treatment*), deport, detained by the police, disability and dump (*as in fly-tipping*).

E   is for Ecstasy (*makes users feel they have lots of energy*), ethnic minority, executed and exploitation.

F   is for famine, firearm and forced labour.

G   is for gambling, grant (*money paid by an authority*), and guerilla war.

H   is for hard drugs, heroin, Holy Land (*see also Crusade*) and humiliated.

I   is for immigration, inappropriate touching, indecent remarks, inhuman behaviour, insulting words and Islamic mortgage.

J   is for judge, judiciary and jury.

L is for labour (*as in Vote Labour*), legal aid and legitimate children (*whose parents are married to each other*).

M is for maternity leave, mental illness, migrate, missionary (*as in Godbotherer, not position*), and molestation (*sexual attack on someone, often a child*).

N is for nationalised (*as in Northern Rock*), naturalised citizen (*as in Captain Hook*), nobility and not-for-profit (*see Nationalised*).

O is for obstructive (*behaviour*), occupy a country (*as in Iraq or Northern Ireland*), offensive (*behaviour*) and off-licence.

P is for paternity leave, persecuted, plague, pluralistic society, pogroms and proportional representation.

R is for racial, racially-motivated crime, racism, rape, recycle rubbish and referendum (*except in the event of a new European treaty*).

S is for scratch card, serious misconduct, slavery (*see Forced Labour*), and strike, to go on.

T is for terrorism, therapist (*psychology*), torture, tow away a car (*see also Clamp*), and treaty (*see Referendum*).

V is for victim and vulnerable people.

W is for welfare benefits.

Y is for Yellow Pages.

*

There was no K, Q, X or Z, but as for the rest: you couldn't make it up.

You might have thought that a publication about Britain which bothered to explain that a baron was a minor member of the aristocracy and that a chieftain was a Scottish clan ruler might have found room for the Queen.

I've missed a few words out, but those I've quoted are what leapt from the page. It does help give you a fascinating insight into the official mentality and what they think constitutes a representative snapshot of modern Britain.

And what a depressing picture it paints. Abuse, adultery, brutality, burglary, cannabis, degrading treatment, exploitation, famine, forced labour, gambling, guerilla war, heroin, inappropriate touching, Islamic mortgages, mental illness, persecution, plague, pogroms, racism, rape, slavery, strikes, terrorism, wheel-clamping.

Who lives in a country like this? David, it's over to yoooooo.

When was the last time we had a pogrom in Britain? Or a plague, or a famine? Why mention the Crusades? As for forced labour, we're paying five million people to sit around on their backsides, claiming benefit. Forced idleness, more like.

There's an unhealthy obessession with child molesting, class, drugs, the victim culture, welfare entitlement and the politics of sex and race, which tells you just about everything you need to know about the new ruling class. The glossary could have been lifted straight from the *Guardian* style book.

After wading through this list, why would anyone want to move here in the first place?

It's more like a brochure for those planning to emigrate.

But before you sell up and head for the airport, I thought I'd have a go at a list of my own.

It may not persuade you to stay, but at least it might provide a more accurate appreciation of what it means to me to be British.

A is for Agincourt.

B is for Bond, James; Bader, Douglas; Botham, Ian; bloody-mindedness and Brylcreem.

C is for Churchill, *The Cruel Sea*, *Carry On*; Connolly, Billy; Calzage, Joe; cricket and chicken tikka massala.

D is for the *Daily Mail*, Dunkirk, Dambusters and *Dad's Army*.

E is for *Ever-Decreasing Circles*, Edinburgh Castle, Ealing comedies, Everton v Liverpool.

F is for 'Flower Of Scotland', the Full English, Frank Spencer, fish'n'chips, and the Finsbury Park Astoria (now the Abu Hamza memorial mosque).

G is for 'God, Harry and St George'; Greaves, Jimmy; and *Get Carter*.

H is for Harry Potter, Harry Ramsden and Hare Krishna; the Horseshoe Bar, Glasgow.

I is for *The Italian Job*, Indian restaurants, *Inspector Morse* and innocence, the presumption of.

J   is for Jagger, Mick; John Lewis; jam and the Jam.

K   is for the Kinks, kebabs and Kinnock falling into the sea at Brighton.

L   is for *The Long Good Friday*; last orders and Liar, Billy.

M   is for Mirren, Helen; Madness, *Minder*, Morecambe and Wise, 'Men Of Harlech' and 'Musn't grumble'.

N   is for Nesbitt, Rab C.; Newcastle Brown and 'Nice to see you, to see you, NICE!'

O   is for the Oval, *Open All Hours* and *Only Fools and Horses*.

P   is for the Proms, Last Night of; *Porridge*, Pete'n'Dud, pantomime, pork pies, Parky and 'Put that light out'.

Q   is for Queen Elizabeth II.

R   is for Remembrance Sunday, Mr Rumpole, reggae, Rangers v Celtic.

S   is for *The Sweeney*, Squeeze, St Paul's; Sutch, Screaming Lord; sausage rolls, 'Stupid boy'; 'Swing Low, Sweet Chariot' and 'Some people are on the pitch, they think it's all over.'

T   is for Trooping the Colour, 'Turned out nice again' and Two Jags getting caught with his trousers down.

U   is for 'Up Yours Delors'.

V   is for Van Morrison, *Viz*, village greens, V-E Day and Vomit Alley.

W   is for Westminster Abbey, Winchester Cathedral, Welwyn Garden City, Wem-ber-ley; Wifebeater and whisky chasers.

X   is for *The X Factor*; and xylophone, Sooty for the use of.

Y   is for 'You'll have had your tea' and 'You were only supposed to blow the bloody doors off'.

Z   is for *Zulu*.

God Save Us All

Lord Goldsmith, the former Attorney General put in charge of Gordon Brown's 'Makes You Proud To Be British' committee announced that he wanted the National Anthem rewritten.

Goldsmith said the traditional version is not 'inclusive' and particularly objects to verse six (did you know there was a verse six?) containing the line: 'Rebellious Scots to crush'. Presumably he would like 'Flower Of Scotland' revised, too, since it refers to sending home the English army 'tae think again'.

Meanwhile, a Welsh Labour MP says the Union flag should be redesigned to include the Welsh Dragon. Why not go the whole hog and chuck in a Muslim Red Crescent and the eagle from the Polish flag?

Actually, when it comes to 'God Save The Queen', the Sex Pistols got it right thirty years ago in their apocalyptic hit single of the same name: 'There is no future . . . in England's dreaming.'

Still, I thought I'd give Goldsmith a hand in bringing the National Anthem up to date and making it more inclusive. Please stand.

God save poor Gordon Brown
Caught with his trousers down
God help him now.
Send him your sympathy
Brought low by infamy
Donors and lost CDs
God save our Gord.

All faiths we do embrace
The whole of the human race
Can settle here.
Big on diversity
And inclusivity
Banned the Nativity
God help us all.

Our land ancestral
Now multicultural
All welcome here.
No need to integrate
We will just celebrate
You can live off the state
No questions asked.

If you're a terrorist
Or fundamentalist
We'll take you in.
Give you a council home
Money and mobile phone
Health care and a car to own
No need to queue.

Mullahs from Pakistan,
Jihadists, Taliban
Please come on down.
Feel free to murder us
Blow up a train or bus
We promise not to make a fuss
God help us all.

Forgive us our racist sins
And for filling our wheelie bins
With the wrong kind of waste.
Though it's a mystery
We hate our own history
Even banned Christmas trees
God help us all.

Land of the Rising Scum

The development of an underclass of people, cut off
from society's mainstream, living often in poverty, the
black economy, crime and family instability, is a moral
and economic evil – Tony Blair, 1996

The first time it properly dawned on me that the game was
up was in Blackpool, where I was covering the Labour Party conference.

As I made my way from the Clifton Hotel, opposite the main
pier, past Yates's Wine Lodge towards the Winter Gardens, at
approximately 9.30am, I had to step into the road to avoid a family
walking four-abreast on the pavement in the direction of the
seafront.

They were all breakfasting on fish and chips from polystyrene
containers, washed down with what I seem to remember was Irn-
Bru, in the case of the children, and Special Brew, for the parents.

The whole family – mum, dad, son, daughter – was dressed in
matching turquoise shell-suits and imitation designer-label trainers.
They all had earrings. Each wore a baseball cap.

The father's cap was distinguished by a plastic dog turd stuck
to the peak, beneath a logo which proclaimed:

SHITHEAD

I can remember thinking to myself, as I watched them window-
shopping at the pork butcher's: 'What chance have these kids got?'

The other thought which occurred to me was, given that the
children were aged, at a guess, eight and six, and this was late
September: why weren't they at school?

Now I know what some of you are thinking. Don't rush to
judgement, Rich. They could have been a blameless, sophisticated
couple, who had taken their children out of their fee-paying con-

vent school for the day to treat them to a field trip to study the varied marine life to be found in the Irish Sea off Blackpool, and had decided to dress down for the occasion.

Feeding them fish and chips for breakfast was simply a way of giving them an authentic working-class day-trip experience to broaden their horizons and drum home the message that not everyone starts the day with organic muesli from Waitrose.

The novelty baseball cap could have been an ironic, postmodern take on the nature of unbridled consumerism or a witty protest about societal stereotyping.

Then again, they could just have been scum.

You know what? I've just thought about it again. I'm going with scum. Sorry, but there's no other word for it.

For all I know, those children could have grown up to become brain surgeons. My guess, though, is that they're both living on benefits in some scruffy council garret, halfway up a burned-out tower block, surrounded by raggedy children who look pretty much like they used to on their jolly boys' outing to Blackpool. Only the fake designer labels have changed.

We've always had what sociologists prefer to call an underclass. But not on this scale and never so visible.

Labour was born out of a burning desire to improve the lot of the working class. In its early years it wasn't just about pay and working conditions, it was about access to decent housing and education. In 1997, Labour still aspired to that noble goal. Or at least said it did. This was Harriet Harman, then Social Services Secretary:

> We are determined to tackle the scandal of one in five households of people of working age having no work. Work is the best form of welfare for people of working age. We will be exploring the scope for the tax and benefit systems to act as an incentive to move off benefit and into work. We want to tear down the barriers that keep people out of jobs and trapped on benefit.

But under Blair and Brown social mobility has gone backwards. Labour's lumpen proletariat has been condemned to a desolate life on sink estates, slumped on sofas, gawping at daytime television, stuffing themselves with fast food, using welfare payments to subsidise their drink and drugs habits.

Five million people of working age have not done a day's work since Labour came to power. Official figures show that three million in England and Wales had no job between 1996 and 2001, while a further two million had never had a job. And these figures did not include the millions who were not working, but nor were they registered as unemployed.

Those stuck on incapacity benefit, lone parents and youngsters not in education or employment have been branded NEETS. But there's nothing neat about it.

While Britain was importing hard-working plumbers, bricklayers and manual workers from overseas, our government was spending billions paying British citizens to do absolutely nothing.

I remember a television report about foreign fruit pickers working in East Anglia for a minimum wage and sleeping three to a room in Peterborough. Outside the labour exchange, the film crew met a local youth who had just signed on for his unemployment benefits.

Clad in designer threads and supping a can of super-strength lager, he was asked why he wouldn't take a job as a fruit picker. If Poles and Slovakians were prepared to work for under £6 an hour, why wouldn't he?

Bold youth just laughed and said he wouldn't even get out of bed for that kind of money.

Which begged the question: if he wasn't willing to work, why was he allowed to claim out-of-work benefits?

One case in particular lifted the stone on Britain's burgeoning underclass. In 2008, a young girl called Shannon Matthews went missing from her home in Dewsbury for twenty-four days.

She was eventually found living under her 'uncle's' bed, where she had been kept doped up on painkillers and antidepressants. It turned out this was an attempt by her 'family' to cash in on the circus surrounding the highly publicised abduction of Maddie McCann in Portugal. They hoped to sell their story to the papers for £50,000 and pocket thousands more in 'reward' money donated by the public.

Further investigation discovered there were around three hundred members of Shannon's extended 'family' living nearby. Family is such a loose concept on these sink estates.

Her thirty-two-year old mother Karen was like a modern version of the Old Woman Who Lived in a Shoe. She had seven children by five fathers and referred to two of them as 'the twins' even though they had different dads. She had never had a job in her life and received £400 a week in benefits.

At the time of Shannon's disappearance, the mother was living with twenty-two-year old *Little Britain* lookalike Craig Meehan, who was described as Shannon's 'stepfather'.

In what sense would that be, then?

Meehan wasn't married to Karen Matthews. By no stretch of the imagination was he anyone's 'stepfather'. At best, he was a live-in lodger who slept with Shannon's mum.

But what should worry us all is that the way the Meehan/Matthews clan chose to conduct their lives is far from unusual any more.

Labour has spent a fortune shoring up single motherhood, rather than supporting traditional two-parent familes. Predictably, it is the children who have come off worse.

These 'new poor' aren't poor in any financial sense. They are showered with benefits, have mobile phones, iPods, computers, plasma TVs. They're well clothed, they don't go hungry and their bills are paid by the state.

But they suffer the most appalling moral poverty because they have been abandoned by the schools, abandoned, in most cases, by their fathers, and left to fend for themselves in a feral parallel universe.

They've had no family stability, just a procession of 'uncles' and 'stepfathers' who stay long enough to get their mothers pregnant again before shuffling off in search of greener pastures.

One of the curious features of such 'communities' is that, while they often display callous indifference towards their children, they are also capable of exhibiting the most ghastly sentimentality – especially when there's a suspected 'peed-io-file' on the manor, or something happens to one of their bay-bees. The lynch mob is never far from the surface when it comes to hunting down the local 'nonce'.

When Shannon went missing, I speculated that the mawkish mob marching in support of her 'family' would turn nasty if anyone close to her was arrested. They would probably torch the house.

After Karen and her gormless boyfriend had their collars felt, police boarded up the house and toured the estate handing out leaflets pleading with the local lowlife not to take the law into their own hands.

In the same week Shannon went missing, a three-year-old child and a three-month-old toddler were stabbed to death allegedly by their mother.

Outside the house, neighbours were interviewed by TV reporters. Of the two women I saw, one was wearing a grey hoodie and the other had her hair pulled back in a Croydon facelift, a stud through her nose and so many earrings in her left lobe it looked like a curtain rail. Both appeared old beyond their years, a legacy no doubt of cheap cigarettes and super-strength lager.

In Hackney, east London, a teenage girl was gang-raped for not showing sufficient 'respect' to a local yobbo. It barely makes the newspapers any more.

Little Britain's horribly accurate portrait of the underclass was accused by the Guardianistas of cruelty and making fun of a 'vulnerable' section of society. Maybe they've got a guilty conscience, but I shouldn't think so. The truth is, the leftist bien pensants have built a land fit for Vicky Pollards.

In the TV show, Vicky Pollard swapped her bay-bee for a Westlife CD. Karen Matthews dumped her first child because her then boyfriend wouldn't give her £5 for a packet of fags.

Britain seems to have cornered the market in welfare layabouts, drug addicts, feral gangs of obese children and hideous, drunken scrubbers, littering the gutters of even our more genteel suburbs.

The women are the worst of the lot, giving birth to a procession of bay-bees by different, transient fathers and expecting – nay, being encouraged by – the state to pay for their upbringing.

The government's preferred solution is to keep on throwing money at the problem, hiring legions of social workers and 'parenting skills advisers' to keep the scum in check, while importing hundreds of thousands of immigrants to do the jobs our indigenous idle are paid not to do.

Frankly, I see no immediate prospect of things getting better any time soon. By and large, the drugged-up welfare cheats on sink estates are left pretty much to their own devices because officials are frightened to confront them.

Local authorities in London have written off £50 million in council tax they couldn't be bothered to collect. Labour decided long ago that the white working classes were no longer worth the effort. I shouldn't imagine Shannon Matthews' slattern of a mother has ever paid a penny in council tax in her entire life.

We're on to second- and third-generation scum now, sustained by a patronising and 'non-judgemental' welfare juggernaut. Never forget that this hasn't happened by accident. This is the country the politicians wanted.

Labour promised a New Jerusalem. They've delivered Little Britain.

Vicky Pollard JP

Lucy Tate, a nineteen-year-old law student from Yorkshire, was appointed Britain's first teenage magistrate after the government lowered the age of qualification from twenty-seven to eighteen to make the courts more representative of the communities they serve.

She joined the bench in Pontefract, dealing with offences ranging from criminal damage to minor assaults.

Lucy seemed to be a bright, well-balanced young woman, with a normal range of interests for someone her age.

It was said that she lacked the necessary wisdom and experience of life. Frankly, I'd rather she sat on the bench than a fortysomething *Guardian* reader who thinks all criminals are victims and society is the real villain.

But if the idea is that everyone should be judged by their peers, I'm not sure Lucy fits the bill. For a start, she still lives at home with both her parents, she has a steady boyfriend and hopes to marry when she finishes her degree course.

That's not a profile which will apply to most of those coming up before her charged with everything from criminal damage to being drunk and disorderly.

If the government wants the bench to be truly representative, they'd have been better off appointing a single mum on benefits with a string of absentee boyfriends.

We now take you over to Darkly Noone Magistrates' Court where Vicky Pollard JP is presiding . . .

CLERK OF THE COURT: Are you Myleene Kayley Jackson, of Abu Hamza Towers, Darkly Noone?

MYLEENE: Why, who's askin'?

MS VICKY POLLARD JP: *'Course she is. Awight, Myles.*

MYLEENE: Awight, Vicks.

CLERK: Would you please let the defendant answer for herself, Your Worship?

VP: *Yeah, but, no, but everyone on the Gaza Estate knows Myles, innit?*

CLERK: If we might proceed. Miss Jackson, you are charged that on the seventh day of August you did steal six packs of Marlboro Lights, four bottles of Smirnoff Ice, three Twix bars and a jumbo packet of Prawn Bhuna flavour kettle chips, the property of Bunglawala's Multimart. How do you plead?

VP: *Not guilty.*

CLERK: Your Worship, the defendant must enter her own plea.

VP: *Yeah, but, no, but she weren't there, were you, Myles? And if Tracey says she was, then she's a lyin' cow.*

CLERK: Miss Pollard, this is most improper.

VP: *This is soooo unfair. I can't believe you said that, people's always picking on Myles.*

PROSECUTING SOLICITOR: Your Worship, if I may, PC Hollis, of Darkly Noone Police, will testify that he caught the defendant red-handed. The cigarettes were stuffed down her leggings and the rest of the contraband was concealed in her double buggy behind her children . . .

VP: *Beyonce and Jamal . . .*

PROSECUTING SOLICITOR: I am obliged to you, er, madam.

VP: *Her babbies gotta eat, ain't they?*

CLERK: Miss Pollard, I really must remind you . . .

VP: *Shut UP! Don't you be givin' me evils.*

CLERK: With respect, Your Worship, we must have a plea from the defendant.

VP: *Why you goin' on about this fing what you know nuffin' about?*

PROSECUTING SOLICITOR: Your Worship, if I may draw your attention to PC Hollis's statement . . .

VP: *That Hollis, he's a perv, I saw him gropin' Tracey round the back of the arcade, it were sooo disgustin', that's why he let her off robbin' a whole rack of scrunchies out of Accessorize . . .*

CLERK: If we could proceed . . .

VP: *Don't say nuffin', Myles. I told you she didn't do it.*

PROSECUTING SOLICITOR: How can you be so sure, Your Worship?

VP: *'Cos she got them from me in a swop for a Chris Langham video, what she nicked out of MVC.*

PROSECUTING SOLICITOR: And where did you get these goods from?

VP: *Oooh, my God, I sooo can't believe you're accusing me, I didn't do it and if Meredith says I did she's a liar and anyway she's three months gone by that boy with the gammy leg off the caravan site...*

PROSECUTING SOLICITOR: Miss Pollard, are you saying you stole the items in question?

VP: *Yeah, but, no, but, shut UP! I never done nuffin' and anyone who says I did is well gonna get beatens. Just because I ain't no stuck-up law student like that Lucy Tate, how many ASBOs has she got?*

CLERK: I think, Your Worship, this might be an appropriate juncture to adjourn for lunch.

VP: *I'll have a Smirnoff Ice, a Twix and a packet of Prawn Bhuna kettle chips from the Multimart. You can nick 'em when Bunglawala's out the back downloading porn off the internet. And him applying to be a magistrate, too . . .*

'If I Could Talk To The Taliban'

After a flying visit to Afghanistan and calling on all his experience of a five-minute photo-opportunity with the troops in Helmand Province, a mere sixty miles from the front line, the Prime Minister announced that he has a cunning plan for ending the war. As the headline put it: 'BROWN: TALK TO THE TALIBAN'.

Some of you may have realised already where I'm going with this. I wonder whether Gordon is aware that there are forty-seven different languages spoken in Afghanistan.

So, with apologies to the great Leslie Bricusse – laydeez and gennulmen, will you please welcome Gordon Brown as Dr Dolittle with his version of 'If I Could Talk To The Taliban'. Try to imagine Rex Harrison with chewed fingernails and a Scottish accent.

If I could talk to the Taliban, just imagine it,
Chatting with the chaps in Pakistan,
I could be rapping with al-Qaeda,
And all the foreign fighters,
In the Tora Bora, east Afghanistan.

If I could talk to the Taliban in Arabic,
Or the dialect of deepest Kazakhstan,
Try a phrase or two of Farsi,
A word of Gujarati,
I'm sure that I could make them understand.

We could converse in Ashkun or Tajiki,
Learn a little of the lingo of Pashto,
If people ask me: 'Can you speak Turkmenistan?'
I'd say: 'Of course I can, can't you?'

If I could meet Mullah Omar in Jalalabad,
Try a little Brown diplomacy
If I could reason with the Taliban,
Reach out to the Taliban,
Plead and get down on my knees to the Taliban,
And hope they don't behead me!

If I could speak man-to-man to Sheikh bin Laden,
In the distant mountains of the Hindu Kush.
Or maybe somewhere nearer,
A live debate on Al Jazeera,
I'd promise that I wouldn't tell George Bush.

If I spoke the native tongue of Pashtun tribesmen,
I could guarantee that I would end this war.
Give a massive grant to Helmand,
Well, it always works in Scotland,
I'd even let them have sharia law.

If I consulted with Algerians and Chechens,
In a safe house in east Uzbekistan.
'Where's Osama?' I could ask,
'Is he up the Khyber Pass?'
They'd say: 'No, infidel, he's in Londonistan.'

If I could parlay with jihadis in Pershawi,
And negotiate with the Yemenis,
If I could talk to the Taliban, give asylum to the Taliban,
Mobile phones, council homes, long-term loans
To the Taliban, then they would vote for me!

Afghan Millionaire

The Taliban may still be in business and the heroin trade is flourishing once again, but for those who believe that Afghanistan can be transformed into a fully functioning, pro-Western democracy there is evidence that the war has not been entirely in vain.

Who Wants To Be a Millionaire? has finally arrived on Afghan television. It is one of the last countries on earth to produce a local version of the phenomenally successful British quiz show.

More than 20,000 people applied for the chance to win a top prize of one million afghani (about 40p). Here's an exclusive preview of the pilot episode, presented by Chris Talibant.

*

Fastest finger first. Put the following invasions of Afghanistan in descending order by date: the first British invasion; the second British invasion; the Soviet invasion; and, finally, the American-led invasion.

Time's up. The correct answer is: America in 2001; Russia in 1979; Britain in 1878 and, before that, in 1839.

Who could forget the slaughter of 16,000 British men, women and children during the retreat to Gadamak in 1841 and the deaths of 15,000 Soviet troops in the 1980s? Apart from George W. Bush and Tony Blair, that is.

Anyway, fastest finger on the buzzer was Mustapha Karzi, in 4.2 seconds, which is quite remarkable given than he's got two hooks where his hands used to be. Let's play *Who Wants To Be a Millionaire?*

It says here, Mustapha, that your ambition is to hijack a plane, fly it to Britain and claim asylum.

That's right, Chris.

Good luck, mate. Let's see if we can help you win enough to buy your air ticket. Ready to play?

Yes, Chris.

This is for five hundred afghanis. What is the main crop of Afghanistan? Is it

 A) opium;

 B) opium;

 C) opium; or

 D) opium.

I'm not sure, Chris.

Take your time, Mustapha, remember you've got three lifelines. You can go 50/50, ask this lovely audience, or phone a friend.

I think I'll ask the audience, Chris.

OK audience, press your detonators – sorry, I mean keypads – now. Hmmm. One per cent say A) opium; two per cent say D) opium, and 97 per cent say 'Death to the Infidel running dogs of the Great Satan'. It's your call.

Well, Chris, 97 per cent is a large number. But I'm going to go with C) opium.

Final answer.

Final answer, Chris.

It's the right answer. Incidentally, what made you ignore the audience?

They'd have said 'Death to the Infidel running dogs of the Great Satan' whatever the question, Chris.

OK, let's play for one thousand afghanis. Where is the headquarters of the Taliban?

Is it:

 A) Kabul;

 B) Kandahar;

 C) Jalalabad; or

 D) Tipton.

You're smiling, Mustapha. You know this, don't you?

Yes, Chris. It's Tipton.

Certain?

Absolutely, Chris, I met them at a quiz night at a jihadist training camp in Pakistan. They said if anyone asked I was to say they were on a computer course or attending a wedding.

It's the right answer. OK, you're going for two thousand afghanis.

You've got two lifelines left. What is the correct way to kill an adulteress? Is it:

> A) push a wall on top of her;
>
> B) stone her to death;
>
> C) behead the filthy slut; or
>
> D) give her a thousand lashes.

(Audience: STONE HER! KILL HER! BEHEAD HER!)

Sorry, audience, you've had your turn. Mustapha, you can phone a friend or go 50/50.

They all look right to me, Chris. I suppose I'd better go 50/50.

Actually, mate, I wouldn't bother. They are all right. And you've just won two thousand afghani.

Allahu Akhbar!

But we don't want to give you that, Mustapha. The next question is for five thousand afghanis. You don't have to play it, but have a look anyway.

Where is Osama bin Laden hiding? Is it:

> A) Tora Bora;
>
> B) Waziristan;
>
> C) Helmand Province;
>
> D) A council house in Tottenham.

Could be any of them, Chris. Can I phone a friend?

Who would you like to call?

I'd like to call Mullah Omar, spiritual leader of the Taliban.

What, that madman in North Wales?

No, Chris, you're thinking of the Mad Mullah of the Traffic Taliban.

My mistake. We're calling now. Hello, Mullah Omah, this is Chris Talibant, from Who Wants To Be a Millionaire?

Hello.

I've got Mustapha Karzi here. He's on five thousand afghanis, he's stuck and he needs your help.

Mullah, Mustapha here. Where is Osama bin Laden hiding?

If you answer that, you treacherous running dog of the Great Satan, it really will be your final answer . . .

Up the Shatt al Arab

One of the most shameful episodes in Britain's proud naval history came in the last few weeks of Tony Blair's premiership when a party of sailors on routine patrol in the Persian Gulf were taken hostage by Iran. Instead of fighting back, they tamely surrendered. They were then paraded on television in a worldwide propaganda coup.

They looked like a Vauxhall Conference football team being led out at Wembley by Nora Batty before the final of the Leyland DAF trophy. Fourteen men kitted out in ill-fitting suits from the local branch of John Collier, John Collier, the window to watch, and a dumpy bird in a Les Dawson headscarf.

Blink and it could have been the Guildford branch of the Manchester United supporters' club arriving back at the airport, complaining about being roughed up by the Italian riot police.

The international image of Britain as Churchillian bulldog was replaced by this bunch of hapless stooges grinning and waving for the cameras like contestants cosying up to Leslie Crowther in the final frames of *The Price Is Right*.

If the British Commonwealth and Empire lasts for a thousand years, no one will ever claim this was their finest hour.

Look, I don't blame the unfortunate human ingredients in this pawn cocktail. They were only obeying orders – which, ludicrously, amount to 'surrender first and apologise later'. The rules of engagement these days have been rinsed in so much fabric softener that I'm astonished our troops are even allowed to carry weapons any more.

Given Gordon Brown's inglorious record of starving the military of the necessary readies, they were probably issued with broom handles and instructed to shout 'Bang, Two, Three' in the face of the enemy, rather like the Walmington-on-Sea Home Guard in 1940.

The hostages weren't to blame for this craven and humiliating episode in our history.

Call me old-fashioned, but that young mother should never have been in the front line. Their commanding officers should have been court-martialled and whoever happened to be Defence Secretary should have been forced to resign.

Blair went on television in full People's Princess mode and uttered pious platitudes about how he stood firm in the face of Iranian aggression, while secretly capitulating. He should have been charged with treason and shot.

Having served their propaganda purposes, the hostages were eventually released. But I despair at what their ordeal and the response to it tells us about the kind of country we have become.

After thirteen years of New Labour, Britain is now a neutered, international laughing stock. The United Nations and our EU 'partners' hold us in contempt.

The feminisation of our entire society has utterly destroyed whatever credibility and moral fibre we once had. I wanted to retch when I saw the father of one of the captured marines cuddling his wife and sobbing on live television in front of a tree festooned with yellow ribbons.

Of course he had every right to be upset, but he shouldn't have shared it with Sky News. His other son looked deeply embarrassed, as if a dog had just peed up against his leg. It was the most skin-crawling moment I have seen since The Mellorphant Man paraded his family in front of a five-bar gate.

And what about the outside broadcasts from assorted pubs around the country, as various friends and relatives showed their solidarity by drinking themselves senseless? All that was missing was Nero and his Stradivarius.

The broadcast media covered the whole affair as if it were an episode of *Big Brother*. Gormless women cackled away about the hostages in the same silly psychobabble with which they discuss 'relationship ishoos'.

One reporter actually moaned about having to give up his seat in business class to make room for the returning heroes. This was hardly the last plane out of Saigon.

The hostages were even given 'sweets and souvenirs' by their captors before being sent on their way. Imagine leaving Stalag 13 with a Lucky Bag.

God knows what the generation who went through World War II would make of it.

'We now take you live to Colditz where Captain Pat Reid and a group of captured RAF pilots are giving a press conference, thanking Herr Hitler for his hospitality and apologising for trespassing in German airspace.'

What made things even worse is that, having been returned home safely, the hostages were then allowed to profit from their ordeal.

Any doubt from which the sailors and marines may have benefited went out of the window the moment some of them sold their stories – although honourable mention must go to those who didn't.

The Ministry of Defence's complicity in this tawdry horror show was treasonable. But it was pretty much what we have come to expect from Labour's Brave New Britain.

Take Faye Turney, the only woman hostage. She was the People's Prisoner. From the off, the hostage saga was covered as if it were an episode of *I'm a British Sailor . . . Get Me Out of Here!*

I wondered at the time how long it would be before she popped up on *Celebrity Fat Club*. I bet they didn't let her get in the dinghy first. This is a woman who was capable of capsizing the *Ark Royal* if she shifted her weight to the wrong buttock

This was not so much *The Great Escape*, more *Carry On Up the Shatt al Arab*, with Turney played by Hattie Jacques.

Think of the fun Kenneth Williams and the crew could have had with that title. Starring Bernard Bresslaw as Ayatollah I'madinnerjacket and featuring lots of double entendres about leading seamen.

The part of the pathetic young sailor who said he sobbed for three days because the Iranians called him Mr Bean would be perfect for Charles Hawtrey.

The MoD's line is that it had to go along with the media circus because otherwise the captives would only have resigned and sold their stories.

Why didn't the MoD fly them to a remote base on Cyprus and debrief them for a few days before giving them a couple of weeks' compassionate leave and then quietly return them to their duties?

A discreet, dignified silence would have enhanced not only their reputations, but helped repair some of the damage to the good name of the Armed Forces as a whole.

The day Faye Turney sold her story to the *Sun* and *Tonight with Trevor McDonald*, for a reported £100,000, was the day the navy died of shame. Or, at least, would have been were there any shame left in the world. We have become the kind of nation where the highest form of duty is to emote on prime-time TV.

It is impossible to exaggerate the deep feeling of embarrassment and disgust felt by all decent members of the Armed Forces, past and present. You only had to check out the weblogs. The army and RAF can barely contain their contempt for the conduct of those who run the so-called Senior Service these days – not just for allowing fifteen sailors and marines to be caught up the Shatt al Arab without a paddle in the first place, but also for the way in which they have compounded that catastrophic blunder since their release.

We may like to think of the First Sea Lord as a Jack Hawkins figure standing ramrod straight on the bridge, but my guess is that he's just another New Labour apparatchik straight from the *Guardian* school of government, with a degree from the Alastair Campbell college of news management.

I kept harking back not just to the tens of thousands of dedicated, courageous career servicemen and women performing such sterling work around the globe, but also to the veterans of previous wars.

In my study, there's a photo of my dad, aged about nineteen, in his Royal Navy uniform. I never found out what he did in World War II until shortly before he died. Unlike Del Boy's Uncle Albert, most of my father's generation didn't talk about their wartime escapades.

Suffice to relate that his was a story of great courage, although not by any means exceptional. I never thought I'd say this, but as I sit and watch this demeaning spectacle unfold, as British sailors cash in on a couple of weeks of discomfort like kiss'n'tell call girls, I'm glad he's not around to see it.

Writing about the hostages returning from Iran clutching their goody bags, I wrote: 'If you come across a miniature bronze statue of I'madinnerjacket and a hand-tooled copy of the Koran as a job lot on eBay in a couple of years, you'll know one of the hostages has fallen on hard times.'

Within a couple of weeks, the *Mail on Sunday* reported that Lance Corporal Mark Banks, of the Royal Marines, was selling off the shiny suit he was given while in Iranian custody.

On eBay.

Makes you proud to be British.

Keep Calm and Carry On

Keep Calm and Carry On. That simple, stiff upper lip slogan, beneath a King George V crown on a red background, has become one of Britain's bestselling wall posters, adorning homes and offices all over the country. It was designed during the war by the Ministry of Information, but never made it into circulation.

It can be found on everything from tea towels and T-shirts to mugs and mouse mats. Thousands are being shifted every week. With Britain facing the worst economic crisis since World War II, we're still taking inspiration from the Blitz spirit.

Meanwhile, despite mounting outrage, the government refused stubbornly to make any contribution to the commemoration of the sixty-fifth anniversary of D-Day, which was the last chance for the survivors of the Normandy Landings, all now well into their eighties, to pay their respects to fallen comrades. Only when Gordon Brown realised that President Obama was going did he relent.

Which got me wondering what would have happened if this lot had been in charge back in 1944.

This is the BBC Home Service. Here is the news, and this is Alvar Lidell reading it. At 0630 GMT this morning, Allied forces began an invasion of occupied Europe. No British service personnel were involved.

While American, Canadian, Free French, Polish and Empire divisions stormed the beaches of Normandy, absorbing heavy casualties, the government defended its policy of non-engagement.

The Prime Minister told the House of Commons that on the advice of the Health and Safety Executive, ministers had decided that the inclement conditions in the English Channel, which caused the Meteorological Office to issue a Severe Weather Warning at 0900 hours yesterday, had made any waterborne crossing too dangerous.

Admiralty officials report that they are unable to meet the new legal requirement of one trained lifeguard to every two soldiers per landing craft, and are therefore unable to put to sea. There is also a shortage of qualified Royal Navy captains, owing to them all being away on diversity awareness courses.

In addition, the presence of barrage balloons and anti-aircraft artillery along the coast of northern France could leave the Air Ministry exposed to the threat of legal action from members of the RAF in the event of injury, stress, hurt feelings or death.

It would be inadvisable to proceed with any invasion until a full risk assessment had been carried out by the War Office, especially to ascertain whether the noise generated by machine gun fire, land mines, mortars and hand grenades falls outside 'safe' decibel limits and required the compulsory wearing of earmuffs.

There was also the danger of passive smoking to be taken into account, as well as the high levels of cholesterol and salt contained in fried breakfasts served to air crew before they embark on bombing missions. Saturated fats are a killer, especially in wartime.

Concern has been expressed, too, about the lack of hand rails, wheelchair ramps and disabled toilet facilities on Juno Beach, in contravention of the government's barrier-free access policy.

Furthermore, it would be inappropriate to proceed with battlefield operations until the completion of the official investigation into institutional racism in a number of British regiments, including the Welsh Guards and the Argyle and Sutherland Highlanders. An interim report from the Equalities Commission has described the Black Watch as 'hideously white'.

The Prime Minister said the desirability of liberating Europe had to be balanced against the very real problem of managing diversity on the home front.

Opposition to the war has been mounting since a dossier which claimed Germany could launch an attack on Britain in forty-five minutes was exposed as a work of fiction, drawn up for the previous Prime Minister by Mr Campbell, former head of the Ministry of Propaganda.

In recent weeks, there have been a number of violent anti-war demonstrations in towns and cities around Britain. In Walmington-on-Sea, a group of radical Nazis jeered a parade of Desert Rats returning from El

Alamein. They screamed 'murderers' and 'baby-killers' and waved banners reading: 'Blitzkrieg all those who insult Hitler'.

Police arrested a local butcher, Mr Jones, who reacted to the demonstrators by throwing a pork chop at them and telling them to go back to Berlin. Jones, a World War I veteran who serves as a corporal in the Home Guard, was found guilty of racially aggravated assault and a breach of rationing regulations. He is due to be hanged on Tuesday.

None of the demonstrators was arrested. It was later revealed that one of the Nazis works as a bomb-loader at the local RAF base. The rest live on National Assistance and were granted asylum in Britain after stowing away on boats involved in the evacuation of Dunkirk.

Most are believed by Military Intelligence to have links to Luftwaffe extremists involved in the carpet bombing of Coventry and the East End of London. Their stated aim is to establish a Gestapo state in Britain.

Although the Prime Minister condemned the demonstrators, he said it was important that we didn't overreact. They were a tiny minority who did not represent the vast majority of peace-loving Nazis.

Asked why our sworn enemies could not be rounded up and shot, or at the very least deported, he said it would be in breach of the Geneva Convention on Human Rights. Judges have ruled that internment of enemy combatants is illegal.

Recently a leading Nazi was awarded £60,000 compensation after being incarcerated in a prisoner-of-war camp on the Isle of Man, where he claims to have been tortured by being forced to listen to Vera Lynn records day and night. Adolf Stormtruper is described as a British resident, even though he was born in Munich and was captured fighting with the Panzer Division in North Africa.

The Prime Minister vehemently denied Opposition claims that this was all a smokescreen and the truth was that his own incompetence had bankrupted the country, crippled our armed forces and left Britain uniquely ill equipped to join the liberation.

Before retiring to his bunker, the Prime Minister insisted that this was a global invasion which had originated in America.

He had nothing to apologise for and was confident of victory. Tomorrow, just you wait and see. Thanks to his leadership, Britain was now leading the world in the manufacture of tin hats.

In other news, boffins at Bletchley Park have cracked the top-secret Enigma code, which directs German submarines towards Allied convoys. The breakthrough came to light after it was left in a railway carriage at Watford Junction.

This is Alvar Lidell. Keep Calm and Carry On.

Banki Hankipanki

At the height of the banking crisis, it emerged that British investors had lost billions in Icelandic banks. To be honest, all I knew about Iceland was that it had been bright enough to stay out of the European Union and had managed to hang on to its fishing fleet, which is what I'd always assumed it did for a living.

Until the world's banking system went belly-up, I had absolutely no idea that this tiny Nordic outpost was considered to be a global economic powerhouse.

Turns out Iceland's economic miracle was all smoke and mirrors and today it's bobbing around in the mid-Atlantic like a dead cod.

Which, in the normal course of events, would be a simple case of 'oh, dear, how sad, never mind'. That's if it were not for the fact that so many punters in Britain fell for the fairy tale.

Some 300,000 people here entrusted their savings to an internet bank based in Reykjavik, which was offering suspiciously higher-than-usual rates of return. I can understand how tempting the deal must have been, but as a general rule I beware Greeks bearing gifts. Or, in this case, Icelanders. If it looks too good to be true, then it probably is.

I'm also highly suspicious of any kind of financial transactions that involve the internet.

Three or four times a week I get invited by someone in Nigeria to allow him to deposit several million pounds in my bank account overnight. For my trouble, he promises there will be a nice little drink in it for me. It is an invitation I have no difficulty declining.

Same with internet banking. I'm sure it was all perfectly legitimate at the time, but there would be no more chance of me investing in an online Icelandic bank than responding to one of those e-mails offering me a bigger penis.

Presumably some people must be gullible enough to tender

their bank details to bogus Nigerians and hand over their credit card numbers to a post office box in Pensacola in the hope of another inch or three in the trouser department – otherwise they wouldn't bother sending them out.

The Banki Hankipanki may not have been in that league but I'd rather put my money where I can see it, or at least in a building I can see. That way, if everything does go the shape of the pear, you form a disorderly queue round the block, kick the door in and ransack what's left in the safe; or rip the paintings off the wall in lieu and hope to recoup your losses on *Antiques Roadshow*.

There are real people to punch in the event of them losing your life savings on derivatives in the Fiji futures exchange. How are you supposed to do any of that if your hard-earned has vanished down an ice-hole in Iceland?

But the real scandal here was that it wasn't just private investors who sank their savings into Iceland and will, fortunately for them, have to be bailed out by their fellow British taxpayers.

Town Halls across the country had been recklessly depositing our council taxes in Iceland, too. And we may never see a penny of it again. Even Scotland Yard had a few bob tucked away there.

None of this would have happened before local authorities started getting ideas above their station. I heard a council officer from Kent on the wireless described as the 'cabinet member' for finance.

I assume he's what we used to call the town clerk or hon. treasurer. These days, every tinpot council official likes to pretend he's an international statesman or big businessman – and pays himself accordingly – just as every jumped-up building society clerk thinks he's Gordon Gekko.

Which is, of course, how we got into this mess in the first place.

Not so long ago, councils would have had their account at the post office next door, not swirling around on the international money markets. Building society managers insisted on a sound record of saving and a 25 per cent deposit before they'd lend you a modest two-and-a-half times salary. They wouldn't have dreamed of doling out 115 per cent loans at a multiple of seven or eight times earnings.

Who could have ever imagined that British taxpayers would end up bailing out the losses of an Icelandic internet bank to the tune of billions of pounds?

Turns out Iceland wasn't so much the Switzerland of the North Atlantic as Fantasy Island.

At least, unlike us, they've got a fishing industry to fall back on.

Peckham Mutual Collapse

While financial institutions crashed and banks had to be bailed out by the government, back in the real economy the effects of the credit crunch were being felt way beyond Canary Wharf and Wall Street. Over in the Nag's Head, Peckham, the punters drowned their sorrows after a difficult week in the market . . .

Evenin', Del Boy. Usual?

Awight, Mike. Malibu and Red Bull, make it a small one.

Small one, Del? You sure?

Times is tough, Mike. Haven't you heard of the credit crunch?

Those wind-damaged wind turbines what you got off Monkey 'Arris not shifting?

Au contraire, Michael. Selling like hot croissants, what with the energy crisis. I've had young Rodney knocking 'em out door-to-door in Notting Hill all afternoon. They're à la mode with your Macaroons these days.

Macaroons, Del?

Keep up, Michael, my son. Don't you read the Speculator? *That's what they call Call Me Dave's little mob. Ever since he stuck a windmill on his chimley, they all want one.*

So what's the problem?

Liquidity, Mike. And speaking of liquidity – same again, please. Luvvly jubbly.

That'll be four pound fifty, plus the century you owe me for Racquel's birthday party booze-up the other night.

Put it on the slate, Michael.

Sorry, Del. No more tick. The brewery's most insistent. They're trying to knock back a hostile takeover from the Far East.

What, Romford?

Further than that, Del. Shanghai. That's why they need all the shekels they can get. Ergo, no slate.

Have a heart, Mike, Trotters Independent Traders is teetering on the brink. New York and Paris have gone. There's only Peckham left.

I thought you said that those windmills was going faster than a man with a gippy tummy in a curry house.

They are, Michael, only I ain't paid for them. And Monkey 'Arris wants his wedge by tonight.

Your troubles is over, Del. Here's Rodney, now. He must have the money he got off the Macaroons.

(Enter Rodney)

Awright, Rodney. Why the long face? Sorry, I forgot. You was born with it.

Leave it out, Del. I need a drink.

What's the matter, Rodders?

It's Cassandra, she's lost her job at the bank.

Bain-marie! She ain't been caught dipping her fingers in the till, has she?

Wash your mouth out with carbolic, Derek Trotter. You should be ashamed of yourself. Cassie ain't like that. She's another unwitting casualty of the global economic meltdown.

What's the global economic meltdown got to do with the Peckham Mutual?

It's gone belly-up, Del. Been taken over by HBOK.

Don't you mean HBOS?

Nah, Del. That's the Halifax and Bank of Scotland. Or, rather, it was, until this morning. Now it's Lloyds TSB.

So what's HBOK?

Hoxton, Brixton, Old Kent Road Savings Bank. Well, it was last time anyone looked. By now, it's probably part of the Timbuktu Investment Consortium.

But the Peckham Mutual has been around ever since Grandad was in short trousers. Mum had her overdraft there all her life, Gawd rest her soul. It even survived that armed robbery at the Elephant and Castle branch, back in 1966. Safe As Houses, that was its motto.

It was safe as houses, Del, until it got over-leveraged in the sub-prime market and packaged everything up in derivatives.

Come again.

Well, Del, it's like this. The Peckham Mutual ended up in this rather negative feedback position where the de-leveraging is feeding a recession which is increasing losses for banks and . . .

Steady on, Rodders. In English, parlez-vous. You sound like that Pesto bloke on Newsnight.

That's who I got it from, Del.

Couldn't they do anything?

The manager wrote to Gordon Brown for help – but that's about as much good as asking Uncle Albert to pilot you round the Cape of Good Hope. Anyway, the government's blown the lot on Northern Rock.

A race horse?

No, Del, though it might just as well have been. It's another bankrupt bank.

But the Peckham Mutual can't be broke. What about the money it's owed? I remember Cassie telling me that it provided all the mortgages when the council sold off the Nelson Mandela Estate to the tenants.

That's the problem. No one has paid them back. Derek, we haven't paid them back. Cassie says we owe thousands.

Temporary cashflow situation, Rodders, that's all.

It's not all, Del. Cassie's boss put all the debts together and sold them to some outfit called Lehman Brothers, only they turned out to be worthless, and now Lehmans has gone pear-shaped and taken the Peckham Mutual with it.

Well then, all our problems are over. If this Lehman wossname's gone under, we don't owe anyone anything any more.

It's not as simple as that, Del. The US government has assumed the loans.

No bother, Rodders. It's not like owing the Driscoll brothers. Anyway, now we've got that money for the wind-damaged windmills . . .

That's just it, Del, we haven't.

What do you mean, we haven't? You better not have spent it. Monkey 'Arris'll be in any minute.

I couldn't sell anything, Del.

Not one? Not in Notting Hill? But I thought windmills was de rigueur mortis up there.

They was, until Lehman Brothers went down the gurgler.

And what's that got to do with our windmills?

They've made five thousand people redundant. And most of them seem to live in Notting Hill. They've been sacking nannies, dog-walkers, anything to save money. So they're not buying wind-mills, neither. It's called trickle-down economics.

Sarko-zy, Rodney. Never mind, we've still got the flat. According to that sort on Location, Location, Location, it must be worth a packet. All we've got to do is sell it and we're out of the woods. This time next year, we'll be millionaires.

Correction, Derek. This time last year, we were millionaires – on paper, at least. There's been a housing crash and the flat's worth less than the mortgage.

Do you think Boycie would lend us a few quid?

No chance, Del. He's gone into receivership – what with the price of petrol and the so-called 'green' tax on 4x4s, no one's buying cars. Marlene's run off with her personal trainer. About the only person with a job round here now is Trigger.

We'll always need road-sweepers, Rodney.

Oh, he's not a road-sweeper any more, Del. He's a Climate Change Enforcement Officer, on twice the wages. Goes round nicking people for putting out rubbish in the wrong bins. Slapped a £20 fine on the van 'cos I didn't switch the engine off at the traffic lights. Here he is now.

(Enter Trigger)

Awight, Del. Wotcha, Dave.

So, Trig, young Rodney tells me you've got a new job.

That's right, Del, I'm in charge of recycling. It's my job to make sure every household has got a kitchen caddy.

A what?

It's like a slop bucket. You put all your food waste in it and the council collects it every other week. Helps save the polar bears.

Hang on, Rodney. Haven't we got a couple of hundred slop buckets left over from the war in the lock-up? Hurry up, bring the van round, before Monkey 'Arris gets here. Credit crunch? What credit crunch? This time next year, Rodders . . .

Mickey
the Mortgage Monster

Some of us saw the financial collapse coming. Back in November 2006, it was reported that banks such as Northern Rock were handing out loans of up to nine times annual earnings and 125 per cent of the property's value. It couldn't last. Here's what I wrote at the time:

My initial attempt to scale the housing ladder very nearly ended up with me flat on my backside before I'd even made the first rung.

Newly married, aged twenty-one, with a child on the way, we urgently needed somewhere to live. Having been brought up to believe that renting was throwing good money after bad, I set off in search of a mortgage.

First port of call was the local building society. After being ushered into the under-manager's office, I was shown the door, then the street, in double-quick time.

They didn't grant loans to anyone who wasn't a member and had no lending history. What I had was a borrowing history – from my mum, from the man who ran the shop where I worked as a paper boy, from whoever was in possession of the office fiver that week.

In any event, even if I had qualified, they would lend only 60 per cent of the asking price.

Next, I tried the bank which received my meagre wages every week and managed my overdraft and car loan.

Sorry, son, we're not in the mortgage business, Barclays told me.

Back in the seventies, the High Street banks were still locked in a Mr Mainwaring time warp and considered common home loans beneath their dignity.

Eventually, I discovered that the local council would grant

mortgages in exceptional circumstances to those willing to take on dilapidated properties.

So I trooped off to the Town Hall and emerged with a £4,000, twenty-five-year mortgage on a turn-of-the-century terrace house with no bathroom and an outside toilet.

I was earning £40 a week, which was equivalent to my monthly repayment.

Twice salary was all the council would lend – at 2 per cent over building society rates – so the car went, along with my wife's savings, and with a few bob from our parents we bridged the gap between the maximum amount I was allowed to borrow and the £4,500 purchase price.

(No, children, this wasn't *Life on Mars*, it was Life on Earth. Or at least Life in Britain, 1975.)

With the help of a modest improvement grant and a retired builder my dad knew, we did the place up and sold it on a couple of years later for a £3,000 profit, which gave us a leg up the legendary ladder.

Over time, the rules eased. The banks entered the mortgage market, joint salaries were taken into account and you were able to borrow up to three times annual earnings.

Even if you stretched yourself to the limit, inflation was guaranteed to ride to the rescue. As wages rose, the burden of debt receded. And, as an added bonus, the value of your house went up.

The Lawson boom of the mid-eighties brought with it Big Bang in the City and a general easing of the financial guy ropes. Welcome to Yuppie Hell. This time next year, Rodney.

Suddenly, the mortgage market was deregulated. Overnight, a whole raft of new lenders entered the market, johnny-come-lately operations with reassuringly traditional names.

There used to be a gelled spiv in a Gordon Gekko suit who propped up the bar in the Old Bell, in Fleet Street, and worked for an outfit with a seemingly respectable name.

He was known as Mickey the Mortgage Monster and he made his commission knocking out huge home loans to hard-up hacks.

Instead of begging the banks for a mortgage, they were now

begging you to take one out. A friend of mine secured – if that's the word – a £200,000 loan on a house in London's upscale Highgate. When I asked him how he'd managed it on a salary of £25,000 a year, he replied: 'I told lies.'

He simply typed a letter on a piece of his newspaper's headed notepaper, claiming he earned £75,000 a year. No one bothered to check.

He calculated he could meet the repayments by juggling all the credit cards being thrust in his direction. I can remember him brandishing his Bank of Kuwait gold card, which he ran up to the limit. When Iraq invaded Kuwait during the first Gulf War, we worked out that his house technically belonged to Saddam Hussein.

Today, he wouldn't have to tell lies. Banks will lend insane multiples of joint income, up to 125 per cent of the property's value, over periods of up to fifty-seven years, no questions asked, guv. (Why fifty-seven, not sixty? Who's selling these mortgages? Heinz? Probably. I see, Tesco are.)

This way complete madness lies. Interest rates are already on the rise again. All bubbles burst.

I've never quite worked out whether house prices have gone through the roof because of a shortage of supply, or because sellers know that there's a lot of easy money sloshing around out there.

And, as any fairground huckster will tell you, there's a sucker born every minute.

Look, I don't want to turn the clock back to 1975 and I'd hate to be in my twenties today trying to get a toe on the housing ladder.

Most people of my generation couldn't afford the homes they live in now if they were starting out today. More to the point, they couldn't afford the homes they started out in.

But the caution of Mr Mainwaring makes more sense to me than the wild, irresponsible abandon of the modern-day lenders and the tomorrow-never-comes financial hedonism of their willing mug punters.

You don't need to have a degree in post-neo-classical endogenous growth theory to know that this drunken-sailor spending spree simply can't be sustained.

I've often wondered what happened to Mickey the Mortgage Monster.

He's obviously alive and well and instead of propping up the bar in a Fleet Street boozer is leaning back in a leather executive chair with his feet on the table of one of our most respected financial institutions.

Northern Rock – Don't Panic!

The run on Northern Rock was nothing new. Back in 1946 there were similar queues outside a bank in Walmington-on-Sea. One small branch stood alone against a complete collapse of the world economic system. This is what happened:

(Enter a flustered Mr Mainwaring, to find his chief clerk, Wilson, mopping his brow)

MAINWARING: What the devil's going on out there, Wilson? I had to fight my way through to the front door.

WILSON: They're our customers, sir.

MAINWARING: I *know* they're our customers, Wilson. What do they want at this time of the morning?

WILSON: They want to withdraw their money, sir?

MAINWARING: What, *all* of them?

WILSON: I'm afraid so.

MAINWARING: How much do they want?

WILSON: All of it, sir?

MAINWARING: *All* of it?

Wilson: Didn't you read the memo from Mr Darling, the chief cashier at Head Office? There's a run on the bank.

MAINWARING: Darling? What happened to Mr Brown?

WILSON: He's not there any more, sir. Something to do with the pension fund. A great deal of money went missing. A chap at my club said it could be as much as £100 billion. Then there was that business with the gold bullion . . .

MAINWARING: My God. Are the police involved?

WILSON: No, sir – the bank promoted Brown to hush up the scandal.

MAINWARING: I always had my suspicions, Wilson. Never trust a man who bites his nails and has his teeth capped. So Brown's responsible for our customers wanting to close their accounts, is he?

WILSON: Up to a point, sir. The final straw was the American.

MAINWARING: I *knew* it. They were three years late for the war. But what have the Americans got to do with the queues outside my bank? The Wall Street Crash was years ago.

WILSON: We've lent them some money, sir. And now they can't pay it back.

MAINWARING: I've never lent an American a penny in my life, unless you count the small overdraft I granted to the GI who got that girl from the fishmonger's into trouble.

WILSON: Ah, yes.

MAINWARING: You're hiding something, Wilson, I can tell.

WILSON: Actually, it was while you and Mrs Mainwaring were on your caravanning holiday at Lulworth Cove.

MAINWARING: Spit it out, Wilson.

WILSON: Well, I was having a drink with Joe, you know, Private Walker, in the Greenspan Arms, and he introduced me to this American acquaintance, who was over here raising money for submarines. Very hush, hush. He said that if the bank could see its way clear to making him a loan, we'd get in back in spades. Safer than the Bank of England, was how Walker put it.

MAINWARING: Why didn't you tell me about this?

WILSON: I didn't want to worry you, sir.

MAINWARING: And the money?

WILSON: Gone, all gone, I'm afraid. After the war, this chap went back to Arkansas and Walker says he hasn't got a forwarding address.

MAINWARING: What about the submarines? They're collateral, you know.

WILSON: Turns out it wasn't *submarines*, it was *sub-prime* mortgages. Worthless.

MAINWARING: You've fallen for the oldest trick in the book, Wilson. Didn't you wonder for a split second why the Americans wanted to borrow money from a bank in Walmington-on-Sea?

WILSON: I'm sorry, sir.

MAINWARING: Sorry? Sorry? Sometimes I wonder how we ever won the war.

(Enter Pike)

PIKE: Mr Mainwaring, Mr Mainwaring! They're breaking the front door down. They want their money back.

MAINWARING: I shall have to take charge of this personally.

PIKE: I've seen all this before, Mr Mainwaring, James Stewart plays this man who runs a Savings & Loan in Bedford Falls and there's a run on the bank and everyone wants their money back but James Stewart can't pay them because his daft uncle has lost it and so James Stewart decides that the only way out is to commit suicide and so he goes to this bridge and he – you remember, Uncle Arthur, you gave me five bob to go to the pictures so you and mum could stay in and listen to ITMA . . .

MAINWARING: Shut up, Pike. It's *your* cretinous uncle who has got us into this mess.

PIKE: What's he talking about, Uncle Arthur? Here, you're not going to commit suicide, are you, Mr Mainwaring, my mum says it's a mortal sin . . .

MAINWARING: Stupid boy. Just open the doors.

(*Enter Jones, Godfrey, Frazer and Hodges at the head of an agitated crowd*)

JONES: Don't panic! Don't panic!

HODGES: Get out of my way. Oi, Napoleon. I've come to draw out my savings. Cough up.

MAINWARING: Don't you take that tone of voice with me, Hodges, you're not the ARP warden any more, just a greengrocer. The war's over.

HODGES: And you're not a Captain any more, just a common or garden bank manager.

MAINWARING: How *dare* you call me common.

HODGES: Hand it over, Napoleon. Eighty two pounds, fourteen shillings and elevenpence ha'penny.

MAINWARING: If you wouldn't mind coming back after lunch.

HODGES: Have you got my money or haven't you?

MAINWARING: I will have this afternoon. We're expecting a delivery of cash from Head Office.

HODGES: Oh, yeah. Pull the other one, Napoleon.

MAINWARING: Look, I have a memo from Mr Darling, at Head Office, promising to make good any shortfall.

HODGES: Who does this Darling think he's kidding. What's a piece of paper worth? Some of us remember Munich.

JONES: Don't panic! Don't panic!

FRAZER: We're doomed, we're doomed, we're all doomed. What are you going to do about it, Mainwaring?

PIKE: Mr Mainwaring's going to kill himself, like James Stewart in *It's A Wonderful Life.*

MAINWARING: I shall do no such thing, you stupid boy. The money will be here, you'll all get paid. You believe me, don't you, Godfrey?

GODFREY: Actually, I don't, Mr Mainwaring, and neither does my sister Dolly. She's sent you some of her upside-down cakes, but she was most insistent that I return with her nest egg.

MAINWARING: Mr Mainwaring, I've just taken a telephone call from Mr Darling, at Head Office.

MAINWARING: Excellent. Good news, everyone – help's on its way.

WILSON: Actually, it's not, sir. He says he was only acting on Mr Brown's orders and there isn't any money.

JONES: There isn't any money! Don't panic!

FRAZER: We're doomed.

MAINWARING: *(mounting counter):* Now pay attention, men. This is no time for panic. We few, we happy few, we band of brothers, we saw off Hitler's hordes and we will get through this little local difficulty. If we fall, the whole edifice could come crumbling down. We are all that stand in the way of a total collapse of the world banking system.

PIKE: Mr Mainwaring, sir . . .

MAINWARING: For the last time, Pike, I am not going to commit suicide. Anyway, I've seen that film and James Stewart doesn't commit suicide. He's saved in the nick of time by his guardian angel.

WILSON: That's all very well, sir, but where are we going to get a guardian angel from?

(Enter Walker, carrying a large suitcase)

WALKER: Mornin' all. Could I have a word, Mr M? In private like.

(Mainwaring, Walker, Wilson and Pike repair to private office)

MAINWARING: What is it Walker? I'm in the middle of a crisis here.

WALKER: Well, I may just be able to help you there. I've just had a bit of a result with some army surplus and I've come to make a deposit.

MAINWARING: How much?

WALKER: Ask no questions, Captain. But I don't want it through the books, OK? Keep it in your private safe and I might have the answer to your prayers.

MAINWARING: I can't do *that*.

WALKER: Your choice, but do you want the Financial Services Agency all over you like a demob suit?

WILSON: He's got a point, sir. Hear him out.

WALKER: And if you keep this on the QT, I'll lend you, say, fifty quid to get you out of this mess.

MAINWARING: We need more than fifty pounds

WALKER: But I can turn it into five thousand for you.

MAINWARING: That could just be enough to get us through the immediate crisis. What's the plan?

WALKER: There's this horse running in the 1.30 at Epsom, 100-1 outsider, but I know the trainer and he says it's a dead cert.

MAINWARING: It might just work, you know. What's this horse called?

WALKER: It's in the *Evening Standard* racing form. Here, Pikey, I've marked it up.

WILSON: Well, hurry up, Frank. What is it?

PIKE: Northern Rock.

ALTOGETHER NOW: STUPID BOY!!

The Sub-Prime Special

If you think the housing slump in Britain is bad, you should see what's happening in America. Prices in some areas are back where they were ten years ago.

When I was in Florida at the height of the crash, estate agents were advertising: 'Take our free foreclosure tour.' It was an attempt to entice visitors to cash in on all the homes which have been repossessed as a result of the sub-prime mortgage crisis.

We're used to tours of the homes of the rich and famous in Beverly Hills and beyond. But a foreclosure tour smacks of desperation. If Britain really does follow America, it can only be a matter of time before open-topped buses are touring London, with guides pointing out all the bargains on offer.

'Laydeez and gennulmen, welcome, wilkommen and bienvenue aboard the Repossession Express, sponsored by Northern Rock. Simultaneous translation into thirty-eight different languages is available via the headsets provided for a modest charge, plus VAT.

'We are experiencing some turbulence in the financial markets, so please keep your seatbelts fastened at all times.

'As we travel around today, you will observe a large number of empty pubs for sale, as a result of the government's smoking ban, the recent rise in the tax on alcohol and the 100 per cent increase in business rates over the past ten years.

'This is a once-in-a-lifetime opportunity to purchase a slice of British history. For instance, as we make our way along Whitehall, on the right you can see Ye Olde Spinne Doctor, formerly the Red Lion, where legend has it that the theory of post-neo-classical endogenous growth was discovered over a few pints of draft Bass.

'This is now surplus to requirements, since all civil servants have been banned from drinking at lunchtime. It does come with planning permission for conversion into a hostel for asylum seekers.

'We are also delighted to offer for sale several hundred post offices, which have been closed under the government's modernisation programme. These are ideal premises for shops selling fireworks, mobile phones, cut-price cigarettes and booze from Calais, or indeed one of those fine establishments where everything costs a pound.

'Given their prime high street location they are also a perfect proposition for any entrepreneur in the human trafficking community planning to open a sauna and massage parlour.

'But enough of commercial property; we intend today to show you some of the prime residential stock which has come on to the market.

'We begin at Number 1 Carlton Terrace, St James's, the official home of the Foreign Secretary, which is being offered for sale by the Treasury in order to meet a temporary shortfall in the public sector borrowing requirement. It was most recently valued at £20 million, but the Chancellor has indicated that no reasonable bid will be refused, especially if the purchaser is prepared to pay cash.

'Next up is a lavishly appointed grace-and-favour apartment in historic Admiralty House, just off Trafalgar Square, which used to be occupied by a notorious former Deputy Prime Minister who was forced to vacate at short notice after being caught in a compromising situation with his diary secretary. It comes with parking space for two Jaguars.

'Our next property is a mansion in fashionable Primrose Hill, belonging to one of the architects of New Labour. This gentlemen has a history of mortgage irregularities and when he paid £2.1 million for it two years ago, eyebrows were raised at his ability to afford it. His current contract with the European Commission is not being renewed and he is unlikely to be able to make the repayments. The house includes a priceless Philippe Starck toilet bowl and a selection of Brazilian artifacts.

'We are now entering Connaught Square, at the heart of London's vibrant Arab Quarter. On your left is the home of a former statesman, whose name I am unable to reveal for security reasons. It has been subject to extensive renovation, but with the owner soon to be arrested on war crimes charges he will not be able to meet his mortgage commitments and is therefore offering the property at auction for a quick sale. He is also prepared to throw in two flats in Bristol.

'Finally we come to the jewel in the crown, the best address in

London, Number 10 Downing Street. Some elements of refurbishment will be required since there is a hole in the downstairs wall with the adjoining property where someone spent ten years banging on it. The present occupant lives frugally and has not replaced the light fittings and doorknobs which were stripped out by the wife of the previous tenant prior to her departure.

'The property is no longer needed and the deeds have been signed over to Brussels. The occupant, who is believed to be in America seeking a way out of his financial difficulties, is to be evicted. Fixtures and fittings include a recently discovered painting by Whistler called 'The Death of Prudence'.'

The Court of Public Opinion

Having discovered that the government couldn't legally strip disgraced banker Fred Goodwin of his £693,000-a-year pension, Harriet Harman went on television and announced an appeal to the 'court of public opinion'.

Ministers had been told that any attempt to stop his pension would fall foul of their own precious yuman rites legislation.

But that didn't stop Hattie. She declared: 'It might be enforceable in a court of law, but it's not enforceable in the court of public opinion and that's where the government steps in.'

This was an intriguing development. In most other circumstances, this government fights tooth and nail not to give in to public opinion.

When they force through unpopular measures, ministers pride themselves on resisting the wishes of the people who pay their wages. In those cases, the 'court of public opinion' is dismissed as 'mob rule'.

If this is indeed a sincere change of heart then, frankly, I'm all for it. From time to time the government pays lip service to public opinion. They even set up a website to ask us which laws we liked, which we would change and which we would like to abolish.

Sir Terence Etherton, the High Court judge who chairs the Law Commission which advises the government on legislation, said: 'We are trying to improve people's lives by making law more up-to-date and fair.'

Sounds great, doesn't it? Just for fun, let's pretend that this was for real and the politicians and the legal establishment really did care what the Court of Public Opinion thought:

Left to the popular vote, the death penalty would be reintroduced tomorrow. Foreign criminals and illegal immigrants would be deported immediately with no recourse to appeal.

We would be allowed to use deadly force against intruders in our own homes and there would be a mandatory minimum five-year sentence for burglary.

The motorway speed limit would be raised, most of the yellow lines by the roadside erased and the M4 bus lane decommissioned.

We wouldn't have round-the-clock pub opening or super casinos. The 'human rights act' and the Treaty of Rome would be repealed, along with the panoply of ridiculous elf'n'safety regulations.

Weights and measures laws would be amended so that green-grocers couldn't be fined or sent to prison for selling fruit and veg in pounds and ounces.

The law on trespass would be strengthened to prevent 'travellers' setting up illegal caravan sites on private land.

Fines of £1,000 for putting the wrong kind or rubbish in the wrong kind of sack would be scrapped, and it would become a legal requirement for local authorities to empty the bins at least once a week.

NHS administrators responsible for the MRSA epidemic would be charged with manslaughter and jailed.

Catholic adoption agencies would not be forced by law to hand over children to gay couples.

All limits on the importation of duty-free goods from abroad would be abolished.

There'd be police stations open day and night in every high street and bobbies on the beat. Serial burglars, car thieves and anyone carrying an offensive weapon in public would face automatic, exemplary prison sentences.

Ludicrous elf'n'safety laws would be scrapped and the legions of five-a-day co-ordinators and diversity managers would have their contracts torn up and be told to get a proper job.

Those preposterous windmills scarring the landscape would be torn down; speed cameras would be dismantled and traffic humps would be bulldozed flat.

Over in the Court of Public Opinion Jacqui Smith would be convicted of stealing, for misrepresenting her sister's back bedroom as her 'main' residence for parliamentary expenses' purposes and all those MPs caught fiddling their allowances would be doing hard time.

Peter Mandelson would have been banged up for dishonestly obtaining a mortgage. He certainly wouldn't have been handed a first-class return on the gravy train, elevated to the peerage and appointed to a key role in government.

Tony Blair would find himself accused of war crimes after sending troops to Iraq on the basis of a dodgy dossier. The Court of Public Opinion would have convicted him of selling honours and taking bribes from Formula One.

In the Court of Public Opinion, Two Jags would have been found guilty of GBH after punching a punter on the campaign trail.

In the Court of Public Opinion, Gordon Brown would be convicted of criminal negligence for selling off Britain's gold reserves at car boot sale prices. He could always ask for a separate count of stealing £100 billion from private pensions to be taken into account – sentences to run consecutively.

Guilty as charged. Take them down.

Hattie should be careful what she wishes for. Once ministers start resorting to the Court of Public Opinion to get their own way, they're on dangerous ground.

Soon we'll get round to asking why we need politicians at all. Why not just pass laws by pressing a button on our Sky remote?

Most politicians, and Hattie in particular, wouldn't last five minutes. Her ruthless, vindictive attempts at social engineering would be laughed out of the court.

That's why there was never the remotest chance that any change in the law put forward by the paying public will be implemented.

It was just another gimmick. Sir Terence admitted that new legislation would be brought forward only if it finds favour with the Lord Chancellor and other ministers.

If the public really did have the power to change legislation, the government would pass a law against it.

Proof of Identity

As the government pressed ahead with its expensive, unwanted and useless ID card system, proof of identity rapidly became the new elf'n'safety.

These barking-mad rules are being used to infantilise us. Once jobsworths seize on a ridiculous way to make our lives as inconvenient as possible, they milk it for all it's worth. And it has spread from the public to the private sector.

We've had pensioners forced to prove their age when buying knitting needles. People have been asked to prove they are over twenty-five before buying spoons, because they are classified as 'drug paraphernalia'.

Supermarkets refuse to sell alcohol to people under twenty-five – even though the law says you have only to be over eighteen.

Some stores won't even sell booze to people who can prove their age – if they're with someone who looks under twenty-five. Mums with their children have had bottles of wine confiscated at checkout.

Christine Middleton, from Edinburgh, was out shopping for Hogmanay with her daughter at her local Co-op; usual stuff – chicken, turkey, sprouts, two bottles of wine (one red, one pink champagne).

When the champagne went through the bar code scanner, an alarm went off.

The checkout girl asked Christine's daughter how old she was. After discovering she was seventeen, she confiscated the two bottles.

Christine pointed out that the wine was for her, not her daughter, and sent for the manager. Still no joy.

The manager said that her daughter could, in fact, be a local hoodie who had persuaded Christine to buy booze on her behalf. Christine remarked that 'pink champagne and a cheeky wee

Rioja' weren't exactly your average hoodie's gargle of choice.

But the manager still wouldn't serve her and, with an impatient queue getting restless behind her, she was forced to withdraw, empty-handed.

Here are some more examples.

★

At the Lichfield branch of Marks & Sparks, thirty-year-old Oliver Butler was told that unless he could produce his passport he couldn't buy two bottles of mulled wine.

They wouldn't accept his paper driving licence either.

Rightly, he points out that you don't see many under-age binge-drinkers swigging M&S mulled wine by the neck down your local shopping precinct. Alcopops and extra-strength cider are more their preferred beverage.

★

At the Dagenham branch of Morrisons, Tessa Sparrow's twenty-four-year-old daughter was prevented from buying a can of furniture polish because she couldn't prove she was over eighteen. They said she might be a solvent abuser.

Charming. Do they think every fresh-faced young woman who tries to buy a can of Mr Sheen is a glue-sniffer?

★

In Eltham, south London, Julie Cooper's son was asked for ID when he attempted to buy a pencil sharpener from a pound shop. Apparently, as a result of the epidemic of knife crime, anything with a blade can only be sold to an adult over eighteen. Presumably, that includes the skates at the Streatham ice rink, too.

I know there are a lot of wicked people south of the water, but I've never heard of anyone being sharpened to death.

★

I've never heard of anyone being scooped to death, either. But at Asda, in Halifax, a customer was forced to prove she was over eighteen before they would let her buy a set of spoons. When she asked why, she was told it was possible to murder someone with a spoon.

*

Lori Trott was refused knitting needles and a ball of wool at Beales department store, in Bedford, because she couldn't prove she was over eighteen – even though she admits to being the 'wrong side of fifty'.

What did they think she was going to do – rustle up a quick balaclava and hold them up at needle-point?

*

David Barlow, from Exeter, tells me that when his twenty-seven-year-old daughter went into Tesco to buy a spatula, she was asked to provide ID to prove she was over eighteen as part of a new anti-stabbing initiative.

I've heard of people being stabbed with scissors, steak knives and barbecue forks. People will always use what falls to hand. One of my favourite stories was about a man stabbed with an antler in a Glasgow pub after an Old Firm game. His assailant snapped it off a deer's head on the wall.

But I've never come across anyone being stabbed with a spatula. Maybe the government has declared war on spanking.

*

A thirty-year-old woman from Leeds was asked to prove she was over eighteen before Morrisons would sell her a chunk of whisky-infused cheddar cheese. A po-faced Morrisons spokesman said: 'We take our responsibilities very seriously.'

Where do they find these people? Who ever heard of someone getting legless on a truckle of cheddar?

*

Ann Maconaghie, of Ballymoney, County Antrim, responded to a website advert for a children's 'Farmyard Friend' cutlery set from Lakeland, the kitchenware company.

This consists of a knife, fork and spoon with pictures of farm animals, ducks and chicks on the handles and is designed to go with a pair of egg cups emblazoned with the logos 'cluck' and 'quack'.

It is described as 'suitable for age 3+'.

Lakeland promises: 'Quack, moo and hoppity hop. Kiddies will go quackers for this cute cutlery set.'

So you might wonder why the advert also prominently displays the warning that 'age restriction applies' and the set is not to be sold to anyone under eighteen.

Perhaps they fear that three-year-olds might log on and buy a set with a view to a little light stabbing in the nursery playground.

Cluck, moo and, indeed, quackers.

*

Janet Lankester went to renew her driving licence at her local Post Office. They refused to accept her state pension certificate as proof of identity because they said she didn't look old enough and demanded her passport.

Since she doesn't travel abroad, Janet has no need of a passport. She had applied for a new EU-style photo driving licence only because her old paper licence, while still perfectly valid, was rejected whenever she attempted any financial transaction, no matter how trivial.

Apparently, this is down to new money-laundering regulations – just in case a white Englishwoman of pensionable age turns out be an al-Qaeda banker, or Bernie Madoff decides to hide the $50 billion he stole from investors in an account in one of our few remaining sub-post offices.

*

In Bedworth, Warwickshire, forty-nine-year-old Maurice Harris was forced to prove he was over eighteen before Tesco would sell him a bag of party poppers. Explosives, innit. They probably thought he was going to blow himself up on the bus on the way home.

*

In another branch, at Flitwick, Bedfordshire, Mail reader Kevin Foster tells me his forty-eight-year-old wife was asked to prove she was over eighteen before she could buy a cut-price T-shirt.

The reason? It had a Guinness logo on the front.

*

At first glance, this all seems laughable, especially after a flurry of reports that grown men and women are being refused whisky-infused cheddar cheese and knitting needles without proof of identity.

The idea that supermarkets are accusing law-abiding adults of being glue-sniffers and purveyors of illicit hooch to under-age hooligans is not only risible but deeply offensive.

It would be easy to put all this down to the good old British jobsworth mentality and the ridiculous modern 'if it saves one life' excuse for lowest-common-denominator law enforcement. But scratch the surface and it soon became apparent that there was something far more sinister going on.

First, proof of identity is not just the new elf'n'safety. It has been seized upon gleefully by the 'consumer protection' nazis.

Whenever I write about this madness, those who work in supermarkets e-mail me to say they have no option because they are operating in a climate of fear.

That's why they go to such ridiculous lengths, like insisting you have to be over twenty-five to buy alcohol, even though the legal age is eighteen.

Shopkeepers and checkout assistants tell me councils are running a reign of terror, threatening to prosecute anyone who doesn't ask for proof of identity, even if the customer is in a bath-chair pushed by his great-grandchildren.

Behind all this insanity, you won't be surprised to learn, is yet another job creation scheme.

Here's a typical advert from the *Guardian*, for Underage Sales Enforcement Officers from an agency which supplies local authorities.

'You will work . . . organise and implement test purchasing on establishments who have previously been investigated and inspected or are under suspicion of selling products with a minimum age limit: i.e. cigarettes, alcohol, etc.

'You will also be required to maintain the councils' databases including inputting complaints and writing up investigation notes.'

Pay is £13 an hour. There's always a drink in it for someone, if not for the poor, harassed mum trying to buy a bottle of Pinot Grigio.

The pounds and ounces police who hounded greengrocer Steve Thoburn to his death for not using metric measures have discovered a new weapon for throwing their weight about.

Town Halls are increasingly mounting covert operations against supermarkets and corner shops, sending undercover agents to buy everything from booze and cigarettes to glue and steak knives.

In some cases, these are under-age children who look over eighteen. In others, they are fresh-out-of-college, twenty-one-year-old Guardianista recruits who could pass for sixteen in a good light.

If a checkout assistant doesn't ask for proof of identity, the heavy mob moves in and prosecutes. It's not enough that someone actually is under-age.

Suspicion is enough. If they don't demand ID, supermarkets face fines of thousands of pounds and the assistant can get a criminal record. Little wonder they decide it's not worth the risk.

Dig deeper and you discover the dead hand of the government's determination to force through its unpopular, unworkable and hideously expensive ID cards scheme, to extend the surveillance state and expand the punishment culture.

Word has clearly gone out to councils and government departments to make people's lives as difficult as possible without photo ID.

Why else would a state-run post office refuse to accept a state-issued pension book as proof of identity for a state-issued driving licence?

Putting pressure on supermarkets to inconvenience customers in the most ridiculous of circumstances is part of the plot. The government clearly figured that eventually we'll become so frustrated that we'll gratefully accept a 'one-stop' state identity card.

Of course, ID cards won't stop terrorism, illegal immigration or organised crime. But next time someone like Janet Lankester goes to the post office to collect her pension, you can guarantee she'll be turned away if she has left her ID card behind the jar on the mantelpiece.

Eventually you'll be fined for not carrying your card at all times and failing to produce it on demand to any police officer or government official will result in immediate arrest.

Britain has become a country where you won't even be able to buy a can of furniture polish without the state's permission and without the state knowing exactly where you bought it, when you bought it and how you paid for it.

Little by little, slice by slice, this is how freedom dies.

'Madman drummers bummers'

There's no escape from New Labour's yuman rites and diversity tyranny, not even behind bars. Being banged up for a serious crime doesn't prevent even hardened villains benefiting from the com-pen-say-shun culture. Legal aid is lavished on cons with the most bizarre and unwarranted grievances.

More than £20 million has been paid out to convicted prisoners making frivolous claims under the yuman rites act – everything from being refused heroin to the wrong kind of toilet paper. And two hundred prisoners were awarded £10,000 each after complaining that they were refused recreational drugs in jail. All of this happened under so-called 'hard man' Home Secretary, John Reid.

After it was revealed that a prisoner in the West Midlands had been running a pub while he was out on day release, it was time for another visit to Slade prison to investigate the increasing insanity in our prison system under Labour. Fletch is in his cell, when Mr Mackay enters . . .

Something I can do for you, Mr Mackay?

You can put that filthy cigarette out for a start, Fletcher. Don't you know our new lady governor has declared Slade a smoke-free zone?

I'd love to Mr Mackay, but I can't.

What do you mean 'can't'?

No offence, Mr Mackay, I'd give up if I could, really I would, but, you see, I'm addicted.

We'll soon cure you of that, Fletcher.

I've tried those patches, Mr Mackay, they don't work.

Willpower, man, that's what you need. Now give me that packet of cigarettes.

Sorry, Mr Mackay, no can do.

Are you refusing to obey the legitimate order of a senior prison officer?

Not at all, Mr Mackay. I'm just exercising my yuman rites.

What on earth are you talking about, Fletcher?

It's like this, see. I'm addicted to nicotine and you have no right to stop me smoking.

Who says so?

The Home Office. It's right here in this newspaper. See for yourself. The government is giving £10,000 each to 198 heroin addicts who were stopped from taking drugs while in prison. So unless you fancy bunging me ten grand, I'd leave those Woodbines where they are.

You're having me on, Fletcher.

It's all here in black and white. Ministers have agreed to an out-of-court settlement of £2 million. Apparently, it was a breach of the addicts' yuman rites.

When did taking heroin become a human right?

Articles 3 and 14 of the European Convention on Human Rights ban discrimination, torture or inhuman, degrading treatment and punishment. Oh, and Article 8 enshrines the right to a private life, so if you don't mind I shall have to ask you to leave.

I'm not going anywhere, Fletcher. What's this got to do with you smoking?

Nicotine's a drug, innit? So you have no authority to stop me smoking, not unless you want my brief all over you.

Human rights for prisoners? I've never heard anything so absurd.

It's all down to that Wicked Wossname woman, what's married to Tony Blair. Serves you right for voting Labour.

I didn't vote Labour, I voted SNP.

So did McLaren.

How did he get a vote?

Postal vote, Mr Mackay, we all did. Very big on your postal voting, Labour.

But prisoners can't vote.

That's where you're wrong, Mr Mackay. Yuman rites, again.

What?

Judges at the European Court of Human Rights in Strasbourg ruled that prisoners are just as entitled to vote as all them on the out. I wish I'd come up before them and not old Hang 'Em High Hoskins at Wood Green. I wouldn't be in here, I'd be sitting at home reading the *Racing Post*. I might even be in line for a bit of compensation, seeing as the Old Bill wouldn't fetch me a bacon sandwich when I refused to come down off that roof.

But you were breaking into a factory at the time, Fletcher.

That's as may be, Mr Mackay, but I was technically in custody, they had the place surrounded and, according to PACE, all prisoners are entitled to proper meal breaks. So I should have got my bacon banjo. I read that the Old Bill sent up a party bucket of fried chicken to one bloke on a roof. He might have been throwing tiles at the time, but he still had his yuman rights.

This is madness. There won't be anyone taking heroin in Slade prison, not while I'm in charge.

Too late, Mr Mackay. Young Lenny's down Crack Alley right now, getting his fix.

Crack Alley?

That's the shower block to you, Mr Mackay.

Where did Godber get heroin from?

Genial Harry Grout – he's got the concession in this nick, along with the snout, the booze and the pornography. He gets the heroin from a cousin of one of those Afghan hijackers on E Wing.

What pornography?

Some serial rapist in solitary downloads it off the internet and Genial Harry distributes it. Internet access is another yuman rite.

Incidentally, Fletcher, have you seen Lukewarm lately?

He's getting a conjugal visit from his boyfriend. Well, I say boyfriend, they're actually married, so to speak.

Lukewarm married? When did that happen?

While you and Mrs Mackay were dipping your toes in the sea on your annual two weeks in Largs. The lady governor let Lukewarm out for a civil partnership ceremony. We all went to the reception afterwards at the pub 'Orrible Ives runs, next to the cattle market.

Ives runs a pub?

Yep, does a decent cask ale and a very tasty pickled egg.

But Ives is supposed to be in here, serving eight years.

Oh, he comes back most nights. Not every night, mind you, not since he got breathalysed for the second time. He doesn't want to end up in prison, does he?

How on earth does Ives get to run a pub?

Day release, Mr Mackay. It's all the rage. I was just reading about a prisoner at Hewell Grange nick, in Redditch, who has opened his own pub in Sutton Coldfield. The prison thought he was working as a driver. He was halfway through a six stretch, so they figured he should be reintegrated into society, seeing as he was no danger, like.

What was he in for?

Stabbing someone in the neck.

Ye gods. They should have locked him up and thrown away the key. Never mind human rights, I'd bring back the birch.

Steady on, Mr Mackay. You're beginning to sound like that Scottish bloke, politician, never off the new plasma TV in the snooker room. John Reid, that's him. Come to think of it, you look a bit like him, too. Now if you don't mind, I'll be getting back to my newspaper. You don't have a light on you, do you?

*

When I was dreaming up that spoof in 2007, I thought I'd pretty much covered the waterfront.

I had prisoners being let out to run pubs; drink and drugs freely available; pornography downloaded on to prison laptops by serial rapists; heroin addicts being paid millions in compensation for being denied their fix; prisoners getting postal votes in general elections; and Lukewarm allowed out to marry his boyfriend in a civil partnership ceremony.

I didn't have to make it up. Most of this lunacy was based on actual cases.

But even my warped imagination didn't stretch to lifers fathering children by artificial insemination. Or being given £27,000 in legal aid to demand the right to do so.

But a few weeks later, along came convicted murderer Kirk Dickson and his wife, Lorraine, who took their right to start a family to Europe's highest court.

Dickson, thirty-four, was serving a life sentence for murder after kicking a man to death in the street in 1995 because he refused to hand over his cigarettes. He met Lorraine Earle, forty-eight, through a prison pen-pal scheme while she was doing twelve months for benefit fraud. They were married after she was released in 2000. Bless.

Like any loving couple, they wanted an ickle bay-bee, even though Dickson was still behind bars with no prospect of release for at least another ten years.

When the governor of Blundeston prison, in Suffolk, where Dickson was doing his time, refused a request to authorise sperm donation, they hired a solicitor to fight their case. Their application landed on the desk of the then Home Secretary David Blunkett, who ruled against them on the grounds that their relationship had never been tested outside prison.

Blunkett was also concerned that the father would not be present for much of the time the child was growing up. But Lorraine's biological clock was ticking frantically and the couple weren't taking 'no' for an answer. When both the High Court and the Court of Appeal threw out their claim, they headed for Europe.

They maintained that their yuman rites were being violated – specifically their right to a private and family life.

Dickson forfeited his right to a family life when he kicked forty-one-year-old George Atkins to death. Why should he be legally entitled to a privilege which he so brutally denied his victim?

In an interview his wife said: 'I know some people think that Kirk should have thought about whether he wanted children before he committed murder, and others think I shouldn't have married someone serving a life sentence if I wanted another child.'

Another child? Oh, yes, I forgot to mention that Lorraine Dickson already has three children by her first husband. It was failing to declare maintenance payments from him when making fraudulent benefits claims which got her banged up in prison in the first place.

She was already bankrupt and had previous convictions for

deception and conspiracy to defraud. She claimed her only income was £15 a week from Tarot card readings.

Mad, as well as bad.

Eventually the case came before seventeen judges sitting in Grand Chamber of the European Court of Human Rights in Strasbourg.

And, needless to say, they won.

The Eurojudges ruled that it was unlawful to stop jailed Dickson donating sperm for his wife to use in IVF treatment as it breached their right to marry and raise a family.

In the wake of this crazy decision, the Home Office had to overhaul its policy of refusing to allow conjugal visits.

So when I imagined Lukewarm getting conjugal visits from his civil partner in Slade prison, I was ahead of the game. Next time I visit they'll probably have been allowed to adopt a baby.

The Home Office is already making provision. This advert appeared in the *Guardian* recently:

'Lead Project Worker, Play In Prisons Project, £20,406 a year. The successful candidate will provide maternity leave cover for the Play In Prisons Project Manager and then work alongside the manager on her return.'

Following the verdict, ministers also lifted the ban on prisoners donating sperm for use in IVF treatments.

Time for your IVF donation, Fletcher. I want you to deposit your sample in this test tube.

What, from here?

*

In that same spoof, as well as Lukewarm's gay marriage, I had Genial Harry Grout as a heroin baron.

Shortly afterwards it was revealed that not only were the prison authorities turning a blind eye to heroin use, they were issuing inmates with Steradent tablets so that they could keep their syringe needles clean.

Oh, and homosexuals were given the right to view gay porn in prison following another yuman rites ruling. Lukewarm must think all his Christmases have come at once.

But never in my wildest imagination could I have made up a woman prisoner doing life for killing her baby suing prison authorities for refusing to let her have a Native American drum so she could talk to dead animals.

After she was sentenced, the woman, who hails from Birmingham, announced she was a Red Indian.

As you do.

Last time I looked, there wasn't a Cherokee encampment under Spaghetti Junction. I haven't spotted any reports of tepees being pitched on the halfway line at Villa Park.

There are plenty of Indians in Birmingham, but to the best of my knowledge none of them is Red.

I'm told Red Robbo is still knocking around, but he's never claimed Apache ancestry as far as I know. Mind you, it's a while since I was last in Brum. Given the scale of immigration, maybe there's a lost tribe of Seminoles camped out in the Lickey Hills, petitioning to turn the old Longbridge car factory into a reservation, complete with casino.

Anyway, this madwoman now styles herself Chaha Oh-Niyol Kai-Whitewind and claims, inevitably, that her yuman rites are being violated by the prison authorities at Low Newton, in Durham.

She not only wanted a drum, she claimed she was entitled to potions, spell books and a peace pipe to allow her to practise her religion, which she describes as 'Shamanic Paganism'.

Minnie Ha-Ha wrote to the prison governor stating: 'I do not believe in violence. I have respect for all life and individuality. This prison, like many others, has an unwritten policy of pagan persecution.'

Her respect for human life obviously didn't extend to her twelve-week-old son, Bidziil, whom she strangled to death for refusing to breastfeed.

She is, of course, stark, staring bonkers. The only thing she needs in her cell is extra padding. Imagine being in the next cell when Loved By The Buffalo, or whatever she calls herself, is up all night doing a rain dance.

How long before some old lag in the Scrubs claims to be the Last of the Mohicans? Give it time: they'll have their own happy hunting ground on the playing fields at Ford Open.

If you think this is a bit far-fetched, it was also reported that the Home Office is considering building special prisons for Muslims, so that convicted terrorists don't have to mix with filthy infidels.

We could always arrange a transfer to Guantánamo Bay, where they would feel more at home.

Why stop there? Why not separate nicks for Rastafarians, complete with steel drums, complimentary ganja and a drive-by shooting range?

Or jails where traditional East End gangsters can celebrate their culture; sipping gold watch round the old joanna, singing 'Knees Up Muvva Brahn', sawing the barrels off a pair of matching Purdeys in the workshop and feeding each other to the pigs on the prison farm?

Tucked away at the end of the story about the Birmingham Blackfoot was the following admission from the Prison Service:

There are 282 prisoners in England and Wales registered as pagans who can worship in their cells or in dedicated communal areas of the prison. Certain religious artifacts may be allowed in their cells, but each is subject to risk assessment. These artifacts include items such as a hoodless robe, a flexible twig and rune stones.

Stand by for day trips to Stonehenge for Druids, human sacrifices on B Wing, and Roman orgies in the shower block.

There's a Springsteen song, 'Blinded By The Light', which begins: 'Madman drummers bummers and Indians in the summer.'

Sounds like the roll call at Parkhurst.

Paedos on Viagra

If I'd written a spoof column about a serial paedophile given Viagra on the NHS and then being freed by a court after he was convicted of molesting an eleven-year-old girl, you'd think I'd finally taken leave of my senses.

Steady on, Rich. You've gone too far this time, even by your standards. We all know things are bad, but this is *Fantasy Island* stuff.

Sadly not.

Roger Martin appeared at Peterborough Crown Court in August 2008 and pleaded guilty to 'inappropriately touching' a girl who was cleaning his sheltered accommodation to earn some pocket money.

Martin, seventy-one, has a string of convictions for assaults on minors, dating back to 1978 when he was caught having sex with a fifteen-year-old babysitter.

It was revealed in court that he was being prescribed Viagra by his GP to treat diabetes. The probation service said it had no powers or any inclination to stop him taking the drug.

Spokesman John McAngus said: 'We could not and would not restrict the use of prescription medication, be it Viagra or anything else. What we do is our utmost to help sex offenders address their offending behaviour.'

And despite his history of molesting children and the likelihood of Viagra enhancing his sex drive, the pre-trial probation report stated that Martin posed a 'relatively modest' risk of reoffending.

His barrister pleaded for leniency, arguing that his client 'wouldn't be able to cope' with a spell in prison and should be treated in the community.

Reluctantly, Judge Nicholas Coleman agreed to impose a non-custodial sentence because of Martin's age and ill health, even though there is nothing to stop him continuing to take Viagra and reoffending.

After being released, Martin said his Viagra use was 'a personal thing really'.

He added: 'I live on my own and I don't have any female company and I don't think I'm doing anything wrong.'

Try telling that to his eleven-year-old victim.

In a case like this, it's difficult to know where to start.

There have always been some dodgy characters in Peterborough. When I lived there, everyone knew the neighbourhood nonce and where he lived.

Parents would warn their children about him. His nickname was a dead giveaway. He was called Frank the Bummer.

Frank used to hang around the lido and invite children to swim between his legs. But that was about as far as it went, to the best of my knowledge. If he had more carnal urges I'm not sure he ever did anything about them.

Had he ever been caught molesting a child, he wouldn't have got away with a bit of community service. The community would have built a gibbet in Cathedral Square and strung him up.

If he'd presented himself at the NHS surgery seeking something to put lead in his pencil, his doctor would have known all about him and called the police.

In those days, GPs lived and worked, and had often grown up, in the same town as their patients. That's not always the case today, with mega clinics and many doctors newly arrived from other parts of the country and from overseas.

Patients don't always see the same doctor twice. GPs have to rely on the records in front of them. Martin was not obliged to disclose his sex convictions.

So it would be harsh to blame the doctor, although we might question why he prescribed Viagra for diabetes, rather than insulin.

It isn't clear whether Martin's probation officer knew he was taking the little purple pill. But even if he did, he thought it was none of his business.

Why was there considered only a 'relatively modest' chance that Martin might reoffend, given that he was already on probation when he carried out his latest assault?

I've always assumed that someone who commited a crime while on probation went straight to jail without passing Go.

And what about the judge who acquiesced to a plea for a non-custodial sentence because Martin 'wouldn't be able to cope' with a prison term?

Tough. He should have thought about that when he was attacking an eleven-year-old girl.

The judge told him: 'You appear to persist in applying for the sexually stimulating drug Viagra and you continue to be prescribed it.' So why take the risk that he might attack another child?

Martin's been at it for thirty years. He's hardly likely to stop now. The safest place for him is behind bars. If he needs treatment, let him get it in prison.

All the individuals are culpable in this case, but it's the system which is rotten.

The doctor could have probed more thoroughly into Martin's reasons for wanting Viagra before writing him a repeat prescription.

But GPs are pressurised to get patients out of the door as quickly as possible to meet central targets, so he probably settled for the line of least resistance.

The modern probation service is staffed by paid-up Guardianistas and seems designed to serve the best interests of their criminal 'clients' not the safety of the wider public.

And as a result of the government's failure to build enough prison places, judges are under pressure to hand down community sentences wherever possible. Maybe that's why Judge Coleman took the soft option and set Martin free.

Even the language used is 'non-judgemental'. Child molesting is downgraded to 'inappropriate touching'.

Paedos on Viagra.

Sounds like an old Frank Zappa album.

I'm Mandy, Buy Me

On the day Peter Mandelson was forced to resign in disgrace for the second time, back in 2001, I can remember writing that he wouldn't be out of work long. He'd either get his reward in Brussels or the House of Lords.

Even I didn't imagine that one day he'd achieve both. Nor that it would be his sworn enemy Gordon Brown who'd bring him back from Brussels and swath him in ermine.

That would be the same Gordon Brown who has been foaming with hatred for Mandelson ever since he switched sides and supported Tony Blair for the leadership when John Smith died.

Brown came into office promising to draw a line under the spin, sleaze, dishonesty and division of the Blair years. It was always nonsense, but enough people fell for it.

Yet he recalled into his Cabinet the living embodiment of all those deadly sins.

Short of Call Me Dave making Jeffrey Archer his new Tory party treasurer, it is difficult to think of a more outrageous political appointment.

Putting this odious, discredited creep back into one of the great offices of state was an affront to any definition of decency.

The only consolation to be drawn when Blair handed Mandelson a first-class ticket on the Brussels gravy train was that at least the most malignant tumour on Britain's body politic had been cut out.

If the average human body is around 70 per cent water, then Mandelson is 90 per cent spite. There has been no more malevolent influence in Westminster in a generation.

Mandelson gloried in his self-styled image as the 'Prince of Darkness'. Except he wasn't very good at it.

There's a line in the movie *The Usual Suspects* about how the greatest trick the devil ever pulled was to convince people he didn't exist. But whenever one of Mandy's diabolical schemes fell apart, as they inevitably did, the trail always led back to his door.

As the posse rounded the corner, there was Mandelson with his trousers round his ankles and the smoking gun in his hand.

For a man who was said to be brilliant at operating in the shadows, he loved the limelight. His vanity, along with his capacity for choosing his enemies injudiciously, was his undoing.

Whenever Mandelson pulls a stroke, he can't help boasting about it. Needless to say, in the febrile world of politics his misdeeds always have a way of reaching the ears of those with a score to settle.

How else does he think we found out about his, er, indiscretions, those repeated 'errors of judgement' which were to cost him his Cabinet career not once, but twice?

Yet after he became Prime Minister, Gordon Brown obviously didn't see Mandelson's history of tax avoidance, deception and financial 'errors of judgement' as a barrier to a seat in the Cabinet.

Mandy has never met a wealthy businessman he doesn't like – especially if said businessman is offering him a no-questions-asked personal loan or a substantial contribution to Labour Party funds.

He manages to rival Blair in the freeloading stakes, with an insatiable appetite for holidays and hospitality.

Mandy and Reinaldo had one free holiday in Italy, where they were staying as a guest of a sausage manufacturer. There's a headline for you:

MANDY AND THE SAUSAGE MERCHANT.

And it was also revealed that he'd enjoyed the hospitality of a Russian aluminium tycoon, who was then exempted from EU import duty when Mandelson was trade commissioner.

So no conflict of interest there, then.

Perhaps the most disgusting aspect of his resurrection is the fact that he has been made a life peer. The most nauseating sight I've seen in many a long year was the smug, thin-lipped smile on Mandelson's face as he took his oath, with the cheers of the parliamentary Labour Party ringing in his ears.

It should have been the moment the Lords died of shame. Instead, it was just another day at the New Labour office.

In any decent society, the other peers would have walked out in disgust. That they stayed put tells you even more about them and our rotten political system than the ennoblement of this pernicious popinjay.

When Labour is kicked out of office, it is comforting to think that many of the smug incompetents who have done so much damage to this country will be consigned to the dole queue.

They won't just forfeit their ministerial salaries and perks; some of them will lose their seats in Parliament, too. And with the country by then deep in recession, potential employers will be thin on the ground.

It will be a rude awakening for a generation of Labour MPs who have come to believe they have a divine right to rule. As the last couple of by-elections has demonstrated, there's no such thing as a safe seat any more.

Unless they can secure themselves a well-upholstered sinecure out of the *Guardian* jobs pages, they'll soon discover their lack of real-world skills is a serious handicap:

> 'Get a move on, Hazel, table four has been waiting
> for his poached eggs for over half an hour.'

Of course, the one person round the Cabinet table who doesn't have to fear the humiliation of signing-on at the job centre is Mandelson.

His reward for his year and a half's service to Gordon Brown is a guaranteed lifetime's income from the House of Lords.

He'll be entitled to collect his attendance allowance, currently £82.50 a day, in perpetuity. He'll enjoy the subsidised meals and extensive wine list and receive the attention of liveried flunkies until the day he dies.

Lord Sleaze will continue to receive invitations to garden parties at the Palace long after New Labour is a distant memory.

While his ex-colleagues are eking out a miserable existence eating cat food in front of one bar of an electric fire, his title will secure him a table at the best restaurants, an upgrade on British Airways, and almost certainly a few quid from companies daft enough to think there's something prestigious about having a peer of the realm on their letterhead – even one as reprehensible as Mandelson.

As former Labour backbenchers scour the 'Help Wanted' pages in their local rag, this reptilian recidivist will be found stroking his ermine collar in a plush armchair in the Lords' bar, snapping his fingers to summon a chilled glass of chardonnay and a saucer of Brazil nuts on a silver salver.

While retirees all over Britain are struggling to make ends meet, Mandelson will receive almost as much as the single person's weekly state pension every day simply for turning up at the Lords and signing his name on his way to lunch.

You'll also be pleased to learn that, in addition to his ministerial salary of £130,000 a year, Mandelson will also receive a £30,000-a-year pension from the EU and a generous 'resettlement' allowance to ease his transition.

Why did he need a resettlement allowance? He already owned a £2.4-million home in London. But, then again, the one thing politicians do know how to do is look after themselves at our expense. When he was forced out of government twice, the blow to Mandelson was softened by tax-free 'severance' payments of £11,000 and £12,129 respectively – despite being lucky not to be driven away in a Black Maria.

When he came back, he got a 'golden parachute' payment from Brussels – in other words, taxpayers – of £78,000 a year to compensate him for the drop in wages he will have to endure.

That's the difference between the £182,500 stipend to which he was accustomed as a European Commissioner and the meagre £104,000 he would otherwise have to scrape by on as a member of the British Cabinet.

It's not even as if Mandelson was made redundant. He left of his own volition. So why the hell should he receive a pay-off?

The main reason he was elevated to the House of Lords was because it was quick and easy and avoided the inconvenience of having to fight a by-election, which he would undoubtedly have lost. Gordon has the same approach to elections that vampires have to garlic and crosses, so a by-election was a non-starter.

But surely if there is a technical necessity for a member of the government to have a seat in one of the Houses of Parliament, there is no earthly reason why that individual should keep his seat when his period in office comes to an end.

If Mandelson had any decency he would announce that he will give up his title when Labour is kicked out, or he is forced to resign, whichever is sooner.

But then, decency is not a word you'd ever associate with Lord Sleaze – any more, sadly, than his Friends Reunited romantic buddy Gordon.

They ask not what they can do for their country, but what their country can do for them. Mandelson embodies the sickening New Labour sense of moral superiority and entitlement.

Why does anyone indulge him? No sane person would keep him as a pet. I'd rather have the neighbourhood nonce round for a Gary Glitter-themed children's birthday party.

Commentators who should know better write about him as if he's a proper person. One dopey bird in another newspaper described him as a 'poppet'.

I've lost count of the times I've seen this pygmy described as a 'big hitter'.

I can think of two words beginning with 'b' and 'h' and ending in 'er' which better sum him up . . .

And 'big hitter' they ain't.

*

Footnote: Mandelson was guest speaker at a press charity lunch at Simpson's-in-the-Strand in the week the government was trying to strip disgraced Royal Bank of Scotland boss Sir Fred Goodwin of his pension.

I was there, too. Foolishly, Mandelson agreed to take questions.

My old friend Ramsay Smith, former *Scottish Daily Mail* editor turned PR troubleshooter, asked him: 'Do you think that all public figures who are forced to resign in disgrace should be stripped of their pensions?'

Mandelson started to bluster and protest that he had been cleared of any wrongdoing by two 'independent' inquiries, before adding: 'The only person who still thinks I had to resign in disgrace is Richard Littlejohn.'

Nice to know it gets to him.

Working on a Dream

What sort of work would Mandelson have been out of if Gordon hadn't rescued him from Brussels? Come to that, what are the job prospects of any of New Labour's finest? The scene is an executive headhunter's office in the City of London, the day after the 2010 general election. Enter one ex-minister . . .

Do come in, Mr Mandelson. I understand you're here about the job. Excellent, excellent. What attracted you to apply for this position.

Well, there's the salary, for a start. £145,000 a year, isn't it?

That's correct.

And the £100 a day walking-about money, plus the two chauffeurs, the generous relocation allowance and the mortgage subsidy. Oh, and the entertainment budget, the night life, the first-class foreign travel and all the lobsters you can eat.

Yes, but why exactly do you want this job?

I've just told you.

But do you have any experience of the financial services sector?

Look, I've said all I'm going to say about that business with the building society. It's time to draw a line and move on.

Very well. Why did you leave the Cabinet before you went to Europe?

I was forced to resign in disgrace.

And the time before that?

I was forced to resign in disgrace.

Er, thank you, Mr Mandelson. Close the door on your way out.

*

The vast majority of his fellow MPs wouldn't be so lucky if they found themselves thrown out on their ear by an ungrateful electorate.

According to a report from Leeds University, ex-politicians struggle to find gainful employment out here in the real world.

Only a handful of Mandelson's Labour colleagues stand a chance of earning anything like the money to which they have become accustomed at Westminster – call it a hundred grand, plus perks, depending on how much they lie on their mileage claims.

The rest can dream on.

Most of them will end up crawling back under the public sector stone from which their little snouts once emerged. And just as well for them, since private companies which have to make their living in the harsh climate of competition have no need of a washed-up party hack with delusions of grandeur and an over-developed entitlement complex.

That's the problem with the political class. Politics is all they're fit for. Take the Cabinet, from the top down.

Gordon Brown has never had a proper job in his life, unless you count a brief stint in television and a spell as a university lecturer, which is what you go into if you can't face the prospect of something more challenging.

Not for nothing did George Bernard Shaw remark: 'Those who can do, those who can't teach.'

Had Gordon called an election and lost his seat, what would his future employment prospects have been?

Forget the memoirs and the lecture circuit. What if he'd had to get a real job?

Given that he'd been Chancellor for ten years, you might have thought that City firms would be queueing up to offer him something.

But then look more closely at his record. Over the past decade he ran up Enron-style levels of debt and wrecked the best pension system in Europe, while picking all our pockets by stealth.

If he'd been a company secretary caught presiding over record losses while at the same time creaming off the pension fund on a scale which would have embarrassed even Robert Maxwell, he'd be writing his memoirs in Ford Open.

Not even Northern Rock would give him house room.

Jack Straw. Lawyer. Worked as a barrister for two years when Grocer Heath was Prime Minister in the early 1970s before becoming Barbara Castle's bagman. Would you want this third-rate crawler on your defence team? Precisely. We're not talking Mr Rumpole here.

Des Browne. Another lawyer, currently running both the MoD and the Scottish Office. Would you trust him with anything more taxing than a little light conveyancing?

Alastair Darling. Gordon's grey glove puppet. Looks like the dead one from Randall & Hopkirk, without the jokes. Yet another lawyer.

Geoff Hoon. Ditto. Was once Visiting Professor of Law at the University of Kentucky. That might just help him get a job behind the counter at KFC.

Jacqui Smith was a schoolteacher. It's back to Bash Street for her.

Alan Johnson. Former postman. At least he went on to run the posties' union, the UCW, unlike Peter Hain, the Cuprinol Kid, who worked there as 'head of research'. When I knew Hain, his job was to go to the bar for Alan Tuffin, Johnson's predecessor. Apart from that, Hain's only claim to fame is digging up cricket pitches. Still, his ability with a shovel could come in handy on the Crossrail project.

Ruth Kelly. Worked on the *Guardian*. I rest my case.

Then there's Tory turncoat Shaun Woodward, who used to produce Esther Ranzen at the BBC. Specialist subject: amusingly shaped vegetables and dogs that can say 'sausages'.

Yet politicians behave as if they are God's Chosen People, with a divine right to do what the hell they like.

They lavish pay, pensions and perks on themselves and treat the paying public – and genuine public servants – with contempt.

Look at the supercilious, insolent manner with which Tony Wright MP (another bloody lecturer) and his committee of gargoyles treated the admirable Yates of the Yard over the cash-for-honours scandal.

Wright isn't fit to polish Yates's truncheon. His attitude was: so what if the government was selling gongs? Everyone does it, so push off and mind your own business, you uppity little Plod.

They really don't think the rules apply to them, whether it's fiddling their expenses or jumping the queue for the Commons tea bar.

Any firm going to the market on a false prospectus would be prosecuted to the fullest extent of the law. Yet Gordon Brown thinks it perfectly acceptable to renege on manifesto promises – such as a firm commitment to hold a referendum on the European constitution. How do these people sleep nights?

Judging by Gordon's saggy, saddlebag boat race, they don't.

According to the Leeds University report, once they're rumbled many MPs suffer 'nervous breakdown, divorce, heart disease, alcoholism, depression, serious debt and even suicide'.

Good.

(Meanwhile, back at the headhunter's)

I'm sorry, Mr Prescott, the vacancy for a Director of Acquisitions and International Investment at Manhattan Pacific Holdings has been filled. Have you ever thought of becoming a ship's steward?

Murder on a Corfu Yacht

Mandelson was soon up to his old tricks. The great political scandal of the summer of 2008 was the clash between Mandelson and shadow chancellor George Osborne over what happened on a Russian billionaire's yacht off Corfu. Osborne accused Mandy of pouring poison into his ear about Gordon Brown. Mandelson retaliated by alleging that Osborne had tried to solicit an illegal contribution from the billionaire.

The cast list of The Corfu Connection read like something out of an Agatha Christie novel. Grand panjandrums, Russian oligarchs, media moguls, upper-class twits and exotic same-sex lovers are the stuff of fiction. The only missing ingredient was Hercule Poirot – which is a pity, since it would take the great detective himself to unravel this unsavoury melange. You can just imagine the scene as he calls all the players together in the drawing room of that multi-million-dollar yacht.

Mesdames et monsieurs, you are probably wondering why I've asked you here this morning.

Damn right I am, Poirot. I was due to have a Brazilian this morning.

Silence, s'il-vous-plaît, Lord Mandelay. I am aware of that. When I was having my moustache waxed in the ship's sâlon de coiffeur I observed your personal assistant making the appointment. But be patient, mon ami. All will be revealed in due course. There has been a breach of protocol, most serious, which I am duty bound to investigate.

What are you talking about, Poirot?

I refer to a dastardly attempt at political assassination, Monsieur Rothschild, one which requires the application of Poirot's little grey cells. Ze body of George Osborne was found washed up on the beach, close to the Taverna Agni. Is that not correct, Captain 'Astings?

Absolutely, Poirot, he must have fallen over the side after the party last night. He was knocking back the old shampoo and looked decidedly dodgy on his feet. At one stage he stumbled on to the dance floor and crashed into the delightful Miss Murdoch and that pushy public relations chappie tripping the light fandango.

Indeed, as you rightly observe, he was a little – 'ow you say? – Brahms and Liszt. But I do not sink he fell overboard.

What, pushed you mean?

Not exactement, more like stabbed in the back.

But why would someone do that, Poirot? He seemed like a decent enough chap, went to school with old Buffy Arbuthnot.

Appearances can sometimes be deceptive, 'Astings. Monsieur Osborne has been telling tales out of school. When I was dining at the Taverna Agni the other evening, I overheard a conversation between him and you, Lord Mandelay.

Now look here, Poirot, I should warn you that I am a personal friend of your author . . .

Not so fast, Lord Mandelay. Poirot does not intimidate easily. I distinctly heard you pouring pure poison into the ear of Monsieur Osborne about a third party, none other than the Prime Minister, Monsieur Gordon Brown.

That was supposed to be a private conversation. If word of what I said gets back to London, my chances of returning to government will be nil. I'll be ruined.

Precisement, Lord Mandelay. Why would anyone want to reinstate someone who called into question his sanity, especially one like you with a great deal of what Inspector Japp calls 'previous'? Zat is a mystery, I fear, beyond the powers even of the world's greatest detective.

What are you insinuating, Poirot?

I shall tell you. All is revealed in *The Great Notting Hill Mortgage Swindle*, by Miss Christie, and its sequel, *The Curious Case of the Stamp Duty Scam*. Then there was *The Mystery of Reinaldo's Visa* and *The Hinduja Scandal*.

You seem to know an awful lot about me, Poirot. Have we met before?

Indeed, we have, Lord Mandelay. I was a guest at the ambassador's residence in Bruxelles when you were living in the Rue des Jeunes Garcons. Perhaps you don't remember being introduced to me.

Probably not. I only talk to important people like myself.

Ah, bien. I also know that you like to avail yourself of the hospitality of rich men and have flown here directly from the home of a prominent manufacturer of saucisson in Italy.

Why are you bringing all this up now, Poirot? You should be concentrating on young Osborne tapping up our host for fifty thousand smackeroos.

That is a red herring, Monsieur Rothschild, n'est pas? And well you know it. Poirot heard you in the library suggesting to Monsieur Osborne that a donation from Monsieur Deripaska could be laundered through a manufacturer of gentlemen's horseless carriages in the North of England, which would have been a matter most illegal. But he didn't fall for it and your attempts to discredit him are most despicable. What would your dear grand-pere make of it? Osborne is guilty of a folie de jugement but his sins pale into insignificance compared to those of Lord Mandelay.

I'm warning you, Poirot, back off or you're finished. I shall have Alastair Campbell destroy you. Some of my closest friends are newspaper editors. Does the name Dr David Kelly mean anything to you?

Ah, oui. The unfortunate doctor. The Ministry of Defence declined Poirot's offer of help in that case, otherwise I am sure my little grey cells could have proved he was murdered most foul.

I have friends in very high places, Poirot.

Indeed you have, Lord Mandelay, and you are not averse to doing them favours in your capacity officiel.

For your information, you interfering French mountebank, I can maintain personal friendships with people who have direct financial interests in the decisions I take. It says so in The Times, *no less.*

I am Belgian, not French. So you can explain, peut-être, how you came to lower import tariffs on aluminium while at the same time enjoying the hospitality most extensive at the expense of our host, who, par coincidence, just happens to be the biggest aluminium baron in Russia.

No conflict of interest, there. We're just good friends.

I have had Miss Lemon checking the files and have discovered that as commissioner at the Communité Européenne, you lobbied most hard for Montenegro to be admitted to the World Trade Organisation.

I'm a great believer in trade.

Vous êtes known bien for it, Lord Mandelay. But is it also pure coincidence that your two bons amis, Monsieur Rothschild here et Monsieur Deripaska – on whose magnificent yacht you are currently staying – are both investing heavily in Montenegro?

I say, Poirot, it does sound a bit rum.

More than a petit rum, mon cher 'Astings. Much more than the storm in a tea shop which is the story of Monsieur Osborne not accepting a loan which he didn't solicit, n'est ce pas? The attempted assassination of Osborne was just another clumsy effort to conceal a calumny most serieux. And, once again, Lord Mandelay, you have been caught out. It has taken the little grey cells of Poirot to reveal the true picture. Inspector Japp, arrest them all.

Gilbert and Sullivan Revisited

For all their fine words about equality, Labour ministers behave like old-fashioned aristocrats, with a particular penchant for fancy titles.

Peter Mandelson's ludicrous array of job descriptions makes him sound like the tinpot dictator of a banana republic (which is pretty much what he is, I suppose).

It all began with the EU's deciding its foreign minister would be known as the 'High Representative' – which sounds like something out of a Gilbert and Sullivan opera. This got me wondering what the great composers would have made of the political scene had they been around today.

CAST

Ruler of the Queen's Nav-ee (Rtd) – Tony Blair
Major-General – Gordon Brown
Posh Spice – Harriet Harman
Ginger Spice – Hazel Blears
Baby Spice – Yvette Cooper
Scary Spice – Ruth Kelly
Old Spice – Tessa Jowell
Policeman – Sir Ian Blair
Yum-Yum – Peter Mandelson
The Mikado – Two Jags

ACT ONE

(Blair prepares to leave Downing Street for the last time)

When I was a lad I served a term,
As an office boy in Derry Irvine's firm.
I peeled his bananas and fetched his booze
And I carried his briefs and polished his shoes.

(Chorus)
He carried his briefs and polished his shoes.

I polished up his shoes so carefully
That I became the Ruler of the Queen's Nav-ee.

He polished up his shoes so carefully
That he became the Ruler of The Queen's Nav-ee.

For polishing shoes I became well known
And soon I had an office of my very own.
'Twas there I met my dear Cher-ee
But they wouldn't let me practise down the Old Bailey.

They wouldn't let him practise down the Old Bailey.

Forget the Bailey, said Cher-ee
For you can be the Ruler of the Queen's Nav-ee.

Forget the Bailey, said Cherie
For he could be the Ruler of the Queen's Na-vee.

As a barrister I couldn't make my mark
So I thought I'd have a go at this politics lark,
And though my dad was an old Tor-ee
Cherie told me Labour was the one for me.

He joined the Labour Party just to please Cher-ee.

I even joined the CND
But I still became the Ruler of the Queen's Nav-ee.

He even joined the CND
But still became the Ruler of the Queen's Nav-ee.

Before too long I'd got my feet
Under the Cabinet table in 10 Downing Street.
And while I told the occasional lie
People thought I was a straight kinda guy,

People thought he was a straight kinda guy.

Although I'd never been to sea
Now I was the Ruler of the Queen's Nav-ee.

Although he'd never been to sea
Now he was the Ruler of the Queen's Nav-ee.

I bombed Iraq and Afghanistan
Though Osama was hiding out in Pakistan.
Stood shoulder to shoulder with the USA
On the strength of Ally Campbell's dodgy doss-ier.

On the strength of Ally Campbell's dodgy doss-ier.

We didn't find any WMD
But I remained the Ruler of the Queen's Nav-ee.

They didn't find any WMD
But he remained the Ruler of the Queen's Nav-ee.

For the past ten years I've had some fun
From cash-for-passports to Formula One.
But they still can't lay a glove on me
When it came to selling honours, I blamed Lord Lev-ee.

When it came to selling honours, he blamed Lord Lev-ee.

If you think you're glad to see the back of me,
Wait till Gordon is the Ruler of the Queen's Nav-ee.

So Tony Blair's getting out of town
We're lumbered with that miserable Gordon Brown.

ACT TWO

(Enter the Spice Girls)

Four little babes with big ambitions
Pert and jostling for positions,
Filled to the brim with righteous zeal
Four little BABES, ARE WE !

(Audience) Get off!

ACT THREE

(A Policeman's Lot, New Scotland Yard)

When a Brazilian's not engaged in his employment,
He's well advised not to wander on the plot.

On the plot.

And he'd better stay away from Stockwell station
Or he's more than likely to get himself shot.

Himself shot.

Our policies are tolerant and di-verse
But when constabulary duty's to be done

To be done

And when it comes to picking out a proper target
A policeman's shot is not a lucky one.

Mind how you go.

ACT FOUR

(The coming of Gordon Brown)

(Enter Spice Girls again)

We'll tell you who we want.
Who we really, really want,

(Audience) Get on with it!

We'll tell you who we want.
Who we really, really want,

(Audience) Is there much more of this racket?

We'll tell you who we want.
Who we really, really want,
GORDON!!

(Audience) Get off!

(Enter Gordon, with stealth-like tread)

I am the very model of a New Labour Prime Minister,
Though some might say the way I got the job was rather sinister
Because I stole your pensions, you might think me hypocritical
But I know the figures back to front, both fiscal and political.

I'm very well acquainted, too, with matters international
Sometimes under Tony Blair we haven't been that rational
Frankly, on occasions our decisions have been risible
But when the blame's been handed out, I've made myself invisible.

When the blame's been handed out, he's made himself invisible
When the blame's been handed out, he's made himself invisible
When the blame's been handed out, he's made himself invisible

Oh, I've been waiting thirteen years, since the deal made in Granita
And now I'm here in Number 10 the feeling's so much sweeter.
It's such a thrill to be PM it warms my zones erogenous
The growth that I'm experiencing, neo-classical endogenous.

It's such a thrill to be PM it warms his zones erogenous
The growth that he's experiencing, neo-classical endogenous.

I know I've been around for years, I should have been in *Life on Mars*,
But if I hadn't entered politics, I could have been a movie star.
I'm sexy and I'm masculine, like the actor Philip Glenister.
I am the very model of a New Labour Prime Minister.

He's sexy and he's masculine, like the actor Philip Glenister.
He is the very model of a New Labour Prime Minister!

(*Audience*) Bring back Tony Blair!

Snouts in the Trough

The biggest political scandal of my lifetime was the exposure of the wholesale abuse of parliamentary expenses and allowances. It only exploded properly in May 2009 when the *Daily Telegraph* bought confidential details of MPs' claims from a Westminster mole. The story went on to dominate the front pages of every newspaper for over a month.

But it had been bubbling away for years. Back in October 2004, I wrote about how MPs and peers were lining their pockets at tax-payers' expense. Even the MPs knew they were in the wrong. Here are the edited highlights of that column.

Later this week, the government is to publish a list of MPs' expenses. It would appear that a number of members have been rushing to repay money which has been, er, claimed in error.

In other words, they want to get in sharpish before they get their collars felt.

I am reminded of an episode of *Minder* in which Arthur broke into a warehouse to replace a consignment of dodgy wine before Mr Morley could charge him with half-inching it. Some MPs are claiming up to £120,000 a year in exes. Fiddles are rife.

There are legendary stories of Scottish MPs travelling four and five to a car and then all claiming the cost of a first-class rail ticket back to their constituencies.

They must have got the idea from their student days, when it was all the rage to see how many people you could cram into a Mini.

There's a tale doing the rounds in Westminster about a West Country MP who pays his children's school fees by falsely claiming to drive back and forth to Cornwall every weekend.

The other outrageous scamboli is the housing allowance, worth up to £20,900 a year, which was intended to help provincial MPs pay for accommodation in London during the week.

In principle, it sounds fair enough. Until, that is, you learn that it is also being claimed by MPs who live in Outer London.

Northern Ireland minister Barry Gardiner represents Brent North, yet claims for another home in Westminster, only a few miles down the Bakerloo line.

Quite why he needs a second home near the factory is beyond me. Red Ken (then London Mayor Livingstone) lives in Brent and manages to struggle in to work at the Glass Goolie most days without feeling the need to have a second drum on the river.

But if Gardiner thinks a flat in town is essential, that's a matter for him. He shouldn't expect the taxpayer to pick up his mortgage payments.

You might think this is borderline graft. But the real scandal is the Cabinet ministers who claim the allowance, even though they are provided with grace-and-favour homes.

To his credit, David Blunkett, the flying swordsman of Sheffield, refuses to take it. Others, including Two Jags, refuse to comment.

We do know that Speaker Michael Martin does claim the full allowance on his flat in London, despite living in some splendour in his official residence at the taxpayers' expense.

And that's not all. Like many MPs, Gorbals Mick has also got his missus on the payroll.

Mrs Gorbals is said to have received around £100,000 to work on constituency matters for her husband, even though there is little evidence that she actually does anything.

Not so long ago, much to the delight of Labour backbenchers, former Tory leader Iain Duncan Smith and his wife Betsy had their names dragged through the mud over similar allegations before being declared innocent.

But when it's one of their own, there hasn't been a peep from Labour. That's probably because most of them are at it, to one degree or another.

When the list is published we should also be entitled to know the names of those MPs who have been scrambling to cover their tracks by repaying money to which they were not entitled before they get found out.

And if any of them are discovered to have been engaged in a systematic fiddle, then it should be a matter for Plod.

Let the fraud squad have a look at the books and see how many of the claims stack up. Other industries, including this one, scrapped their Old Spanish Practices years ago.

At the very least, MPs' exes should be subject to independent audit, not an in-house whitewash. A couple of high-profile scalps should put the kibosh on the scams.

Where better to start than the Speaker? It's time to stop Gorbals Mick taking the Michael.

*

That was a full five years before the *Telegraph* blew the lid off every cough and spit of this criminal racket. No wonder Gorbals Mick spent £200,000 of taxpayers' money on legal fees trying to keep details of this organised graft from the prying eyes of the press and the paying public.

I'm not claiming any special insight. The stories were widely known, but the scandal remained buried, despite sterling digging by the *Mail on Sunday* in particular. And as recently as May 2008, I was back on the case.

According to parliamentary expenses smuggled out under the radar last Friday, Tony Blair remortgaged his constituency home in Geordieland for £300,000 – twice what it was worth. He then claimed back the interest payments from the British taxpayer.

Someone please explain to me which bit of this isn't stealing.

Even by the standards of Northern Rock, a 200 per cent mortgage is stretching it. Did Blair go to Peter Mandelson's financial adviser?

Yet those newspapers which have bothered to report this scam have given it little prominence, as if a former Prime Minister trousering hundreds of thousands of pounds which rightfully belong to someone else is no big deal.

In her grubby little book, the Wicked Witch says that the Blairs paid just £30,000 for the house in Trimdon. So how the hell did they manage to raise a loan secured on the property for ten times that amount?

By all accounts, it's still only worth £250,000. Isn't that what they call negative equity?

If they can find a building society stupid enough to lend them that kind of money, fine. But why should the rest of us have to pick up the bill for their interest payments, or part thereof?

At the time, the couple were also negotiating to buy their £3.5 million house in London's Arab Quarter. Were taxpayers stumping up the deposit through Tony's exes?

Whichever way you cut it, this was a massive abuse of the system. So why does no one else seem to give a damn?

Blair's spokesman says: 'Everything was done in accordance with the rules.' That tells you all you need to know about the rules.

It turns out we also bought them a new kitchen, complete with Aga for £10,600 and a dishwasher for £515. Oh, and we picked up the gas bill, too.

None of this money will have to be repaid when they eventually sell up.

Still, the Blairs' boot-filling is par for the course. We've also been charged for Margaret Beckett's herbaceous border and Barbara Follett's window cleaner.

And when Gordon Brown's not polishing his moral compass, he's submitting a claim for his subscription to Sky Sports and Sky Movies.

Since when was it part of a Prime Minister's job to have free access to *Pirates of the Caribbean* and Doncaster versus Leeds in the Third Division play-off final?

More to the point, what was going through Gordon's head when he filled in his expenses form?

This is someone who prides himself in being a financial genius, a political collosus, taking the right long-term decisions to get us through the global turbulence, etc, etc, etc.

When he was whacking in a claim for whatever it costs to watch Sky Movies these days, didn't it occur to him for a second that this extravagance might not play too well in the Crewe and Nantwich by-election?

The fact that none of these claims is illegal proves that the system itself is as bent as a nine-bob note.

It also helps explain why politicians haven't got a clue what goes on in the real world. They never have to put their hands in their own pockets.

As someone said, Gordon Brown knows the price of a barrel of oil, but not the cost of a tank of petrol. He doesn't even pay for his own television licence. Or his own light bulbs, come to that. What kind of cheapskate claims for light bulbs?

At this point in an article of this type, I'm supposed to say that, obviously, our politics are Persil white when compared with – fill in your own other country.

But then you read that Labour MPs Anne and Alan Keen have bought a flat at Waterloo using £175,000 of taxpayers' money – even though they have a home just nine miles away near their neighbouring west London constituencies. It would be cheaper to get them a limo home from Westminster every night. They're also claiming £876.57 a month for their £430,000 life insurance premiums.

These are the kinds of details which Gorbals Mick spent £200,000 of our money trying to prevent us finding out.

It's fashionable and sophisticated to pretend that our politics are pure as the driven snow.

MPs' snouts-in-the-trough expenses prove that's a lie.

*

And then it just went away again, until a year later when the mole started hawking a stolen CD containing the details of the expenses around Fleet Street. Books could be written about the wholesale dishonesty of our political class. Books *have* been written, the best of which was by my *Daily Mail* colleague Peter Oborne.

The claims for duck houses, the porticos, the moat dredging are the stuff of legend. The leaked material confirmed everything we knew, everything we suspected, and much, much more. I'll just mention a few cases, which stuck in my craw.

Back in 2004, I wasn't far wide of the mark but I had no idea of the scale of the stealing. And nor did anyone else at the time.

The first indications that something sensational was about to erupt was when Home Secretary 'Jackboot Jacqui' Smith was revealed not only to be claiming that her sister's front bedroom was her 'main' residence in order to maximise her expenses, but had also submitted claims for a kitchen sink and pornographic movies watched by her husband Richard Timney.

This flagrant abuse came to light after it was revealed that Smith claimed £67 for a cable television subscription – including access to the Playboy Channel, the Adult Channel and Television X, listed euphemistically as 'additional services' to spare the subscriber's blushes.

Purely in the interests of research, you understand, I visited the Television X website to check out the schedule. In alphabetical order, it starts with 'Anal Boutique' and goes downhill from there. Suffice it to say, the line-up specialises in what we in the trade call 'acts too disgusting to be described in a family newspaper'.

Now, there is a charitable argument that any man married to a 'Blair Babe' should be entitled to pornography as a basis for negotiation. But whether the British taxpayer should have to pay for it is another matter altogether.

Jackboots said she knew nothing about the porn channels, which were wrapped up in her internet account. The BBC, quick to leap to her defence, assured us she has given her husband a 'good earbashing' (which I believe can be found under 'E' on the Television X website and costs £4.95 for the full half-hour).

She may not have known, but he certainly did. And Timney was not some naive house-husband, idling away the lonely nights while high-flying wifey is keeping the world safe from international terrorism. Timney is a full-time politician, paid £40,000 out of the public purse to be Smith's adviser – in which capacity he has been known to write to their local paper singing her praises, while not actually mentioning that he's married to her.

He will have been well aware what 'services' were being claimed on her expenses – he filled them in. Maybe he genuinely believed that claiming for dirty movies was legitimate. After all, if Gordon Brown can claim for his Sky Sports and Sky Movies subscription, it's only a short stretch to the Playboy Channel.

In any event, Jacqui Smith signed the expenses claim. Even if it was an 'oversight' she put her name to it and she accepted the money. Were we to believe that the Home Secretary is so slapdash that she signs anything shoved in front of her, without bothering to read it?

In the scheme of things, a few quid for some filthy films is a mere bagatelle when viewed in the context of the £100,000 Smith fraudulently claimed from the taxpayer by pretending that her sister's box room in Southwark is her 'main' home.

As I pointed out the moment this scandal broke, the Home Secretary had a perfectly serviceable grace-and-favour house in Belgravia at her disposal. It's a short, chauffeur-driven hop from her department and, befitting the holder of one of the four great offices of state, is a great deal smarter than a scruffy terrace in south London, which from the outside looks one step up from a squat.

But if she lived rent-free in Belgravia, she wouldn't be able to fiddle her expenses. Listing her sister's address as her 'main' residence means she was able to lavish a small fortune on her real family home in Redditch, all courtesy of the mug taxpayer.

Even if you ignore the filthy movies, she claimed for everything from the kitchen sink (literally) to two washing machines, two DVD players and two flat-screen TVs. She even charged for an antique fireplace – and the coal to go in it – and a patio heater.

None of this has anything to do with the execution of her duty as an MP.

Next it was revealed that Tony McNulty, the Labour MP for Harrow East, also a Minister of the Crown, had claimed £60,000 from the taxpayer by falsely registering his parents' house in Harrow as his 'second home'.

Caught stealing from taxpayers, employment minister McNulty cites the 'Nuremberg' defence. Translation: I was only obeying orders.

This was disingenuous garbage and he knew it. No one forced McNulty at gunpoint to fiddle his parliamentary expenses. Labour whips didn't put him up against a wall and tell him that unless he claimed £60,000 in parliamentary expenses his political career was toast.

McNulty wasn't compelled to pretend that his parents' house in his Harrow constituency was his 'second home'. He hasn't lived there since 2002, when he remarried and moved in with his wife, six miles away.

If he thought trousering tens of thousands of pounds for a house he doesn't live in wasn't exactly kosher, he was at liberty not to do so.

For somebody who never seemed to be off television and cultivated a reputation for straight talking, I can't ever remember seeing him on *Newsnight* denouncing this outrageous scam.

Instead, he had us believe, risibly, that he was under some kind of moral obligation to rob the taxpayers of money for expenses which he hadn't incurred – that somehow it would be letting the side down if he didn't. Rude not to.

That was the defence wheeled out by MP after MP as their misdeeds became public.

In the middle of the maelstrom, there was at least one refreshing moment of honesty.

Leytonstone Labour MP Harry Cohen actually admitted to screwing every last penny out of the parliamentary money tree.

He didn't claim he actually lives most of the time at his weekend cottage and adjoining caravan on the Essex coast, just that he lists it as his 'main' residence for the purpose of maximising his allowances. He said quite openly that he regarded the extra bunce as part of his salary and remained unrepentant.

The rest of them dissembled and obfuscated to disguise their guilt, hiding behind the excuse that what they were doing was within the 'rules'.

Although this happened on Labour's watch, the Tories and Liberals were equally guilty.

*

Take Julie Kirkbride, the MP for Bromsgrove, and her MP husband Andrew MacKay, caught claiming expenses for a non-existent second home.

She should have taken the hint when someone lobbed a brick through her constituency office window.

Yet she still protested her innocence, even though the paying public didn't want to listen to her sophistry, no matter how hard done by she considers herself.

And it is the self-pity which is so nauseating. She wrote a ludicrous, self-serving, self-justifying piece in *The Times*, effectively protesting that she was only being victimised because she was a working mum.

It reminded me of the Wicked Witch's lachrymose plea of mitigation when she was revealed to have used a convicted con man to buy two cut-price flats.

Have you noticed how these tough-as-old-boots feminists always resort to the tearful 'poor little woman' card when they're rumbled?

Kirkbride for the Defence was a classic of its kind:

'Like millions of women . . . mother who works . . . wife and mum . . . demanding hours . . . networks to ensure my child enjoys security . . . consistency and comfort . . . growing boy . . . soon need his own space . . . elderly mother . . . keeping the family together . . . hugely upsetting . . .'

Cue violins, Kleenex, large glass of chardonnay. And jumbo-sized sick bag.

Oh, do piss off, pet.

In television interviews, she painted a heart-rending picture of having to hand over her young son in a lay-by off the M40 so she could meet her commitments to her constituents.

'Mummy, Mummy, don't leave me.'

'Sorry, darling, but the people of Bromsgrove need me. Don't forget to clean your teeth.'

Priceless. For everything else, there's the Additional Costs Allowance.

Unlike millions of other working women, Kirkbride led a hugely privileged and lavishly-rewarded life.

Out in the real world, working mothers aren't able to charge the taxpayer for their childcare. They often have to balance their desire to return to work with the crippling cost of nurseries, which can eat up most of their pay packet.

They can't put in a bill for employing their sister as a private secretary or obtain a repayment-free £50,000 mortgage to allow their independently wealthy brother to live in as a full-time babysitter.

Yet all this – and more – Miss Kirkbride considered to be her entitlement.

Between them, she and her husband claimed £170,000 in second-home expenses over the past few years.

MacKay had to go when it was revealed he didn't actually have a second home, just the houses he shares with his wife in London and her constituency.

MacKay should have been helping the fraud squad with their inquiries, not hanging on until the next election. As for his wife, she must have known he was fiddling and was therefore complicit in the whole scam. So spare us the innocent little woman routine.

She also claimed £1,000 worth of electrical equipment for her babysitter brother. Allegedly, he doubles as her technical assistant and provides administrative support, as well as changing nappies.

What a saint.

And she billed the taxpayer £1,040 for a professional photo-shoot for her website, in which she can be seen posing provocatively in a cornfield. It's the kind of thing you'd find on an internet dating site for young farmers.

Nice legs, shame about the expenses.

Julie Kirkbride has always prided herself on her humble background. Her lorry driver father died when she was seven and she grew up in a terraced house in Halifax.

Did she stop for a moment to wonder what her working-class dad would have made of her outrageous expenses claims?

Or the millions who, unlike her, still live in terraced houses – as opposed to an apartment carved out of a baronial mansion, with another place in London thrown in for good measure?

Around the time of the expenses scandal, a report was published which showed that 50 per cent of people in Britain earn a shade under £20,000 a year.

That's less than a third of an MP's salary and not as much as most of Westminster's finest claim in allowances.

Miss Kirkbride used to be a journalist. She, above most, should have been aware of the old adage: don't do anything which you wouldn't want to see on the front page of your local paper.

Is it any wonder the people of Bromsgrove demanded her scalp, no matter how effective and popular she's been as their MP? When they read about her expenses claims, they felt betrayed.

It's an indication of just how out of touch the entire political class has become.

*

While the world and his wife, quite legitimately, went chasing two-bob crooks like MacKay and name-any-one-from-a-couple-of-dozen-others, I tried all along to focus on the main event.

And that is the wholesale abuse of the expenses system by ministers at the very top.

What the hell was Alastair Darling doing buying four homes in four years, all of which he charged to the taxpayer? Why did Darling think we should have to pay his stamp duty? Why did he hire an accountant to minimise his tax bill and then stick it on his exes?

He was the Chancellor of the Exchequer, for heaven's sake. He made the rules. Why does he think they don't apply to him?

If he doesn't understand the implications of the tax code, what chance have the rest of us got?

And Darling wasn't alone. Nine members of the Cabinet hired accountants to fill in their own personal tax returns and then claimed the bill on their expenses.

That's something which the Revenue (ultimate boss: A. Darling) specifically prohibits.

But ministers including David Miliband, Hilary Benn, Douglas Alexander and James Purnell all claimed for accountancy services, as did a substantial number of more junior members, trying to sneak them through as part of their office expenses.

As Chancellor of the Exchequer and subsequently Prime Minister, Gordon Brown has never attempted to conceal his visceral contempt for those who try to avoid paying their 'fair' share.

When he was at the Treasury, he raised stamp duty four times in as many years. He has made it his life's mission to abolish tax loopholes, exemptions and allowances.

Brown beefed up Revenue & Customs enforcement, ruthlessly targeting small businesses and the self-employed, taxing 'benefits in kind' and severely restricting the scope of legitimate expenses.

Part of his cunning plan to save the world involved demanding that independently governed states close their offshore tax havens.

Yet all the while he has been a major beneficiary of the biggest onshore tax haven in Britain, namely the House of Commons – where the rules which govern ordinary mortals simply don't apply.

As far as our elected representatives are concerned, irritants like capital gains tax, council tax and taxes on perks are for the 'little people', not for them.

Theirs is a larcenous land of loopholes, exemptions, expenses, allowances and shameless fiddles, which spits in the face of every honest British taxpayer.

*

We all pored over the demeaning details of MPs' expenses claims – from jellied eels and Jaffa Cakes to Two Jags' two toilet seats and Tudor beams.

They exploited the notorious 'John Lewis List' to furnish their homes in style, at no cost to themselves, kitting them out with everything from state-of-the-art plasma TVs to wet rooms and cutting-edge kitchens.

Risibly, every single one of them claimed that this extravagant expenditure is essential for the execution of their parliamentary responsibilities and they are therefore entitled to be reimbursed, in full, by the British taxpayer.

Why the hell should we have been expected to pay for their food and foot the bill for their gardeners and cleaners, let alone treat them to extensive electronic toys and home improvements?

Some of their home makeovers are so lavish I'm surprised they haven't featured on Channel 4's *Grand Designs*.

We're only playing within the rules, they bleat, but even that's debatable. Where, for instance, does it say in the rule book that an MP can't function without a patio heater?

Their argument that the system's at fault and, anyway, everyone takes advantage of it, simply won't wash. Parliament made the rules and Parliament appoints the people who administer them, which explains why practically everything goes through on the nod.

There were so many snouts in the trough that you'd have been forgiven for thinking that a swine flu epidemic had broken out at Westminster.

But however outrageous some of these chiselling claims, the real scandal is far greater.

And it isn't just that MPs avoid paying the 'benefit in kind' taxes which any normal taxpayer would be hit with in similar circumstances.

The capital gains racket is perhaps the worst of all. Tax evasion is a crime, but MPs seemed to think they were above the law.

Just you try 'forgetting' to pay your taxes and see how sympathetically you are treated. Under Gordon and Darling, tax loopholes, allowances and exemptions have been ruthlessly eradicated.

(You try telling the Revenue that a new bathroom is essential to your profession and see how far it gets you.)

It is the cynical way in which they manipulated the system to their maximum advantage, chopping and changing the designation of their 'main' and 'second' homes at will.

This allowed them to make multiple claims for furnishings and avoid capital gains tax when they come to sell.

The rules say an MP's 'main' home is where he or she spends

most of their time. Yet the Balls-Coopers, Westminster's expenses 'golden couple', designate their house in London as their 'second' home, even though they live there practically full-time and their children go to school round the corner. That lets them claim 'double-bubble' expenses.

Ed Balls claimed that generous allowances were essential if politics wasn't to be confined to 'rich people with trust funds'. That doesn't mean MPs should expect to live as if they've all got trust funds, courtesy of the taxpayer.

Or keep the profit when they sell houses bought for them by the taxpayer.

Hazel Blears changed her 'second' home three times in a year, pocketing a £45,000 profit along the way.

Geoff Hoon played the system with such expertise it has allowed him to build up a £1.7 million property empire.

You might expect Gordon Brown – Mr Hair Shirt Moral-Compass himself – to be above all this money-grubbing sleight-of-hand, given his hatred of loopholes and tax avoidance.

Er, not quite.

How dare Brown stand up and condemn others when his own sticky fingers were elbow-deep in the till?

Brown has never given a convincing explanation of why he found it necessary to claim for two different second homes, while living in the same grace-and-favour flat at public expense for the past twelve years.

When he was Chancellor, he had a free apartment in Downing Street and a bolt-hole flat nearby, which he bought in a fire sale from the estate of the late crook Robert Maxwell – appropriately, you may think, given that Gordon appears to have modelled his pensions policy on Captain Bob's.

Until shortly before he became Prime Minister, Brown designated his bolt-hole as his 'second' home for the purposes of claiming allowances, which included paying his brother six grand for 'cleaning services' – as you do.

With all the accounting acumen for which he is legendary, he even spread the cost of a new £9,000 kitchen from Ikea over two financial years, which allowed him to stay just within the maximum second home allowance limit.

When he inherited Number 10, he followed the example of any shrewd businessman looking to keep as much of his own hard-earned as possible – he put the flat in his wife's name.

This left him free to switch his house in Scotland to his 'second' home. Consequently it, too, was extensively renovated at the expense of taxpayers, who also picked up the tab for his gardener and cleaner.

Another bonus is that if he sells the flat when he's kicked out of office, he won't be liable for capital gains tax – which he would have been had it remained his 'second' home.

Cute, eh? No loopholes, exemptions, avoidance or special allowances there, then.

But given that he's lived pretty much cost-free in Downing Street for the past twelve years, we might ask why Gordon has charged anything on his expenses.

After all, just because he can, it doesn't mean he's obliged to.

He's not short of a bawbee or two and is famously parsimonious. And as Prime Minister he's paid £194,250 year and rarely has to put his hand in his own pocket. He's got a six-figure, index-linked pension to look forward, too, and no doubt a few directorships in the pipeline.

So why did he stoop to charging taxpayers for tarting up his house in Scotland and paying his gardener and cleaner, let alone picking up the tab for his light bulbs and Sky Sports subscription?

He didn't have to wait until after whistleblowers and the press had exposed MPs' expenses as a venal, corrupt racket, which officially sanctions systematic lying and stealing, before denouncing it and announcing grandiose 'reforms'.

If he thought the system was bent, he had a dozen years in the two most powerful offices in Britain to do something about it, not milk it for all it was worth.

These blatant fiddles weren't 'errors of judgement'. An error of judgement is going out without an umbrella on a rainy day, or scuffing your alloys taking a corner too fast.

What we're dealing with here is stealing, fraud and deception.

You don't have to be Michael Mansfield QC to establish a prima facie case. Any half-competent conveyancing solicitor could tell you there's sufficient evidence to put before a jury.

I heard from plenty of serving and ex-coppers who tell me that it wouldn't be difficult to prove that some MPs are guilty of obtaining pecuniary advantage by deception.

The 1968 Theft Act, section 17(1), states that someone is guilty of an offence:

a) Where a person dishonestly, with a view to gain for himself or another, or with intent to cause loss to another, destroys, defaces, conceals, or falsifies any record or document made or required for any accounting purpose, or

b) In furnishing information for any purpose produces or makes use of any account, or any record or document . . . which to his knowledge is or may be misleading, false or deceptive.

Sounds to me as if we've got them bang to rights. But if that's too difficult to prove:

Section 15 of the same Act says:

Any person who by any deception dishonestly obtains property belonging to another with the intention of permanently depriving the other of it, commits an offence.

I even published the number of Harrow nick and several *Mail* readers made specific complaints against McNulty. But the CPS and Scotland Yard didn't want to know.

As for Tony Blair, Brown's partner in crime for so many years, we shall never learn the full extent of his claims.

Blair's expenses were, er, 'accidentally' shredded after he stepped down as Prime Minister.

That's the convenient political equivalent of: 'The dog ate my homework, sir.'

It shields Blair from the laser beam of scrutiny to which those MPs he left behind have been subjected.

Today, six years after I first wrote about it, I still look at the scandal of MPs expenses and wonder why no one ever had their collar felt.*

Which bit of this *isn't* stealing?

---

* At the time this book went to press, three Labour MPs and one Tory peer had been charged with criminal offences arising from their expenses claims. McNulty and Smith were not among them. The Tory couple Julie Kirkbride and Andrew MacKay also escaped prosecution. Last thing I heard both were reported to be lining up six-figure salaries as political lobbyists. The real disgrace is not that a handful of MPs were charged, but that most of them walked away scot-free.

Letters to the Editor

Jackboot Jacqui's porn-fan husband, paid £40,000 a year of taxpayers' money to be her research assistant, was discovered writing letters to their local paper in Worcestershire, praising her policies and trashing the Tories.

Since he was using his own name, Richard Timney, and she sticks to her maiden name, Smith, readers probably weren't aware of any connection. His true identity was unmasked after a series of letters was published in the *Redditch Advertiser* on subjects as diverse as ID cards and free bus passes for pensioners.

I couldn't help wondering if this was a one-off, or indicative of a wider trend. So I scoured the letters' pages of a number of other newspapers.

To the Editor of the *Fife Herald*.

Sir, Last week you called our MP, Gordon Brown, a 'big feartie' and suggested he was bankrupting the country to further his own political ambitions.

I can assure you that he is a man of great moral courage and prudence. Only the other day he single-handedly crushed a spider in our bathroom, using his big clunking fist.

As for allegations that he had failed to fix the roof while the sun was shining, I would point out that he spent the whole weekend up a ladder, stretching a tarpaulin over the missing tiles caused by the high winds which started in America.

Gordon is not afraid to take tough, long-term decisions to lead us through the current economic downturn, unlike the Tories who would do nothing.

Just this week he decided we should stop buying Scott's Premium Porage Oats and replace them with Lidl Own Brand Porridge-Style Gruel.

Yours, Mrs Sarah Brown, via e-mail, since our local post office has closed down because of the Tory cuts.

To the Editor of the *Yorkshire Post*.

Sir, In your last edition you suggested that Ms Yvette Cooper MP was involved in an elaborate expenses scam, claiming thousands of pounds for a second home in London, where her sons go to school, while representing a constituency in Yorkshire.

Whilst it is true that she lives and works full-time in London, helping hard-working families – unlike the Tories who would do nothing – she regards Yorkshire as her primary home and this year has spent as many as three weekends in her constituency.

I trust you will correct this outrageous slur, which originated in America.

Yours, Ed Balls, Hackney.

To the Editor of the *Hackney Gazette*.

Sir, In your last edition you suggested that Ed Balls MP was involved in an elaborate expenses scam, claiming thousands of pounds for a second home in Hackney, where his sons go to school, while representing a constituency in Yorkshire.

Whilst it is true that he lives and works full-time in London, safeguarding children and hard-working families – unlike the Tories who would do nothing – he regards Yorkshire as his primary home and has spent as many as three weekends there this year.

I trust you will correct this outrageous slur, which originated in America.

Yours, Yvette Cooper, Castleford.

To the Editor of the *Hull Daily Mail*.

Sir, I write in connection with your campaign to secure a seat in the House of Lords for our long-serving, former Deputy Prime Minister, who is standing down at the next election.

After what that fat bastard's put me through these past forty years, it's me what deserves a peerage. I'd look good in ermine.

Then I could give him the elbow once and for all and he can shove off with that Tracey trollop from the typing pool.

Pauline Prescott, Mrs (for now).

To the Editor of the *Scotsman*.

Sir, I write to protest about your description of Alistair Darling MP as a financial illiterate who failed to see the economic downturn coming.

Following the collapse of Northern Rock, which began in America, he withdrew all our savings from the Royal Bank of Scotland and invested them in high-yield accounts with Lehman Brothers and AIG, unlike the Tories who would do nothing.

How's that for foresight?

Mrs Margaret Darling, Marshelsea Debtors' Prison.

To the Editor of the *Sheffield Telegraph*.

Sir, In the current downturn, which began in America, this is no time for a novice.

What what we need are experienced men in the Cabinet, unlike those wet-behind-the-ears Tory toffs who would do nothing. If bloody Mandelson can make a comeback, why can't I?

Come on, Gordon, gissa job.

David Blunkett, Central Paternity Court, Barking.

To the Editor of the *Notting Hill Gazette*.

Senhor, It is refreshing to see Lord Mandelson restored to eez rightful place at the 'art of govermente.

'Ow long before eez allowed to take eez rightful place on Strictly Come Dancing?

Doddery, he is not.

Lady Reinaldo, Rue des Jeunes Garcons, Rio de Janiero.

Green Shoots

At the height of the expenses scandal, the government kept trying to change the subject. Despite all evidence and contrary to the latest gloomy reports from the Bank of England and the IMF, ministers claimed to detect 'green shoots' in the economy.

The Prime Minister outlined his reasons to be cheerful in a speech at Broadmoor. These are the edited highlights.

'Governor, fellow inmates, it gives me great pleasure to present to you conclusive evidence that Britain is well on the way to recovery.

'Everywhere I look, I see green shoots as a result of our investment. For instance, estate agents report a booming trade in second homes in the Westminster area, giving a much-needed boost to the strategically important property speculation industry.

'Such is the growing confidence that some investors have purchased as many as three flats in a single year. My own Chancellor of the Exchequer, Mr Darling, has given a firm lead, buying and furnishing four different homes in quick succession.

'This has only been possible because of a number of flexible schemes we have made available, including repayment-free mortgages and the ability to reclaim stamp duty from the taxpayer.

'The market has also reacted well to our decision to allow sellers to avoid capital gains tax.

'In turn, this has had a significant knock-on effect in the retail sector, with John Lewis and Ikea reporting record profits across the board.

'Sales of flat-screen televisions and other electrical goods are at an all-time high as consumer confidence returns.

'I was talking recently to the manager of the Leicester branch of John Lewis and he told me that one regular customer had cleaned out his entire stock of silk cushions in a single visit.

'Other stores report a run on everything from sofas and decorative lamps in the shape of elephants to novelty toilet seats and trouser presses.

'Over at Ikea, they are doing brisk business in home improvements, such as wet rooms and stone kitchen sinks. As I take my leadership responsibilities seriously, I recently invested £9,000 in a brand new kitchen, taking maximum advantage of the scheme which allows me to spread the cost to the taxpayer over two financial years.

'All this has had the beneficial effect of combating unemployment and creating British jobs for British workers, especially Polish plumbers and electricians.

'There has also been a strong demand for cleaners since we introduced the scheme which allows householders to split the cost with their brother and then reclaim it in full.

'Across the country, we have created increased employment opportunities for gardeners, some paid as much as £6 an hour.

'Sales of ride-on lawnmowers, barbecues and lawn furniture have also shown a marked increase. This is a direct result of the measures we have taken to combat climate change, which means that for the first time in history it is safe to sit in your garden without running the risk of being burned to a crisp or attacked by polar bears.

'These green shoots are not confined to any one region. Our investment in vital infrastructure has had the dual effect of creating employment and restoring some of the finest buildings in England.

'This has led to a revival in traditional skills, such as stone masonry and carpentry. In Yorkshire, we invested thousands in rebuilding a portico, which had fallen into disrepair. On Humberside, we invested in Tudor beams on a famous turreted mansion and in Hampshire we funded the repair of a magnificent pergola.

'We have embarked on an extensive programme of public works, including tackling dry rot, clearing paddocks, tidying up tennis courts and cleaning swimming pools.

'In Oxfordshire, we were able to get to the root of a wisteria epidemic, which had the potential to kill hundreds of millions of people. In Suffolk, we proved we are tough on moles and tough on the causes of moles.

'Thanks to our investment, the helipad maintenance industry can look forward to a bright future. And I am proud to be able to announce to you today that Britain now leads the world in moat-dredging.

'To those who accuse us scurrilously of not fixing the roof while the sun shone, I would point to the £3000 we invested in repairing an historic leaking roof in Hartlepool for a devoted public servant, Mr Mandelson.

'As for the allegation that we have been throwing taxpayers' money away, nothing could be further from the truth.

'In fact, even as I speak to you tonight, there are men and women queueing up to repay this unparalleled investment.

'In an extraordinary gesture, one lady, a Miss Blears, has written out a cheque for £13,332 to Her Majesty's Government. And only today, another gentlemen has generously returned £41,000. Smaller amounts are coming back every day. So far we have recouped £130,000.

'Ignore the Jeremiahs who talk Britain down. My fellow inmates, where some of you see little green men, I see only green shoots.

'Britain will come out of this global recession fitter and stronger, or my name's not Napoleon XIV.'

A fuller version of this speech can be found on YouTube, keyword: Looney Tunes.

Be Lucky, Son

As the expenses scandal rumbled on there came the revelation that gangland killer Reggie Kray attempted to make a fresh start after being jailed for murder. While not actually repenting his crimes, he did try to turn over a new leaf, according to prison files. It's not certain whether he was sincere or this was just a clever ruse to get out of jail. Reggie, who with his twin brother Ronnie ran a reign of terror in London's East End in the 1960s, sounds like a perfect role model for today's politicians.

Just imagine if Reg was alive today, being interviewed on the *Today* programme and employing what we have come to know as the Gordon Brown defence. It might go something like this.

Good morning, I'm Evan Montague. My guest in the studio today is the East End businessman Reginald Kray, who has just been convicted of murder at the Old Bailey.

If I could just stop you there, Evan, you're being a bit previous.

But you and your brother were both found guilty by a jury.

Look, our old mum brought us up with a firm sense of right and wrong, to tell the truth at all times – except to the Old Bill, obviously.

Are you saying you're not guilty?

It was a right fit-up. Frankly, I'm disgusted at what I heard in that court. My conscience is offended.

With respect, twelve men and women weighed the evidence and reached a unanimous verdict.

That's just one rogue poll, based on a very small sample. It's not what we're hearing on the doorstep.

On the doorstep?

You knock on any door in Vallance Road, Evan, and people will tell you that what they want is for the Kray Twins to get on with the job.

But you run organised crime rackets and are responsible for a wave of violence and murder. Are you denying your involvement in the Whitechapel bullion robbery?

At least we didn't sell off the gold for a quarter of what it was worth.

But it didn't belong to you.

We only rob those what can afford to pay their fair share. We are taking necessary steps to support our community, providing much-needed jobs to help people in these difficult times.

Such as?

Croupiers, strippers, prostitutes. Our record in expanding the service and leisure sector is second to none. We are also financing traditional East End trades, such as armed robbery, safe-cracking and demanding money with menaces.

But that's against the law.

We have acted at all times within the rules.

What rules?

The rules of our organisation. We have a strict code in our world, which we are committed to uphold.

But the public are appalled when they read about some of the things which have been going on.

I'm appalled, too, Evan. And I can assure you today that those who have transgressed will be chastised, starting with the slag what grassed us up to the Daily Telegraph. *We have already taken action to ensure that those guilty of the most serious wrongdoing will not be standing again.*

Not standing for what?

Not anything, Evan. Just not standing. Or breathing, come to that.

So you admit you murdered Jack 'The Hat' McVitie?

I have acted at all times within the rules, as has my brother.

But he murdered George Cornell, shot him in the head in the Blind Beggar, after Cornell called him a 'fat poof'.

Cornell's behaviour was wholly unacceptable. Under our rules, lack of respect is punishable by summary execution. Ronnie done nothing wrong.

That's murder, you both deserve to go prison. No one should be above the law.

Why not? Parliament is. And at least we've got a code of honour. If some of them MPs had stolen from us like they stole from the taxpayer, they'd be propping up motorway flyovers.

But, Mr Kray, the public is demanding that the East End is cleaned up, especially the blood on the pavement outside the Blind Beggar.

And I agree with them. That's why I am getting on with the job. Who better to clean the place up than those what created the mess in the first place?

With respect, Mr Kray, you've had at least twelve years to clean up your act, but you've chosen to steal, kill and get rich on the proceeds of crime.

Respect, I like that. People don't want to dwell on the past, they want to know what we are going to do in the future. Things is going to be different around here from now on.

But you're only saying that because you've been caught red-handed.

I'm glad my old mum can't hear you, son, or I'd have to cut your tongue out. For the record, I didn't go into organised crime to get rich. I'll have you know that me and Ron still live in the same house we grew up in. We've haven't got second homes, or moats, or porticos or duck houses, unlike some people I could name.

Why should we believe you when you say you are going straight in future?

We're getting rid of the old Gentlemen's Club, for a start. We're turning it into a casino. Now that Labour's introduced twenty-four-hour licencing on every high street, there's no profit in spielers. Our scrapyards are well placed to take advantage of the government's scrappage scheme and our counterfeiting department has picked up a nice little contract to help the Treasury with its quantitive easing.

And what next for you, Mr Kray?

I'm thinking of becoming an MP. Who needs the Long Firm game when you can buy a few houses and do them up with taxpayers' money, sell them on and avoid capital gains tax.

What makes you think the public would vote for a criminal as their Member of Parliament?

Silly question, son. Be lucky.

Tehran Television

There was blanket coverage in Britain of the unrest which has followed Iran's disputed election. Gordon Brown even issued a statement calling on the Iranian government to accept the democratic will of the people. But imagine how our own political crisis must have looked from the Middle East. Do we really have any right to sit in judgement on other countries? Here's how Tehran Television might have reported events in Britain.

'Allahu Akbar! Welcome to a special edition of *Eye on the Infidel*, live from London, capital of the hated New Labour tyranny.

The Supreme Leader, Ayatollah Brown, is clinging to power despite receiving only 15 per cent of the vote in last week's elections.

In some conservative tribal regions, the ruling junta's share fell to just 8 per cent, with government candidates beaten into fourth place by fascists and separatists.

Even in lowland Scotland, formerly a Brownite stronghold, Labour was humiliated by nationalist forces.

It represented a new nadir in the fortunes of Labour under the dictator Brown, an ultra-orthodox Presbyterian theocrat, who replaced the despised Bushite running dog Tony Blair in a coup two years ago.

But Brown is refusing to accept the result of the election and has declared himself the winner. He told the official state broadcaster that he was getting on with the job, which is what people wanted him to do.

A clumsy attempt to remove the Supreme Leader by dissidents rallying under the banner of the breakaway Guardianista faction was ruthlessly crushed.

Brown then embarked on a shambolic reshuffle of his Cabinet, in an attempt to purge reformists from key posts. But at least two of the leading dissidents remain in office, a stark illustration of the Supreme Leader's underlying political weakness.

Such is the parlous level of his support at home, he has been forced to draft in from Europe exiled party elders like the twice-disgraced mortgage fraudster Ayatollah Mandelson and expenses baroness Harridan Kinnock to shore up his crumbling regime.

Civil unrest has been mounting since the collapse of the infidel capitalist banking system.

In London, a newspaper vendor was clubbed to death by masked police during violent clashes between security forces and anti-globalisation protesters.

Similar hardline tactics, involving riot shields and baton charges, have also been used to suppress peaceful protests by demonstrators opposed to Labour's totalitarian efforts to eradicate traditional English countryside pursuits.

In the Islamic province of Luton, troops clashed with brave members of local jihadist groups campaigning peacefully for the introduction of sharia law in Britain and an end to the religious wars of aggression against Muslims in Iraq and Afghanistan.

Hundreds of thousands of women have taken to wearing hijabs to express their support for sharia. The burqa is now a common sight in British towns and cities.

Meanwhile, in London, millions of commuters took to the streets after the Underground system was brought to a standstill because of a strike by revolutionary transport workers loyal to the deposed spiritual leader, Ayatollah Redken.

At the heart of this crisis is the fact that under the Supreme Leader's profligate stewardship, the country is effectively bankrupt. Britain's vast oil and gas reserves have been squandered and taxes are soaring.

As well as a run on the banks, there has been widespread looting of department stores, particularly the John Lewis chain, led by members of the ruling elite making off with sofas, plasma televisions and kitchen sinks.

Politicians from all parties have stolen millions of pounds making false expenses claims and used public money to build private property empires and watch pornographic films.

This corruption goes right to the heart of the political establishment, with even the Treasury minister implicated in wholesale tax avoidance. Scandalously, he remains in office, even though the Speaker, Ayatollah Gorbals, has been forced to resign.

Once the home of parliamentary democracy, Westminster is little more than a talking shop, poorly attended and utterly discredited. Most of Britain's laws are now imposed by foreign bureaucrats and judges without any debate.

Freedom of speech has been brutally repressed. Police arrested an Opposition spokesman simply for doing his job.

There is also the question of the democratic legitimacy of the Brown junta. He seized power without an election and has repeatedly demonstrated his contempt for accountability and the will of the people.

Yet rather than acknowledge their anger, he persists in changing the subject and is now considering tinkering with the voting system in a cynical last-ditch attempt to remain in power.

The Supreme Leader has withdrawn into his bunker and is reduced to issuing deranged statements on YouTube.

It is frightening to think that this madman has access to nuclear weapons and has never accepted Middle England's right to exist. He appears to be hell-bent on wiping the United Kingdom off the map and submerging it into an imperialist European superstate.

And yet the British still have the nerve to lecture us on democracy.

My fellow Iranians, we should give thanks that we are in the safe hands of our beloved President Ahmadinejad, peace be upon him. Allahu Akbar!'

Hi-De-Hi

Back in 2001, my novel, *To Hell in a Handcart*, featured a tacky theme park called Goblin's, somewhere in southern England. Disneyland, it wasn't.

The surly, tattooed staff were forced to dress as elves, the rip-off food was poisonous, visitors were wheel-clamped as they drew up at reception, the whole place was run entirely for the convenience of the management and nothing worked properly.

Guests included a party of juvenile delinquents, taken on holiday at taxpayers' expense by their social worker to teach them the error of their ways.

They spent their time fighting, swearing, drinking, taking drugs, abusing employees and fellow campers alike, burgling the chalets and stealing from cars.

Goblin's wasn't exactly meant to be a metaphor for modern Britain, but I can understand why some people thought it might be.

It all came flooding back at Christmas 2008, when I read about the Lapland New Forest experience, otherwise known as Winter Blunderland, a new 'tourist attraction' on the Hampshire/Dorset border.

The staff even dressed like elves. Families who'd paid £30 a head were expecting a snowy Christmas village, an ice-skating rink and a jolly Santa handing out presents.

They arrived to find something which resembled a cross between an illegal gypsy site and a derelict garden centre, with 'Lapland: Way In' Sellotaped on to a traffic cone.

There were mangy 'huskies' covered in mud and tethered to stakes, the ice rink was closed for repairs and, after being forced to stand for up to three hours in freezing temperatures to see Santa, visitors were told that if they wanted their pictures taken with him it would cost them an extra £10.

Most of the toys handed out didn't work. The Nativity scene looked like something 'plonked in the middle of a war zone', according to one witness. Needless to say, tempers became frayed and the elves started brawling with customers.

Santa was punched in the face by a father who had been waiting in line for four hours.

A young girl had to be comforted after arriving at the grotto only to discover Father Christmas out the back having a quiet cigarette.

One of the elves took a blow from a livid mum. Another elf suffered leg injuries when she was rammed by a pram. A security guard said he was called a 'pikey' and punched in the forehead by an irate parent.

After more than two thousand complaints, the park was shut down and local trading standards officers launched an investigation. The RSPCA was also on the case, after reports that dogs, reindeer and donkeys had been ill treated.

It emerged that the erstwhile proprietor of Winter Blunderland was a convicted fraudster, who has served time for tax evasion. Victor Mears and his younger brother, Henry, brought to the theme park industry all their valuable experience of running a scrapyard and a fruit and veg stall.

The Brothers Grim were described as 'a bit like Del Boy but without the nice side' and, working on the tried and tested principle that there's one born every minute, expected to make £2 million from mug punters over the festive period.

Now, you might ask why these unfortunate families didn't cut their losses and turn tail when they saw the entrance to the attraction, which made the approach to a council recycling depot look like the Yellow Brick Road.

But after what, in some cases, must have been an arduous journey along the South of England's congested, pot-holed highways, which heartless parent is going to tell their excited kiddies they're going straight home without seeing Father Christmas?

More than 50,000 people had already paid, up front online.

And seeing the enchanting publicity pictures on the Lapland New Forest website, it's easy to understand how so many were taken in.

Still, if it's metaphors you're looking for, Winter Blunderland was a reasonable approximation of Brown's Britain.

You can just imagine Gordon, dressed up in his Santa suit, with chief pixie Peter Mandelson at his knee, rubbing his hands at the thought of raking in all that lovely money on a false prospectus.

Mandy's even got form for fraud. How much tax have we paid over the years for goodies which have failed to materialise – from a 'world-class' transport network to weekly dustbin collections?

Brown's Britain has been run entirely for the benefit of the management, everything costs an arm and a leg and nothing works properly.

The queues for Santa's grotto equate to those for treatment on the NHS. If you want to see a dentist, or guarantee your children a decent education, it'll cost extra.

Meanwhile, it's not just ice rinks closed in the real world, it's post offices and police stations. Half the country resembles a transit camp for gypsies and illegal immigrants, and there are scuffles breaking out all over.

Oi, you can't park there.

Welcome to Brown's Blunderland, twinned with Goblin's. We are all going to hell in a handcart.

*

A couple of months later came a report that the traditional British holiday camp was enjoying a revival, thanks to the credit crunch.

Almost driven to extinction by the cheap package holiday boom, both Butlins and Pontin's have both invested heavily and bookings rose to a level not seen since the sixties. I checked in to the world-famous Maplins holiday camp, at Crimpton-on-Sea, Essex, to discover what had changed and what modern delights are on offer.

'Good morning, campers. Hi-de-hi! Today's forecast is for heavy rain and freezing temperatures. This is a global cold front, which began in America, and management takes no responsibility for the inclement conditions.

'Our commandant – sorry, guest services manager – reminds you that, thanks to his foresighted programme of investment, Maplins is in better shape to weather this depression than most other holiday camps.

'He utterly refutes all allegations that he failed to mend the roof when the sun was shining. Guests who are experiencing leaks and damp patches in their chalets should address their complaints to the previous management.

'Our ambitious ten-year rolling refurbishment programme is ongoing and when complete every chalet will be equipped with designer stone sinks and the very latest, state-of-the-art wide-screen plasma televisions, currently only to be found in our staff quarters.

'The programme has proved so successful that last weekend we were proud to entertain in our Polynesian Suite a party of MPs on a fact-finding mission. Many of them were so impressed, they have opted to participate in our time-share scheme, which will allow them to designate their chalet as their main home for the purposes of parliamentary expenses.

'Campers are advised that the hole-in-the-wall cash machine next to the gift shop is temporarily out of funds. We apologise for any inconvenience. It should be back in service later today, just as soon as the management has printed some more money.

'Would all our Eastern European visitors who have put their names down for fruit picking and casual labouring please assemble next to the main gate to await transportation to local farms and building sites.

'Those who choose not to work should make their way to the customer services booth where they will be issued with complimentary meal vouchers and free tokens to spend in the amusement arcade. Unfortunately, these concessions are not available to British citizens.

'Maplins' new Healthy Options breakfast menu is now being served in the cafeteria. Campers are invited to help themselves to the all-you-can eat muesli and mango buffet. Fried breakfasts are no longer available and any guest caught trying to smuggle in a salt cellar will be escorted from the camp. Further information can be obtained from our friendly team of five-a-day co-ordinators.

'Proof of identity will be required from everyone under the age of sixty-five in the Jolly Roger fun pub. This is a no-smoking facility and our bar staff have been instructed not to serve any guest with more than three units of alcohol per day. Any pregnant woman who attempts to obtain a second half of lager will be refused service for her own good and asked to leave the premises.

'All guests are required to attend compulsory keep-fit classes. These are held every half-hour in the pole-dancing club, which is situated between the Happy Endings massage parlour and the Tumble Tots crêche in the model village.

'Sunday's Easter egg hunt for the under-fives will set off from outside the twenty-four-hour casino at noon. Entry forms can be obtained from Miss Smith, who can be found under the patio heater outside the sex shop.

'We also regret that, on the advice of health and safety and our insurers, the swimming pool has been drained and the diving boards dismantled. Fishing is no longer permitted, on the instructions of the European Union.

'The dodgems have been decommissioned because they are unable to comply with modern crash safety regulations and the cost of installing air bags, traffic humps and speed cameras was prohibitive. The helter-skelter has been closed because it has no wheelchair access.

'Ditto, the Haunted House, which is being converted into a hostel for asylum seekers.

'We also apologise to older campers that, unfortunately, the bowls tournament has had to be postponed indefinitely, owing to the illegal gypsy camp on the bowling green.

'The good news is that we are able to offer lucky heather at half-price and rides on stolen lawnmowers for the kiddies.

'And the boating lake is due to be reopen, once it is cleared of Tamil Tigers.

'There will be no glamorous granny competition, not only because it is both sexist and ageist but also because these days some grannies are only thirty.

'Our annual beauty pageant has also been abandoned, on the advice of our diversity directorate. It was felt that the contest objectivised vulnerable women and encouraged rapists and that the swimsuit section discriminated against campers who wear burqas.

'The knobbly knees competition has also been ruled inappropriate. Instead it will be replaced in the Jade Goody Theatre by Maplins' Got Talent, hosted by TV's Piers Morgan.

'Alternative entertainment is available in the lecture hall, which tonight features a call for worldwide jihad from Sheikh Omar Bakri, live by satellite.

'And our popular karaoke nite goes ahead as planned. Earmuffs will be provided to comply with anti-noise regulations. Knives must be handed in at the door.

'Maplins Radio stars Russell Brand, who will ring up the elderly gentleman in Chalet 86 and tell him he has just had sex with his wife, with hilarious consequences.

'We regret that Maplins' mosque will remain closed until further notice while our Redcoats investigate claims that a number of guests were plotting to blow up the Agadoo Disco and Nite Klub. Our chief security officer, Mr Quick, has tendered his resignation after details of the operation were discovered in a carriage on the miniature railway.

'All security inquiries should now be addressed to Mr Yates. He is particularly anxious to hear from any campers who may have witnessed an alleged assault on a camper by one of our Redcoats during the anti-globalisation demonstration outside the Housey Housey bingo hall.

'Campers are advised to take advantage of the free condoms and morning-after pills available from reception. Due to an unforseen outbreak of MRSA, the first aid station has been closed and we are therefore temporarily unable to offer quickie abortions on demand.

'Here at Maplins we take our commitment to the environment seriously and are determined to cut our carbon footprint accordingly. With climate change in mind, we are attempting to generate all our electricity on site, from the windmill on the crazy golf course. We apologise for the frequent power cuts we have been experiencing.

'If you are checking out today, please be aware that our all-inclusive rate does not include access to pornographic films on demand, which must be paid for individually. Yes, that means you in Chalet 69, Mr Timney.

'Don't forget to pay your £50-a-head departure tax to Mr Darling at the cashier's desk. And if you are leaving, please remember to take all your rubbish with you, since the waste bins in the chalets are only emptied once a fortnight. Thank you for choosing Maplins.

Hi-de-hi!'

Praise Be to Gord

Every time Gordon Brown has been caught out, he has hidden behind his son-of-the-manse act.

He talks about his 'moral compass' and reminds us that his father, the late John Brown, was a Church of Scotland minister.

So I suppose it was inevitable that he managed to wangle a special guest appearance on *Songs of Praise*, affording him another chance to parade his piety.

Gordon chose Psalm 23, The Lord Is My Shepherd, and a couple of his favourite hymns. He also held forth on the subject of 'courage'. Yes, honestly.

I'm surprised the BBC didn't just let Gordon conduct the whole service. It might have gone something like this:

Dearly beloved, today's lesson is taken from the holy Book of Balls, the chapter which deals with the very real challenges of post-neo-classical endogenous growth syndrome.

It is about a Good Samaritan who devotes his life to saving the world and a rich man who passes by on the other side of the road. Let us begin by singing our first hymn.

> All things bright and beautiful,
> All schools and hospitals,
> All our public services,
> Call Me Dave will close them all.
>
> Each surgery we've opened,
> Each council house for rent,
> Will soon be turned to rubble,
> By Mr Ten Per Cent.

All things bright and beautiful,
All schools and hospitals
All our public services,
Call Me Dave will close them all.

The nurses in starched aprons,
The bobbies on the beat,
The teachers in the classrooms,
The sweepers of the streets.

All things bright and beautiful,
All schools and hospitals,
All our public services,
Call Me Dave will close them all.

The smiling dinner ladies,
The workmen in their huts,
The midwives and the matrons,
Will fall to Tory cuts.

All things bright and beautiful,
All schools and hospitals,
All our public services,
Call Me Dave will close them all.

Diversity advisers,
Co-ordinators, too,
They're going to rob the many,
For tax cuts for the few.

All things bright and beautiful,
All schools and hospitals,
All our public services,
Call Me Dave will close them all.

(*Congregation*) Praise be to Gord!

Please be seated. People often say to me: 'Prime Minister, you were never elected.' And I say unto them, Our Lord was not elected, either, but he was the right man for the job.

The tough choice we face today is between what Jesus would have called 'investing' in people and doing nothing.

Ask yourself this: when having to choose between feeding the five thousand and healing the sick, or cutting inheritance tax for a handful of multi-millionaires, what would Our Lord have done?

Let us pray.

> Our Leader,
> Who art in Downing Street
> Gordon is thy name.
> Thy will be done
> In Cabinet
> As it is in Parliament.
> Give us each day
> Our additional costs allowance
> And lead us out of recession.
> Forgive us our expenses
> But never forgive those who conspire against you.
> Lead us not out of Europe
> And deliver us from Cameron.
> For you are in office
> But not in power.
> Amen.

When I read my Bible each night as I lie awake in bed, worrying about how I can help hard-working families, I am struck by how many of the challenges I face – treacherous disciples, for instance – would be familiar to Our Lord.

As we all know, Jesus chased the moneylenders out of the temple. But he didn't have to cope with a global financial crisis, caused by reckless moneylenders in America.

While I have chased some out of the temple – Sir Fred Goodwin, for instance – I could not risk the entire temple falling down.

So I have nationalised the temple and lent the moneylenders £1.3 trillion. Although Jesus had many great gifts, such as the ability to turn wine into water, he did not have quantitive easing.

There is a lesson here we would all do well to reflect upon, particularly those who would stand back and do nothing.

If I may quote the great hymn:

> *We plough the fields and scatter,*
> *The good seed on the land.*

Another example of the way in which Labour governs for the many, not the few.

(Congregation) Praise be to Gord!

Our final reading this morning is Psalm 23.

The Lord Mandelson is my shepherd,
I shall not resign.
He maketh me to lie in the House of Commons,
He guideth me through leadership challenges,
He restoreth my job,
He leadeth me down the path of selfishness,
For his own sake.

Yea, though I walk through the valley of the mountain of debt,
I will take no blame.
For this is a crisis,
Which is global,
And began in America.
He prepareth excuses for me in the presence of mine enemies,
He annointeth my head with guile,
His prize is to runneth the country.

Sure, shame and dishonour shall follow him all the days of his life.
But he will dwell in the House of Lords forever.

Let me leave you with this thought: it takes as much courage to break your promises as it does to keep them. Sometimes it is more courageous not to tell the truth than to speak it.

As we sing our last hymn, a particular favourite of my good

friend President Obama, Mr Darling will be passing among you with the collection plate. All members of the congregation will be expected to contribute 50 per cent of their salary, plus VAT.

And may the Lord have mercy on my soul.

John Brown's body is revolving in his grave,
John Brown's body is revolving in his grave,
John Brown's body is revolving in his grave,
But his son keeps droning on . . .

The Final Curtain

In the week in which Channel 4 pulled the plug on *Big Brother*, it was announced that the curtain was finally coming down on Britain's longest-running unreality show. In its thirteenth year, it has suffered a catastrophic collapse in ratings as viewers have become bored and deserted in droves.

Once hailed as an exciting social experiment, whose sole purpose was 'education, education, education', the series has descended into little more than a repellant freak show.

New Labour has demeaned its contestants and audience alike, coarsened our culture, debased living standards, promoted a climate of bullying and exhibitionism, and lowered Britain's standing around the world. It has become a byword for corruption and incompetence, obsessed with sex, greed and racism.

Back in 1997, more than thirteen million people were glued to the programme, which was hailed for its eclectic, ground-breaking cast.

Housemates included an effete public schoolboy, a former ship's steward, a dour son of the manse, a blind man and his dog, an openly gay public relations man and his exotic Brazilian boyfriend, and a scary, ex-convent schoolgirl who quickly became known as the Wicked Witch.

New Labour was the first series to be broadcast round the clock, seven days a week, 365 days a year. Unlike its close rival, *Big Brother*, it wasn't just the housemates being filmed.

More than four million CCTV cameras were erected all over Britain so that every move of the audience could be captured, too; broadcast on spin-offs such as *Police, Camera, Action!* and *Slappers Go Mad on Malibu*; and used in evidence against people putting their dustbins out on the wrong day.

From the start, the show was mired in controversy, after one of the original housemates, Cookie, was caught having sex with another contestant, a flame-haired civil servant called Gaynor.

Ally, the house bully, a recovering alcoholic and pornographic writer, with a history of mental illness, forced Cookie to leave his wife or face eviction.

Ally was eventually evicted himself after his bullying got completely out of hand and he drove one contestant, a mild-mannered doctor called Kelly, to suicide.

Kelly was found under a tree in the New Labour garden with his wrists slashed. To this day, conspiracy theorists continue to maintain that he was murdered to boost ratings.

Blair, the pretty public school boy, survived an early scare despite accepting a £1 million bribe from a motor-racing tycoon to wear a T-shirt advertising tobacco. Viewers were seduced by his easy charm and his insistence that he was a straight kinda guy.

His emotional reaction when the popular royal housemate, Diana, was killed in a car crash in only the third episode made TV history and proved to be the defining moment of series one.

New Labour's resident village idiot, Two Jags, was captured on film punching a member of the audience during the warm-up to the second series.

He was the clown you loved to hate, always raiding the fridge while the other housemates were asleep.

Ratings went through the roof when another contestant, Tracey, was caught on camera performing a sex act on Two Jags in the diary room. His wife Pauline went through the roof, too.

But viewers began to tire of his antics, which included dressing up as a cowboy and playing croquet in the garden while railing against the 'snobs' who were out to get him.

Then there was Blunkett, the first blind character, who formed a passionate attachment to the only American housemate, Kimberley, drafted in on the strength of her dressing up as Snow White at Disneyland.

Viewers were captivated by Blunkett's descent into madness as he launched a demented paternity suit to prove that he was the father of Kimberley's baby. When he was finally evicted, Blunkett cracked up completely. His sobbing, self-pitying departure was the highlight of the series two finale.

Today, the programme is a shadow of its former self. Only two of the original cast remain, dour Scottish sociopath Gordon and gay PR man Mandy, the self-styled Prince of Darkness.

For most of the show's twelve-year run, Gordon spent his time biting his nails and banging his head against the wall. Whenever there was a scandal in the New Labour house, he always hid behind the sofa, out of sight of the cameras.

After Blair was evicted in 2007 and went on to become a global star, earning millions of pounds a year, Gordon attempted to become the main character, but ratings continued to slump and he soon realised there was nowhere to hide.

He even resorted to a bizarre act of self-abuse on YouTube, in the belief that the audience had migrated to the internet, but it was too late.

Other housemates were drafted in, notably Jackboot Jacqui, a disciplinarian schoolteacher from the Midlands who marked her arrival with an ostentatious flash of cleavage. For a while, the tabloids were fixated upon her breasts and her enthusiasm for punishment.

But she was evicted when it was revealed that while she was living rent-free in the New Labour house, she was claiming overnight expenses for sleeping in her sister's spare bedroom and her husband was downloading pornography and charging it to the programme budget.

The real survivor is Mandy, who has been evicted from the show twice – once for taking out a huge mortgage on the New Labour house without telling the producers and, secondly, for helping obtain VIP passes to the green room for a couple of Indian billionaires.

Last year he made a sensational third comeback as the producers launched a last-gasp effort to breathe life into a tired old format.

But despite being given his own celebrity spin-off series, set on a luxury yacht off Corfu, even Mandy couldn't win back the audience.

As New Labour has resorted to increasingly desperate and

cynical stunts, viewers have stopped watching, the sponsors have dried up and the show has run £1.3 trillion over budget.

The final episode was due to be broadcast in May.

We will all be glad to see the back of it.

'The Times, They Are A-Changin''

More than forty-five years after he released 'The Times They Are A-Changin'', Bob Dylan went back to the top of British album charts in the summer of 2008. Dylan, now sixty-nine, has mellowed over the years. But it got me wondering what kind of anthem he would write today if he was still an angry young protest singer surveying the contemporary British political scene. It helps if you do the voice.

Come gather round comrades wherever you are,
And admit that this time, Gordon Brown's gone too far,
The men in white coats are approaching the door,
The government isn't worth saving,
His performance on YouTube, it was the last straw,
He isn't just mad, he's stark raving.

Come loyal backbenchers and vote with your feet,
The pollsters all say you will lose your safe seat,
It's six-to-four on that you're gonna get beat,
The way that this madman's behaving,
Your party is heading for certain defeat,
For the times they are a-changin'.

Come Cabinet ministers, you all know the score,
Put down your red boxes and run for the door,
Admit that New Labour is dead on the floor,
The roof wasn't fixed and it's raining,
Forget Alan Johnson or Jolly Jack Straw,
It's not just the leader needs changing.

Come Westminster pundits, you all got it wrong,
You told us that Gordon was clever and strong,
But then he turned out to be weak all along,
Though he pretended the world he was saving,
And now that he's finished, you're a-changin' your song,
Because Gordon is drowning, not waving.

The line it is drawn, the curse it is cast,
At the general election, you're gonna come last,
The days of dear Prudence are all in the past,
You've stolen our pensions and savings,
Unemployment and taxes are going up fast,
And we're going to vote Call Me Dave in.

I agree with Nick

We certainly looked on course to vote Call Me Dave in, even though the Tory lead in the opinion polls had dwindled. The smart money was still on an overall Conservative majority of between twenty and thirty seats, but the rigged boundaries and electoral mathematics, both in Labour's favour, made any firm prediction risky.

The BBC and the boys in the bubble were doing their best to talk up a hung parliament, or what the Beeb and the Lib Dems decided to start calling a 'balanced' parliament – a far more agreeable term.

There was also the question of the first televised leadership debates to be factored in. No one could forecast what effect these three beauty pageants would have on the outcome.

They threatened to be uninspiring, sterile affairs, smothered by a catalogue of ground rules and restrictions.

What, I wondered, if they were to take the form of the wonderful 'I look down on him' sketch on class, starring John Cleese and the Two Ronnies, from *The Frost Report*. If you're too young to remember it, you can find the original on YouTube.

GORDON BROWN: I look down on him because he is an upper-class snob who went to Eton.

CALL-ME-DAVE: I look down on him because he is a lying Scottish sociopath who has turned Britain into a basket case.

NICK CLEGG: I know my place. I look down on both of them because I am a Liberal Democrat and therefore morally superior.

GB: I look down on him because he has innate breeding and believes he has a divine right to be Prime Minister, even though he has never had a proper job in his life.

CMD: I do have innate breeding but I look down on him because he believes he has a divine right to be Prime Minister, even though he has never had a proper job in his life.

NC: I know my place. I don't have innate breeding and I have never had a proper job in my life, but I'm never likely to be Prime Minister, either. So I suppose I should look up to both of them, but I don't.

GB: I look down on him because he was a member of the Bullingdon Club.

CMD: I look down on him because he is a bully, who shouts at secretaries and throws mobile phones at the wall.

NC: I know my place.

GB: I look down on him because he is bought and paid for by Lord Ashcroft.

CMD: I look down on him because he is bought and paid for by Lord Paul and Unite.

NC: I look down on both of them, even though my party's biggest donor has been convicted of fraud.

GB: I look down on him because he cynically exploits the death of his child to win votes.

CMD: I look down on him because he cynically exploits the death of his child to win votes.

NC: Some people say I look like Piers Morgan.

GB: I look down on everyone because I saved the world.

CMD: I look down on him because although he boasts about saving the world, he's bankrupted Britain.

NC: I've slept with more than thirty women.

GB: I get a feeling of superiority over them because I'm still going to be Prime Minister after the election, even if that means cutting a deal with the Lib Dems.

CMD: I get a feeling of superiority over him because I went to Eton and because the Lib Dems will support me as Prime Minister. Clegg's a closet Tory who looks up to Mrs Thatcher.

NC: I know my price.

★

I wrote that back in March 2010, two months before the first debate took place. The actual debates were pretty dull, though Clegg's novelty value propelled him briefly into second place in the polls. Brown was reduced to parroting, 'I agree with Nick.'

With hindsight, my 'I look down on him' riff now appears weirdly prophetic, even though it was supposed to be a joke.

Banana Republic

Clegg's price was five Cabinet seats, the watering down of a few Tory promises, a handful of symbolic Lib Dem policies and a referendum on electoral reform.

But for a few agonising days it was touch and go. At the beginning of March, I wrote a column speculating that regardless of the result of the election Gordon Brown would refuse to resign.

He would simply barricade the door of Number 10, while he attempted to stitch up a grubby deal with the Lib Dems.

It was only half in jest. For the past three years, I'd been warning that Brown would have to be dragged out of Downing Street by what remained of his fingernails.

He always believed he had a divine right to be Prime Minister, whatever the wishes of the electorate. So Labour tried to rewrite the result.

In terms of seats and votes, the Conservatives won the election, although fell short of an overall majority. The Tories beat Labour by two million votes and almost fifty seats.

Cameron's Conservatives polled as many votes as Tony Blair managed in 2005 – a share sufficient then to deliver Labour a sixty-six-seat majority. Britain's biased constituency boundaries cost CMD an outright victory.

Labour slumped to its lowest share of the vote since the Michael Foot meltdown in 1983. It lost more seats than at any election since 1931.

Gordon Brown suffered a humiliating defeat by any measure. Labour forfeited the right to govern.

Anyone with a shred of decency would have tendered his resignation the moment the scale of Labour's losses became apparent. But decency is not something we have come to associate with Brown, a man, I would argue, without shame, principle or honour.

While the Tories and Liberals negotiated in good faith, Brown simpy refused to budge while Labour tried to pretend that Britain had rejected the Conservatives and was crying out for a 'progressive' Lib-Lab coalition.

From the moment the exit poll was published after voting ended on Thursday night, Labour's losers began reading like automatons from a script written by Peter Mandelson and Alistair Campbell, two of the most slippery individuals ever to achieve high political office.

The 'line to take' was repeated ad infinitum on the airwaves over the next few days, parroted in the desperate Labour propaganda sheets, the *Guardian*, the *Independent* and the *Daily Mirror*.

In a military coup, the first target is always to take over the television and radio stations. In Gordon Brown's bloodless coup attempt, there was no need. The state broadcaster, the BBC, was already signed up to the cause, only too happy to repeat the lie that the Conservatives had lost the election and that the clear message from voters was that they wanted a new 'progressive' left-wing alliance.

Campbell became a permanent fixture on the BBC, even though he has no official standing. Then, at 5 p.m. on the Monday after his resounding defeat and with Cameron and Clegg's teams locked in negotiations, Brown tried to steal the election and keep Labour in power in perpetuity.

He announced that he was offering the Lib Dems everything they wanted on proportional representation, without the incovenience of a referendum, provided they threw in their lot with Labour – even though together they still couldn't command a majority in the Commons.

His death-bed conversion to the attractions of PR was driven by a lethal combination of self-interest and malice. Brown was attempting to foist on to the British people an electoral system constructed with the single aim of ensuring permanent centre-left government, with Labour as the dominant force.

Even if he couldn't remain in Downing Street, he would at least go down in history as the man who ensured that Britain would never again have a Conservative government.

He also said he was prepared to stand down, but not for at least six months. Britain would then get its second unelected Labour Prime Minister in succession.

It defied belief and threw the pundits into confusion. If no one in Britain knew what the hell was going on, imagine what they made of it abroad.

There was only one place to go. It was time to tune in again to *Eyewitness News*, Palm Beach, for an American perspective:

*

Good morning, America, how are you? This is your favourite son, Chad Hanging, reporting. Let's cross live to London, Englandland, where our special correspondent Brit Limey has been following developments.

Good morning, Chad. I'm standing in historic Piccadilly Square, in downtown London, where people are coming to terms with the results of the election.

So who is the new president of Englandland, Brit?

President Norman Brown, Chad.

I thought he was the old president.

He is, Chad.

So President Brown won the election?

No, Chad, he lost the election. President Brown's Labour Party came second, two million votes behind the Conservatives.

So the Conservatives won?

No, they lost, too. They didn't get enough seats in the House of Lords to form a majority government.

So President Brown got more seats, even though he got fewer votes.

Negatory, Chad. President Brown got fifty fewer seats than the Conservatives.

Then why is he still President?

He's holed up in Number 10 Downing Street, where the Queen lives, and refuses to come out.

Can he do that?

Apparently so, Chad. He can carry on being President until someone else forms a government.

What happens now?

Well, Chad, it's up to the Liberal Democrats to decide who becomes President.

I didn't realise the Democrats were standing in Englandland. Does that mean President Obama could become president of Englandland?

No, Chad. Different party. They're led by a guy called Clegg, who won one of the TV debates. For a while he was the new Susan Boyle.

They're a new party, right?

No, they're an old party. Even older than the Conservatives and Labour.

So the Liberal Democrats won the election?

No, they lost too. They only got fifty-seven seats, which is fewer than they got at the last election in 2005.

How come they get to choose the president, then?

Because they came third.

So this guy Clegg could become president?

No chance, Chad, but he could become Vice President or Homeland Security Secretary.

How so?

He's talking to the Conservatives about forming a coalition.

And where does that leave President Norman Brown?

Clegg's talking to the Conservatives about forming a coalition, too.

If Clegg decides to go with Labour, does that mean Norman Brown could stay on as president?

Not necessarily, Chad. Labour and the Liberal Democrats still wouldn't have enough seats to command a majority. And Clegg says he wouldn't work under President Brown, so Labour would have to choose a new president.

But that would mean that the new president hadn't been elected by anyone.

That's the way it works in Englandland. President Norman Brown wasn't elected by anyone, either.

Tell me more about this Clegg guy, *Brit*.

Well, Chad, he looks like Piers Morgan, from America's Got Talent, *he supports illegal immigration and thinks Englandland should be governed by Europe.*

And what do the people of Englandland think about that?

They hate the idea, Chad, which is why the Liberal Democrats came a poor third in this election.

Yet Clegg still gets to choose the president?

That's right, Chad.

Isn't that like letting the Tea Party pick the president of the USA?

Not really, Chad. The Tea Party is more popular than the Lib Dems and contains fewer wacko nutjobs.

So what happens now?

Clegg seems likely to do a deal with the Conservatives, which would mean a man called Call Me Dave becomes president, even though he didn't win enough seats, either.

Can they do that?

I guess so, Chad. During the election, Clegg promised a more open, accountable, honest form of government. It's the 'new politics'.

Run that by me again, Brit. So under this new, open and more honest politics, the politicians pick the President without asking the voters?

That's a big Ten-four, Chad. All the negotiations have been conducted in secret.

Why don't they just hold another election, Brit?

Because the Labour Party and the Liberal Democrats haven't got any money to fight another election, Chad. The biggest Lib Dem donor is a convicted fraudster who is on the run from the police.

Did they give the money back?

Of course not, Chad. They kept it, arguing that it was the only way they could compete with Labour, who are bankrolled by the unions, and the Conservatives, who are owned by someone called Lord Paddy Ashcroft, who lives in a banana republic called Belisha.

Englandland sounds more like a banana republic than a mature democracy.

Funny you should say that, Chad. There was chaos when the polling stations shut before everyone had voted.

You're kidding me.

I wish I was, Chad. There are also twenty separate police inquiries into voting irregularities, including postal vote fraud. The election has been widely condemned by international observers from as far afield as Kenya, Rwanda and Bangladesh. It looks as if it may have to be re-run in some areas.

And these are the guys who told us we didn't know how to run an election in Florida.

That's right, Chad. You couldn't make it up.

Elvis won't leave the building

When Brown's outrageous attempted coup collapsed, he vanished. After he failed to turn up for the State Opening of Parliament, I even offered a reward for any confirmed sighting of him.

Then I remembered that at one stage during the campaign, Labour became so desperate that it even wheeled out an Elvis impersonator to try to boost Gordon's flagging ratings.

I speculated that the only career option left open to Gordon might be as an Elvis impersonator. Perhaps the reason he had gone missing was that rehearsals were already underway.

We take you over now live to Caesar's Palace and Working Men's Institute in Kirkaldy for an exclusive preview of his forthcoming world tour.

Lay-deez and gen-nul-men. Please put your hands together for the Dunfermline Elvis . . .

Thank you very much. I'd like to start tonight with a very special version of 'Heartbreak Hotel', which began in America.

Well, since my Tony left me,
He's found a new place to dwell
A five-million pad in Connaught Square
And a country house as well.

Oh, Tony, I'm lonely, Tony
Oh, I'm so lonely, Tony,
I'm so lonely, I could cry.

And when he's not in England
He's got somewhere else to live
It's a luxury, six-star hotel suite
In downtown Tel Aviv.

Oh, Tony, I'm lonely, Tony
Oh, I'm so lonely, Tony,
I'm so lonely, I could cry.

Well since my Tony left me,
My life's been a living hell,
It's not so much 10 Downing Street,
As Heartbreak Hotel.

Oh, Tony, I'm lonely, Tony
Oh, I'm so lonely, Tony,
I'm so useless, I could cry.

You're too kind. This next song is dedicated to Peter. It's called 'His Latest Flame'.

A very old friend,
Came by today,
He was telling everyone in town
About the love that he just found
And Clegg's the name
Of his latest flame.

He talked and talked
And stroked his hair,
Said Clegg was just like Tony Blair
The voting system isn't fair
And Clegg's the name
Of his latest flame.

Would you believe
That yesterday,
I put him in the Lords and he swore to me
He'd be mine eternally
And Clegg's the name
Of his latest flame.

Thank you, lay-deez and gen-nul-men. This one goes out to someone called Nick. It's called 'Devil In Disguise.'

He looks like Tony
Walks like Tony
Talks like Tony
But I got wise
He's just a Lib Dem in disguise
Oh, yes, he is
A Lib Dem in disguise.

He fooled you with his promises
He cheated and he schemed
Heaven knows how he lied to you
He's not the way he seems

He looks like a Tory
Walks like a Tory
Talks like a Tory
But I got wise
He's just a Lib Dem in disguise
Oh, yes, he is
A Lib Dem in disguise.

Thank you so much. It's great to be back in Kirkaldy. 'I'm All Shook Up'.

Oh well, bless my soul
What's a-wrong with me,
I'm grinning like a monkey
With dysentery.
The pollsters keep-a telling me
The game is up
And my nails
They're all chewed up.

Uh-huh-huh, huh, yea-yea, yea.

My hands are a-waving
In the wrong place
A stupid rictus smile plastered
On my face.
After thirteen years
Looks like I'm out of luck
And my nails
They're all chewed up.

Uh-huh-huh, huh, yea-yea, yea.
I'm all washed up.

OK, everybody, let's rock!

 Warden threw a party at the Wandsworth Jail
The place was full of MPs who began to wail
Everything they did was within the rules
Even claiming public money for their swimming
   pools
Let's rock, everybody, let's rock,
Everybody in the whole cell block
Was dancing to the duck house rock.

Number forty-seven said to number three
Hey, man, aren't you that corrupt MP
Flipped your second home to avoid CGT
Come on and do the duck house rock with me.
Let's rock, everybody, let's rock,
Everybody in the whole cell block,
Was dancing to the duck house rock.

Sadly that's about all we've got time for this evening. I want to
leave you with a song about love's labour's lost. Or maybe that
should be Labour's lost love. Goodnight.

When no one could understand me,
When everything I did was wrong,
He gave me hope and consolation,
Now even Mandelson has gone.

He's no longer here to lend a hand
Or put me on YouTube
It's no wonder,
No wonder I'm screwed.

And when I smile, the kids are frightened
The markets plunge when I'm around
I've lost the country a small fortune
I have even trashed the pound

I'll guess I'll never know the reason why
They hate me like they do
But it's no wonder
No wonder I'm screwed.

Meet the New Boss . . .

So much for the 'new politics'. Within a few short weeks, two of the Lib Dem Cabinet members were mired in scandal.

It has always been said that when it comes to scandals, with Labour it's money, with the Conservatives, it's sex. The Lib Dems managed to combine both.

David Laws was forced to resign as Chief Secretary to the Treasury because he trousered £40, 000 of taxpayers' money in second-home expenses which he funnelled to his gay lover.

His feeble excuse was that he wished to keep his relationship private. Fair enough. In that case he shouldn't have claimed anything. He doesn't need the money, by all accounts, having made enough in the City to retire when he was just twenty-eight.

Obviously he didn't know that he was going to turn up in such a high-profile job (he was, after all, a Lib Dem) but he must have known that his claims were dubious. He had plenty of opportunities to pay back the money by slipping a cheque under the door of the Fees Office.

Laws stepped down from the Treasury but continued to sit as an MP. In the spirit of the 'new politics' surely he should have offered himself immediately for re-election. After all, he didn't steal from the government, he stole from the taxpayers, including his own, constituents.

I've never understood why disgraced ministers forced from office are allowed to continue as MPs.

Laws' replacement was wet-behind-the-ears Danny Alexander, who only five years ago was press officer for the Cairngorms and brought to the job two weeks' experience in the non-job of Scottish Secretary. He hardly seemed qualified for the onerous task of cutting Britain's debt mountain.

There was also the fact that Alexander avoided paying Capital Gains Tax when he sold his flat in London by designating it as his main home – even though for the purposes of claiming parliamentary expenses totalling £37,000 he had maintained it was his second home.

That's precisely the kind of behaviour which cost Hazel Blears her job in the last Labour government. She was forced to write out a cheque to Revenue for the tax she had avoided.

As chief secretary, Desperate Dan will now be responsible for trying to implement the Lib Dem manifesto commitment to raise CGT to 40, or even 50 per cent – even though he played the system to avoid paying it himself. Naturally, he insists he acted within the rules.

Next up was Chris Huhne, the Minister of Windmills, who was discovered to be having an adulterous relationship as hilarious as any former Labour or Tory 'sleaze' scandal.

I'd already christened him Chris Whohe, on the grounds that despite his monumental self-importance, no one in the real world had ever heard of him.

When the pictures of his mistress were published, she looked familiar. I recognised her from the days when we both used to work for Sky News.

Funny, I thought to myself, I always had her marked down as a lesbian. Turns out I was half-right. Carina Trimingham is bisexual. Even though she was sweating up the sheets with Huhne, it wasn't all that that long ago since she married her lesbian lover in a civil partnership ceremony.

Takes all sorts. According to profiles, among the many jobs she's had over the past few years was working as press officer for AC/DC.

That would explain it. You couldn't make it up. Seeing as she also worked for *Top of the Pops*, it's probable that the AC/DC in question is the Australian group who once released an album called Dirty Deeds Done Dirt Cheap rather than the Campaign for Bisexual Equality.

But, these days, who knows? If you asked a cartoonist to draw you a comedy lesbian from central casting, Carina Trimingham is what you'd get – all spiky haircut and Doc Martens. Chuck in a boiler suit and she's Millie Tant, straight from the pages of *Viz* magazine.

When Huhne was just another irrelevant Lib Dem MP, news of his extra-marital relationship would barely have troubled the scorers. As soon as he accepted ministerial office a in the coalition government, he stepped up a division.

Huhne put his private life on offer when he paraded his family for public approval at the recent general election.

He even published his wedding snaps from twenty-six years ago and boasted: 'Family matters to me so much' – even though he was already up to his neck in an affair with a bisexual woman twelve years his junior.

When he was rumbled, Huhne wrote off a quarter of a century of marital bliss with a curt, one-sentence statement in a shameful attempt to seize the moral high ground.

No contrition, no word of regret, no apology for the hurt he has caused his family.

Huhne peddled a false prospectus to the electorate. If he had left his wife and taken up with Miss Trimingham *before* the election, it would have been out in the open and voters could have made up their own minds.

Of course, being a Liberal Democrat he couldn't even get the adultery right. Most MPs who go over the side keep the wife and kiddies in the constituency and the mistress in London. Huhne kept his family in London and slept with Miss Trimingham at his home in Eastleigh.

As a former journalist himself, Huhne must have realised that the headline 'Married Minister in Lesbian Love Triangle' would prove irresistible.

Most probably, Huhne thought he wouldn't get caught. None of them do. But once the rumour mill started churning this was a headline waiting to happen.

The Lib Dems are the original AC/DC political party. They swing both ways, from sandal-wearing socialists to free-market, wet Tories.

Most of them hate each other more than they hate their opponents, which is why whoever tipped off the press about Huhne would have done so with malicious relish.

Huhne's behaviour isn't surprising, it's depressingly predictable, although a minister leaving his wife and running off with a lesbian is a novelty.

In all other respects it was a rerun of an old Labour scandal, which saw the late Robin Cook forced by Alastair Campbell to choose between his wife and his mistress.

Just like Cook, Huhne gave his missus the elbow. Meet the new politics, same as the old politics.